Yale French Studies

MW01285710

Claude Lanzmann after *Shoah*

MICHAEL G. LEVINE AND JARED STARK   1   Editors' Preface: To Transmit a Question: Reflections on Lanzmann's Work after *Shoah* (1985)

I. *The Shoah after "Shoah"*

JARED STARK   19   How to See Nothing: *A Visitor from the Living* (1997)

JUDITH KASPER   41   Revolt as a Study in Precision: *Sobibor, October 14, 1943, 4 p.m.* (2001)

ALEXANDER GARCÍA DÜTTMANN   58   "I was a report": *The Karski Report* (2010)

SARA GUYER   68   Testimony beyond Justice: *The Last of the Unjust* (2013)

STUART LIEBMAN   85   *Four Sisters* (2018) and Claude Lanzmann's Holocaust Film Project

II. *"My homeland is my film"*

BRAD PRAGER   101   Israeli Soldiers in the Eyes of the Beholder: *Tsahal* (1994)

MICHAEL G. LEVINE   123   "Yes, this is the place": Lanzmann between *Napalm* (2017) and *Shoah*

III. *Lanzmann par lui-même*

FRANÇOISE MELTZER   139   Time and the Hare: Lanzmann's Autobiography

CLAUDE LANZMANN   156   Self-Portrait at Ninety: An Interview with Franck Nouchi and Juliette Simont

Yale French Studies

Michael G. Levine and Jared Stark
  Special editors for this issue
Alyson Waters, *Managing editor*
Editorial board: Pierre Saint-Amand (Chair),
  Morgane Cadieu, Thomas C. Connolly,
  Jill Jarvis, Alice Kaplan, Maurice Samuels,
  Christophe Schuwey
Assistant editor: Sophia Helverson
Editorial office: Humanities Quadrangle,
  320 York Street, 3rd Floor
Mailing address: P.O. Box 208251, New Haven,
  Connecticut 06520-8251
Sales and subscription office:
Yale University Press, P.O. Box 209040
New Haven, Connecticut 06520-0940

Designed by James J. Johnson and set in Trump
  Medieval Roman by Newgen North America.
  Printed in the United States of America.

ISSN 044-0078
ISBN for this issue 978-0-300-26221-6

Alyson Waters edited 56 issues of *Yale French Studies* with unflagging excellence. Under her leadership, YFS explored a rich diversity of topics—from Surrealism to Francophone cinema, from Baudelaire to Marie Chauvet, from *noeuds de mémoire* to the *bande dessinée*. She helped editors develop their concepts for issues, vetted translations, made sure the journal kept a balance of periods, topics, and authors, and led our editorial meetings with lucid good humor and discernment. Alyson has been more than an editor: she has been the curator of our intellectual life for 29 years.

Anyone who has been through a copy edit with Alyson understands that the qualities that have made her an award-winning translator have also ensured that the articles appearing in YFS are free of Gallicisms, typos, and infelicities of any sort. She's been a wonderful mentor to the graduate student assistants who have learned the art of editing from her.

We will miss her, though we take consolation in the prospect of her many new translations to come.

MICHAEL G. LEVINE AND JARED STARK

Editors' Preface:
To Transmit a Question: Reflections
on Lanzmann's Work after *Shoah*

Claude Lanzmann was a man obsessed with questions, the smaller
the better. "Was the weather very cold?" "From the station to the
unloading ramp in the camp is how many miles?" "How long did the
trip last?" Like the Holocaust historian Raoul Hilberg, whom he admired greatly, Lanzmann feared that to begin by asking the big questions would run the risk of coming up only with small answers. The
small, precise questions he posed were a way of working concretely,
of slowing the impulse to sum up and conclude, of chipping away at
fashionable pronouncements and received truths, of making inroads
into the silence he encountered in those with whom he spoke. His obsessive questioning enabled him bit by bit to forge a path, to discover
a method where none seemed to present itself. Reflecting on the construction of *Shoah* in a seminar he gave at Yale on April 11, 1990, he
recalled that it "happened to me to be stuck for days, even for weeks
. . . because I am a stubborn man. When you climb a mountain, when
it is a *première* on the north face, you have to invent the way because
there is no way already made."[1]

   The questions Lanzmann relentlessly posed to himself and others
also raised the related question of cinematic transmission. Speaking
in the same seminar, he recalls walking around Auschwitz without a
camera during the making of *Shoah*, asking himself: "At which moment did it start to be too late?"

> Of course, when the gates of the camp are passed it is already too late.
> It is too late when the gates of the crematorium are . . . , but here it
> was already too late. When they were on the train it was already too

   1. Claude Lanzmann, "Seminar with Claude Lanzmann, 11 April 1990," in "Literature and the Ethical Question," ed. Claire Nouvet, *Yale French Studies* 79 (1991): 83.

YFS 141, *Lanzmann after "Shoah,"* ed. Levine and Stark, © 2022 by Yale University.

late. When they boarded the train in Drancy or in Salonika it was already too late. When was it not too late? How will this story be helped? I know that I was obsessed with these questions. I was asking myself: "How to transmit these questions? How to transmit these feelings to the spectator, to the viewer of the film?"[2]

As the cadences of this passage and the insistent repetition of the phrase "too late" suggest, to transmit a question for Lanzmann was above all to hold it open and to brood over it, to pursue it to the point of obsession, to find within it other more difficult and ever more precise questions. This was also his way of reaching out to the spectator. "How to transmit these questions? How to transmit these feelings?" Such "how to" questions also remained for him perpetually open. As their juxtaposition and parallel phrasing imply, they remained above all to be posed in terms of one another. How to transmit a question as though it were a feeling? How to feel one's way by holding on to an open question, to a question that, in opening, repeatedly gives way to others?

Posed time and again, the question of the "how to" was negotiated by Lanzmann each time anew, each time as though for the first time. If anything, this questioning only intensified after *Shoah* was hailed as a masterpiece, as a decisive work of historiography as well as cinematography. In the twelve years it took to make the film, Lanzmann engaged in extensive research and traveled widely, tracking down and interviewing Holocaust survivors, bystanders, and perpetrators on three continents. Of the 230 hours of footage created during those years, nine and one-half became *Shoah*. What remained led to yet other questions. How could or would he make films after *Shoah*? What would become of the unused footage, much of which contained otherwise untold or only partially told stories?

This volume of *Yale French Studies* charts the different paths Lanzmann took after the release of *Shoah* in 1985 until his death on July 5, 2018, at the age of ninety-two. The first section looks at the five films he made drawing on the outtakes from *Shoah*, beginning in 1997 with *Un vivant qui passe* (*A Visitor from the Living*). This first experiment in making new films from the unused footage was followed by *Sobibor, 14 octobre, 1943, 1600 heures* (*Sobibor, October 14, 1943*,

---

2. Ibid., 89. Ellipses in the original.

4 p.m.) (2001), *Le rapport Karski* (*The Karski Report*) (2010), and *Le dernier des injustes* (*The Last of the Unjust*) (2013). The last of this group of films, *Les quatre soeurs* (*Four Sisters*), reached French theaters just one day before the director's death.

The second section turns to a different but related trajectory in Lanzmann's work: films not centrally devoted to the Holocaust and not drawing on the *Shoah* outtakes: *Tsahal* (1994), along with its short companion piece, *Lights and Shadows* (2008), and *Napalm* (2017).

The last section focuses on Lanzmann's strong impulse to tell his own story, a drive embodied in his 500-page autobiography, *Le lièvre de Patagonie* (*The Patagonian Hare*), published in 2009, and in his last major interview, a wide-ranging discussion with Franck Nouchi and Juliette Simont titled "Self-Portrait at Ninety," which appears here in translation for the first time, from the volume *Claude Lanzmann: Un voyant dans le siècle*, edited by Simont and published by Gallimard in 2017.

While *Shoah* and, more recently, its outtakes have been the subject of a substantial body of scholarship, Lanzmann's later films and writing, with a few notable exceptions, have received little attention, and nowhere in a single volume. What emerges in and across the essays we present here is a Lanzmann *after* Shoah, a filmmaker who sought to forge new strategies and invent new languages when dealing with recalcitrant material, unsolved artistic questions, and the many testimonial encounters that continued to haunt him; a writer who had to reckon not only with the fame, prestige, and critical authority *Shoah* had given him, but with the way the term "Shoah" itself came to replace "Holocaust" as the name for the destruction of European Jewry; and a contradictory, "non-integrated" public intellectual whose different sides would come out in very different ways depending on the cultural context in which his work was received.

A TREASURE

In the seminar he gave at Yale in 1990, published in an important volume of *Yale French Studies*, edited by Claire Nouvet and including an early version of Shoshana Felman's groundbreaking study of *Shoah*, Lanzmann provocatively responded to a question about the unused footage: "You want to know my deep wish? My wish would be to destroy it. I have not done it. I will probably not do it. But if

I followed my inclination I would destroy it. This, at least, would prove that *Shoah* is not a documentary."[3] The creation of the Claude Lanzmann Shoah Collection at the United States Holocaust Memorial Museum, which now houses the 220 hours of outtakes and has digitized and made them widely accessible, along with the five films Lanzmann himself made drawing on this footage, evidence a shift in perspective. Indeed, by the time of "Self-Portrait at Ninety," what he had previously wished to destroy had become a "treasure":

> What I realize today with great lucidity is that I was putting together a *treasure*, in the Greek sense of this word. All those years as I was accumulating an immense quantity of material I was a kind of archeologist, completely possessed and fascinated by what I was discovering. That discovery did not really have as an end the making of a film. What I wanted above all was for everything to be gathered, saved, saved from time, which passes and causes everything to be forgotten.

How to understand this "treasure," this storehouse? Two recent studies of the outtakes have viewed them largely as a resource for developing a critique of Lanzmann and of *Shoah*.[4] What they seek to demonstrate is how Lanzmann relegated voices, perspectives, and histories with which he was "less comfortable" to the "cutting room floor" because they did not seem to align with his own authorial agenda.[5]

We take a different approach. As Lanzmann returns to the unused footage created during the making of *Shoah*, another history opens up and becomes possible, one that leads him to recognize something new in what he had been doing. Such a return allows him to revisit his own past much in the way that his films excavate the silences of history. This includes revisiting *Shoah* itself, viewing it not only from the perspective of what allegedly had to be excluded for it to

---

3. Ibid., 96.

4. We refer to Jennifer Cazenave, *An Archive of Catastrophe: The Unused Footage of Claude Lanzmann's* Shoah (Albany: State University of New York Press, 2018) and *The Construction of Testimony*, ed. Erin McGlothlin, Brad Prager, and Marcus Zisselsberger (Detroit: Wayne State University Press, 2020).

5. McGlothlin and Prager suggest that what determines what was included in and excluded from *Shoah* is "that there were certain narratives with which Lanzmann was . . . less comfortable" in their "Introduction," to *The Construction of Testimony*, 9. Cazenave argues that "the unused footage of *Shoah* calls on us to reintegrate into the narrative of the Holocaust heterogeneous voices and histories captured by the camera but ultimately left on the cutting room floor" (*Archive of the Catastrophe*, 6). See also, in this volume, Judith Kasper's critique of Gary Weissman's approach to *Sobibor*.

coalesce as a unified work, but also as an essentially unfinished and unfinishable film. As such, it might be viewed in Benjaminian terms as an "original" that will have called for its translation, that will have made a place within its own surprisingly fault-ridden structure for the supplement of translation, the supplement of a certain "after."

Lanzmann gestures in this direction in remarks made during a panel discussion of *Shoah* at Yale on May 7, 1986. "The last image of the film," he recalls, "is a rolling train."

> You know, this was a real question, the question of the end . . . . When does the Holocaust really end? Did it end the last day of the war? Did it end with the creation of the State of Israel? No, it still goes on. These events are of such magnitude, of such scope that they have never stopped developing their consequences . . . . When I really had to conclude I decided I did not have the right to do it . . . And I decided that the last image of the film would be a rolling train, an endlessly rolling . . . train.[6]

While it is clear that Lanzmann intended the ending to be seen as open, what is less clear is the nature and indeed the temporal structure of that openness. The essays gathered in this issue seek to explore this structure, endeavoring, on the one hand, to address the later films on their own terms and, on the other, to view them as translations of a certain excess of the original, as translations of precisely those elements that kept *Shoah* from coming to a close. It is our contention that the later films are "after" *Shoah* only to the extent that they make contact with a certain otherness of the original, only to the extent that they invent new ways of working with previously unmetabolized historical energies, with what Lanzmann refers to in the introductory scroll of *The Last of the Unjust* as the persistence of a certain specter. Speaking specifically about the conversations with Benjamin Murmelstein he had recorded in Rome in 1975, he says:

> These long hours of interviews, rich in first-hand revelations, have continued to dwell in my mind and haunt me. I knew that I was the custodian of something unique but backed away from the difficulties

---

6. Qtd. in Shoshana Felman, "The Return of the Voice," in Shoshana Felman and Dori Laub, *Testimony: Crises of Witnessing in Literature, Psychoanalysis, and History* (New York: Routledge, 1992), 241-42. Ellipses in the original.

of constructing such a film. It took me a long time to accept the fact
that I had no right to keep it to myself.

THE SHOAH AFTER *SHOAH*

On one level, what remained other to *Shoah* and acquired a central
role in the later films based on the outtakes are a number of crucial
historical perspectives and themes that, as Lanzmann noted repeatedly, were not supported by the "architecture" of *Shoah*. As Stuart
Liebman writes in his essay in this volume on *Four Sisters*, "*Shoah*
did not attempt to offer a comprehensive history of the Holocaust, as
is sometimes claimed." Lanzmann's focus in *Shoah* on the machinery of extermination, with surviving members of the special detach-
ments, the *Sonderkommando*, as his central witnesses, along with
the rejection of voice-over commentary and the decision to include
the process of translation as part of the work, led to a film that, in
its already epic length, could not address all of the questions that
Lanzmann had investigated in compiling the "treasure" of which he
spoke. Among the topics that *Shoah* keeps open and that become central to the later films are the administration of the ghettos by Jewish
Councils (*The Last of the Unjust*, the *Bałuty* chapter of *Four Sisters*);
revolts in the camps (*Sobibor, October 14, 1943, 4 p.m.*, *The Merry
Flea* in *Four Sisters*); the silence of the international community (*A
Visitor from the Living*, *The Karski Report*); and women's experiences
in the ghettos and camps (*Four Sisters*).

Not only did these historical themes prove impossible to integrate
into the architecture of *Shoah*, but the architectural metaphor itself
seemed, in the context of various structural innovations, to be in
need of revision. As Brad Prager notes in his essay here, with the making of *Tsahal*, Lanzmann's first three films—*Pourquoi Israël* (1973),
Shoah (1985), and *Tsahal* (1994)—come to appear as elements in a
trilogy, thus retroactively transforming the seemingly self-supporting
and autonomous architecture of *Shoah* into a part of a narrative
continuum—one that, moreover, is not itself complete since *Sobibor*
(2001), is later added to this group. In a similar vein, Liebman suggests that, in light of Lanzmann's films after *Shoah*, his *oeuvre* as a
whole comes to appear as "a Renaissance polyptych altarpiece." Further metaphors emerge in this volume's discussions of Lanzmann's
later films. This is due at least in part to a marked difference in
form: in contrast to the first three, they are much less wide-ranging

and polyphonically composed, with each film focusing instead on a single interview and a single protagonist. New metaphors emerge, for example, in Judith Kasper's way of viewing Lanzmann's film on Yehuda Lerner and his unforgettable account of the uprising in Sobibór as a tragic drama, albeit a critically revised and interrupted one. Both Jared Stark and Alexander García Düttmann, in their respective readings of films dealing with reports made to the international community during the war, see Lanzmann reworking the very notion of a report. Thus, Stark in his discussion of *A Visitor from the Living* speaks of the film as a counter-report to the blind and falsified one prepared by the Swiss doctor Maurice Rossel, who, as a delegate for the International Red Cross, issued a favorable review of conditions in the Theresienstadt ghetto. In his essay on *The Karski Report*, which draws on parts of Lanzmann's interview with the Polish envoy not included in *Shoah* and in which Karski speaks of his encounters with Roosevelt and others following his clandestine visit to the Warsaw ghetto, Düttmann takes on the voice of the witness, making him speak in an eerily mechanical way in order to lay bare the dilemmas that underlie the very attempt to deliver a precise report—for Lanzmann as well as for Karski. *The Last of the Unjust*, in Sara Guyer's reading, is not so much the cinematic presentation of a testimony as a critical reflection on the substantial risks of the testimonial turn in the humanities. And as Liebman notes, each of the four chapters of *Four Sisters* assumes what for Lanzmann was the unusual form of a "life story." In contrast to the contrapuntal structure of *Shoah*, in which testimonial fragments focused on a central event are made to break into and through one another, *Four Sisters* allows each woman to present her experience of the *univers concentrationnaire* in the context of life before and after the war. Each woman's testimony is allowed its own space, each is given a film of her own. Yet this seeming autonomy is complicated by the arrangement of the individual units into what Liebman describes as a "suite." Or as Lanzmann himself, emphasizing a different kind of sisterly bond, puts it, "A profound unity reunites these women without family ties."[7]

What these various metaphors demonstrate is not only a significant departure from the "architecture" of *Shoah* but that each film

---

7. "Quatre Soeurs: Interview de Claude Lanzmann avec Serge Toubiana," *frenchtouch2*, January 23, 2018. http://www.frenchtouch2.fr/2018/01/quatre-soeurs-entretien-de-claude.html

following it presented a unique set of challenges that could be met only by forging a unique approach, a new way of traversing the "north face." It required what Lanzmann would describe on numerous occasions as the "invention of a language." Elements of the cinematic language he developed in *Shoah* persist in the later films: a focus on voices of extraordinary testimonial power; a preoccupation with the face of the witness often juxtaposed with empty landscapes or what Lanzmann calls "non-sites of memory"; the use of props and staged scenes that enact without illustrating the past; and always, the small, precise questions. It would appear, however, that the "laws" Lanzmann had given himself for the making of *Shoah* needed to be broken or modified if he were to invent a new language for each film. His fervent rejection of archival images, for instance, is countermanded in the opening shot of *Sobibor* and at various moments in *The Last of the Unjust*, *Napalm*, and *Four Sisters*. Reverse shots of Lanzmann begin to appear in *A Visitor from the Living*, foregrounding the filmmaker himself in new ways and posing new questions for a cinema of testimony, as Stark observes. We see Lanzmann staging himself not only as a historical witness but also as a reader in Guyer's incisive analysis of the opening of *The Last of the Unjust*. Consecutive translations, integral to the form of *Shoah*, are edited out in the *Noah's Ark* section of *Four Sisters*. Footage Lanzmann had previously rejected from *Shoah* because the witness appeared to be self-consciously acting or playing a role comes in Düttmann's reading of *The Karski Report* to expose a certain element of the *cabotin* or ham as a necessary condition for any attempt to bear witness to the precise event of catastrophe. As we encounter these films based on footage not used in *Shoah*, what we see, then, is that it was not simply a problem of length that led to their exclusion. What Lanzmann says of *Four Sisters* echoes similar statements concerning all of the later films: "If they don't appear in *Shoah*, it's because they required a film entirely of their own. There was no other solution."[8]

VOYANCE

The inventiveness of the later films thus also sheds a different light on Lanzmann's famous dogmatism. Known for magisterial pronouncements and verdicts on Holocaust representation and its lim-

8. Ibid.

its, he appears in his later work to be a filmmaker guided by less rigid precepts. There is, however, one "law," first articulated in *The Patagonian Hare*, upon which he insists for both his journalistic articles and his films:

> I worked on these articles in the same way I worked on my films: in-depth research, distancing myself, forgetting myself, entering into the reasons and the madness, the lies and the silences of those I wished to portray or those I was questioning, until I reach a precise, hallucinatory state of hyper-alertness, a state that, to me, is the essence of the imagination. It is the one rule that makes it possible for me to reveal other people's truth—to flush it out if necessary—to make them real and alive for all time. It is my rule, at least. I consider myself a seer, and I have recommended that anyone who wants to write about cinema integrates this concept of "foreseeing" (*voyance*) into their critical arsenal.[9]

Before discussing this "law" in greater detail, it is important to recall how, for some critics, the post-*Shoah* Lanzmann appeared as an imposing, egocentric figure, as an *auteur* who claimed property rights and godlike authority. Called upon to pronounce judgment on major Holocaust-related works of film and literature—*Schindler's List, Life is Beautiful, The Kindly Ones, Son of Saul*—Lanzmann was no doubt a fierce and opinionated arbiter, famously impatient and unwilling to suffer fools. And yet, while he may have cultivated this persona in public, as the passage cited above suggests, his own writing and filmmaking were guided by a different set of principles, by a self-imposed law that obliged him to practice a certain kind of self-effacement, to put the self in parentheses, and to go so far as to "hallucinate" his way into the other's world, experience, and language. The Lanzmann who testily dismissed the questions posed to him by reporters or audience members, who was quick to find offense in slightly critical comments, or even in praise that he felt to be wrong-headed—the sacred monster he was as a public figure—was somehow at odds with the investigator, the questioner, the writer and filmmaker who felt that everything hinged on a very particular, intense kind of vigilance. What he called "*voyance*"—foreseeing or clairvoyance—may thus be said to name a tension or gap in Lanzmann himself, a mode of

9. Claude Lanzmann, *The Patagonian Hare*, trans. Frank Wynne (New York: Farrar, Straus and Giroux, 2012), 271. Originally published as *Le lièvre de Patagonie* (Paris: Gallimard, 2009), 394-95.

hyper-sensitivity or openness that dwelt upon what could not be integrated, and on what, as such, required his utmost attention.

In the interview included in this volume, Lanzmann returns to the question of integration, of what it means to be integrated or unintegrated, which he had addressed in *The Patagonian Hare* and elsewhere. Although being Jewish was, as he says, "one of the great pleasures of my life," he also insists that he had a need *not to know* about Judaism, not to learn Jewish prayers, not to study Rashi or Levinas, not to know how to say kaddish. Using a phrase that elsewhere suggests his lack of assimilation into *French* identity and nationality, he declares, this time with regard to *Jewishness*: "I am not at all integrated (*Je ne suis pas du tout intégré*)." If Jewishness precludes assimilation into French culture, so too does Frenchness block integration into Jewish culture. Lanzmann's apparent delight in reciting from memory French poetry by Rimbaud, Mallarmé, Leconte de Lille, and Saint-John Perse, which he exhibits at length in the interview with Nouchi and Simont, is paired with a proud admission that he does not know all the words to the Marseillaise.

This lack or refusal of integration, moreover, is linked to the very possibility of witnessing—and, for Lanzmann, therefore also of film-making. "There can be no true creation without opacity, the creator does not have to be transparent to himself, " he writes in *The Patagonian Hare*. "One thing is certain, the role of the witness, which became mine on my first visit to Israel and has constantly grown and reconfirmed itself with time and with each film, required me to be both within and without, as though I had been assigned a precise position."[10] *Voyance*—another version of the demand to "see beyond" that is central to Stark's reflection on *A Visitor from the Living* and that returns in Guyer's reading of *The Last of the Unjust* as a requirement to "un-see" the deceptions that obscure vision—is thus intimately, if paradoxically, linked to opacity. For it would seem that with each film after *Shoah*, as Lanzmann becomes increasingly attuned to and troubled by what remained other to *Shoah*, increasingly captive to and responsible for what could not be integrated into that film, his films increasingly reflect on the "precise position" of the filmmaker himself as witness. In the essays included here that discuss the films based on the *Shoah* outtakes, we see that for the filmmaker to become a witness—to himself, to

10. Lanzmann, *Patagonian Hare*, 231; *Le lièvre de Patagonie*, 337-38.

history, to others—means to occupy a "precise position" which is not simply that of a mediator or of someone indecisively stranded on the threshold. It is instead more dynamic. To be "both within and without," both inside and outside, was to find himself uniquely situated—or rather, uniquely non-situated and non-integrated—and indeed singularly called upon to act on the very limits he occupied, to displace them in such a way as to *take precisely the inside outside*," in Shoshana Felman's formulation.[11] What appears to be a "precise position" is thus not simply a particular attitude toward witnessing. It is also a position in which the very question of what it means to bear witness becomes increasingly fraught. Particularly in *A Visitor from the Living, Sobibor, The Karski Report,* and *The Last of the Unjust,* as Stark, Kasper, Düttmann, and Guyer respectively demonstrate, Lanzmann himself increasingly moves from the one who elicits testimony to the one who bears witness, though in ways that cannot be grounded on a prior knowledge or position but that need to be created each time anew. These moments of imaginative, creative witnessing are central to the readings of Lanzmann's late films presented here, from Stark's discussion of the imagined gaze of the *Muselmann* that Lanzmann discovers encrypted in the otherwise blind testimony of Rossel, to Kasper's insight into the ways Lanzmann's own cinematic precision mirrors the obsessive and necessary precision of Yehuda Lerner's account of the revolt at Sobibór, both in the ways it requires and disrupts precision, to Guyer's provocative contention that what Lanzmann bears witness to in *The Last of the Unjust* is not a previously silenced experience that is brought to life and incarnated in testimony, but rather the experience of a radically destabilizing testimony that "shakes the foundations of judgment and understanding" and that as such requires a reconceptualization of testimony in the "age of post-truth." In each of these cases, the "precise position" that Lanzmann occupies as filmmaker and witness is one that is shadowed by a certain impossibility. It is, as Düttmann shows, a position assigned and a responsibility dictated by the unprecedented nature of any event worthy of the name. "Precision emerges," Düttmann writes, "when it is impossible to put an event or a series of events . . . into perspective on the basis of their recognizability, their identifiability, and their

---

11. Felman, "The Return of the Voice: Claude Lanzmann's *Shoah*," in Felman and Laub, 242. Emphasis in the original.

assimilability, and when a witness must be sent out into absolute darkness—a deadly darkness and a darkness worse than death—so as to report back."

HOMELANDS

It is in light of Lanzmann's remarks and Düttmann's discussion of the paradoxical demands produced by the "precise position" of the witness that we may begin to appreciate the deeper significance of the filmmaker's frequently repeated claim, "my homeland is my film." Such a claim, we contend, is less an assertion of sovereignty than the acknowledgment of a drive to dwell—and to find creative energies—in spaces of dislocation and dispossession. In temporal terms, it is a drive to inhabit in the fullest way possible those moments when the veneer of the everyday, of accepted histories and established chronologies, wears thin and another temporal—or rather *atemporal*—dimension may be glimpsed.

In Prager's reading of *Tsahal*, this dimension is associated with mythical time: *Tsahal*, he argues, along with Lanzmann's first film, *Pourquoi Israël*, and *Shoah*, form a "myth-making trilogy" in which Israel becomes "a nation that exists to prevent a reoccurrence of the Holocaust." While acknowledging Lanzmann's explicit rejection of a teleological history according to which Israel would be the redemption of the Shoah, Prager suggests that in terms of its selection of voices as well as its visual landscape, *Tsahal* aligns itself with "the colonial myth that this land was, prior to 1948, more or less uninhabited." Yet *Tsahal* is also, Prager shows, nothing so much as a self-conscious reflection on the image as such and the way it works both to construct and to interrogate the myth of the nation as homeland. Images such as the famous cover of *Life* magazine featuring an apparently triumphant Israeli soldier after the Six Day War evince an opacity—what Prager calls a "bifocality"—that wrenches the image from any straightforwardly political or ideological meaning.

In contrast to the mythical and mythified temporality Prager sees at work in *Tsahal*, Levine's essay on *Napalm* associates the atemporal dimension of Lanzmann's late films with a moment of rupture—namely, a startling act of self-revelation, a practically wordless testimonial performance by Kim Kum-sun, the North Korean nurse with whom he had an unconsummated affair during a 1958 trip to Pyongyang. If myth suspends time by producing an imagined coherence between past, present, and future, the traumatic temporality that Levine identifies in *Napalm* operates according to an entirely different temporal logic. Such a logic is brought into focus in *Napalm* at the moment when Lanzmann, standing on a bridge in Pyongyang and evoking his meeting with Kim Kum-sun there 57 years earlier, suddenly switches languages and cites words uttered by Simon Srebnik toward the beginning of *Shoah*—"Ja, das ist das Platz" [sic], "Yes, this is the place." The citation invites the viewer to read one location in the place of the other, to consider whether *Shoah* may have had its own beginning in this encounter which will never have been one. In this sense *Shoah* may be said to remain open not only at its end but at its beginning. A film that undoubtedly comes after will have belatedly opened it to a time before.

The films that do not draw on the unused footage from *Shoah*—*Tsahal* and *Napalm*—thus also appear, in often surprising ways, as what we called earlier translations of what could not be contained in *Shoah*. Such translations will have kept it from coming to a close and, even more enigmatically, from ever having a definite beginning. They show that if, for Lanzmann, the Holocaust "still goes on," this is due not only to the sorts of historical aftermaths that are more obviously on display in the films that draw on the outtakes: the enduring traumatic impact on survivors, the unresolved debates about guilt and responsibility, the historiographical and philosophical dilemmas created by a history characterized at once by a totalizing regime of death and by startling resistances and unaccountable exceptions to every rule. This endlessness is also something staged within and for the filmmaker himself. Indeed, in light of the self-conscious role of cinematographer Lanzmann plays in *Napalm* and that Levine analyzes, we see how the films after *Shoah* increasingly foreground the filmmaker's own implication in and production of history.

"SO THAT EVERYTHING REMAINS PRESENT"

Thus even as Lanzmann throughout his later films seeks out moments of witnessing that "incarnate" the past, in which the past is not past but rather (re)lived and experienced in the present, he also increasingly creates moments in which he incarnates himself, in which he seeks to suspend time not only for those he interviews but for himself. We see this most clearly in his 2009 autobiography, *The Patagonian Hare*, discussed by Françoise Meltzer, and in the interview that closes this volume, "Self-Portrait at Ninety." The interview is wide-ranging, touching on Judaism and French national identity, Zionism and antisemitism, Lanzmann's love of poetry and his encounters with celebrated filmmakers, the meaning of 9/11, and his youth in the French resistance. He describes his views on seduction as well as a violently jealous encounter with a woman with whom he was infatuated. Such moments necessarily resonate with several widely-circulated accusations of sexual harassment on Lanzmann's part and with criticisms of the celebration of his image as a womanizer. The interview also leads him to reflect on questions of mortality: friends who have died, and what it means to be ninety. "It's like a barrier," he says, "a limit, that made it very real to me all of a sudden." And yet, as interviewer Juliette Simont observes, Lanzmann's attitude toward dying seems somewhat "peculiar." "There are people," she says, "who are really serene and who, when they reach that age bracket where the statistics are 'against them,' see that as the completion of a natural cycle and not as a scandal." To which Lanzmann replies, "Well, this non-scandal scandalizes me."

Meltzer's essay allows us to see how Lanzmann envisions filmmaking itself as a response to this scandal. For if his project might be understood, on the one hand, as an attempt to transmit the question of when it was too late, of when a death sentence was imposed and became inescapable, on the other hand, the insistent attempt to locate the moment and to connect it with a name—to be able to say, "Yes, this is the place"—constitutes the very possibility of incarnation. This effort to connect a name with a place, Meltzer notes, is for Lanzmann, as for Proust, "often elusive, if not simply impossibly unreal." And yet his life and work seemed driven by the need to create such connections. "Lanzmann's idea of 'incarnation' is a strange one," Meltzer notes. "It is the ability to 'be real' with a place."

How to be real with a place? How to connect a name to a place, how to grasp history in the consciousness of its presence, in its endlessness, rather than as a dead abstraction? How to connect *le lieu et la parole*, site and speech, to evoke one of the original titles for the film that would become *Shoah*? These questions, in the end, are what Lanzmann's images transmit. In "Self-Portrait at Ninety," he recognizes the potentially deadly power of images, the power of the image to destroy. "[E]very image worthy of the name has a crushing presence, it abolishes, in a sense, what has preceded it." Not only *Shoah* but all the films made after it have at their heart, according to Lanzmann, an attempt to resist this abolition: "there had to be recurrences, echoes, so that one image didn't abolish another, so that everything remains present." Just as *Shoah* needed to remain open and endless, so too do Lanzmann's later films themselves continue to ask how to resist the foreclosure, the finality, of the abolishing image, and in this way how to respond to the scandal of death, to death as scandal—to the scandal of an individual death and of a history of death.

In this sense, the image that provides the title for Lanzmann's autobiography is exemplary. As Meltzer notes, the title refers to a moment when, on a trip to Patagonia at the age of seventy, a hare appeared in Lanzmann's headlights. "It literally stabbed my heart with the fact that I was in Patagonia, that at that moment Patagonia and I *were real together*." And yet, if the Patagonian hare gives birth to a moment of epiphany, or to what Lanzmann calls "incarnation," it is because this moment opens itself to other recurrences and echoes: to the hare in the children's story he had memorized by Silvina Ocampo, "The Golden Hare," and that serves as the epigraph to his autobiography, in which a hare "stood illuminated by the sun like a holocaust on the graven plates of sacred history"; to the hares that swarm across the road as he drives with Simone de Beauvoir through a dense Serbian forest, trying to avoid killing them; and finally to those he sees and films at the Birkenau death camp, and who appear to him, as they flatten themselves and crawl beneath the barbed wire fence, as startling images of an impossible escape, of an impossible exception to the rule of death. Indeed, identifying himself with the hare, noting that "If there is any truth to metempsychosis and if I were given the choice, I would unhesitatingly choose to come back as a hare," Lanzmann sees the possibility of escape not just from particular life-threatening situations but, more metaphysically, from the deadening confines of time and of the self.[12] As we reflect on Lanzmann's late films and writing along with the contributors to this volume, we would like to imagine Lanzmann, like the hare caught in the headlights, looking back at the car, the truck, the train, the camera endlessly rolling, endlessly threatening abolition. And we would like to ask, along with Lanzmann, how to stop in amazement, to come to a halt and suspend a death sentence even if it may already be too late, and to be "real together."

12. Lanzmann, *The Patagonian Hare*, 244; *Le lièvre de Patagonie*, 355

I. The Shoah after "Shoah"

JARED STARK

How to See Nothing:
A Visitor from the Living

"I was the eyes, I had to see, and I had to, if you will, attempt to see beyond, if there was something to see beyond."[1] With these words, the Swiss doctor Maurice Rossel defines his charge as a delegate of the International Committee of the Red Cross (ICRC), in Claude Lanzmann's 1997 film *Un vivant qui passe* (*A Visitor from the Living*). But what does it mean to be "the eyes"? Rossel serves as the eyes of an organization whose protocols, combined with Rossel's own biases, produce a failure to see beyond the secrecy and deception of the Nazi "master liars." But in investigating the role of Rossel as a (failed) witness to history, *A Visitor from the Living* also raises the question of the role of the filmmaker and the film itself in being "the eyes," in "seeing beyond." In its efforts to lay bare what Rossel did not see, and to see beyond Rossel's denials, evasions, and bad faith, *A Visitor from the Living* does not simply oppose to Rossel's falsified account of history a full or correct one. Lanzmann's interest, of course, is also to correct a misrepresentation of history. But beyond such a correction, his film invites its viewers to think anew about cinema as a distinct form of historical witnessing rather than simply the repository

1. Claude Lanzmann, dir., *A Visitor from the Living* (1997). In transcribing and translating dialogue from the French, I have consulted the subtitles from the version of the film included on disc six of the *Shoah* Criterion Collection DVD box set (2013); the transcript of the raw footage from the Claude Lanzmann Shoah Collection of the United States Holocaust Memorial Museum (https://collections.ushmm.org/search/catalog/irn100416); and the transcript of the film published as Claude Lanzmann, *Un vivant qui passe: Auschwitz 1943 – Theresienstadt 1944* (Gallimard, 1997). In many cases these various transcripts and translations are incomplete or inaccurate and so have been modified by me accordingly. Other translations throughout are mine unless otherwise noted.

YFS 141, *Lanzmann after "Shoah,"* ed. Levine and Stark, © 2022 by Yale University.

of archived knowledge. What does it mean for the film *as a film* to bring into view the perspective of those who remained invisible to Rossel—in other words, to be their eyes?

This question arises at the point of encounter between two histories: the history of Rossel's (failed) effort to "see beyond" during World War II, and the history of *A Visitor from the Living* itself. The latter includes two moments: the time Lanzmann interviewed Rossel in 1979 and the transformation of the raw footage into a film in 1997. Although Rossel's work as a professional observer and investigator takes place under radically different conditions from Lanzmann's work as a filmmaker, the fact that Lanzmann chooses the Rossel interview as the first of the outtakes of *Shoah* to be made into a film of its own, more than ten years after the release of *Shoah*, suggests that aside from its historical value, there is something in the Rossel interview that speaks to Lanzmann *as a filmmaker*. Indeed, it would seem that what compels him to turn the Rossel footage into a film is precisely that he doesn't seem to know how to do this, that it is a challenge.[2] "I watched what we call the 'rushes,' the uncut material of the Rossel interview," Lanzmann states in an interview. "I found it nonetheless very strong. But it still had to be made into a film. I had nothing, I had absolutely no material. I had only Rossel, that was all."[3] Along with the other films Lanzmann made drawing on the 220 hours of unused footage created during the making of *Shoah*, *A Visitor from the Living* has generally been seen as an "appendix," "addendum," or "satellite" to *Shoah*.[4] But it is more than a mere footnote to *Shoah* because it calls upon Lanzmann to discover a new way to make a film. In important ways, it marks a critical departure from its predecessor.

2. On Lanzmann's attraction to challenges for their own sake, see his "Self-Portrait at Ninety" in this volume.

3. "Deux enfants de *Shoah*," interview with Hélène Frappat, 2003. *Shoah* Criterion Collection box set, disc six.

4. Janet Malcom refers to the film as an "addendum" in "Of One Man Who Saw Evil, and Preferred Not to Focus," *New York Times*, October 7, 1999, qtd. in Sue Vice, "Shoah and the Archive," in *The Construction of Testimony: Claude Lanzmann's Shoah and Its Outtakes*, ed. ErinMcGlothlin, Brad Prager, and Marcus Zisselsberger (Detroit: Wayne State University Press, 2020), 65. Jennifer Cazenave refers to it as an "appendix" in *An Archive of the Catastrophe: The Unused Footage of Claude Lanzmann's Shoah* (Albany: State University of New York Press, 2019), 220; Sue Vice speaks of it as a "satellite" in Vice, "Shoah and the Archive," 65.

A FILM MADE OF NOTHING

The cinematic form of *A Visitor from the Living* is noticeably different from the three films Lanzmann had made previously. Most obviously, it is shorter: 68 minutes compared to the three hours of *Pourquoi Israël* (1973), the nine and one-half hours of *Shoah* (1985), and the more than five hours of *Tsahal* (1994). As such, it invites a different kind of viewing experience and a different kind of discussion, particularly in comparison to the epic length of *Shoah*. As Lanzmann notes in a comment that he insists is "not simply a joke" during his 1990 seminar at Yale, "after nine and one-half hours nobody has the desire to [talk]."[5] But what makes this experiment in brevity possible in the first place is an underlying transformation of method. Rather than a multilingual, polyphonic cast of characters occupying very different and even incompatible positions, the film focuses on a single protagonist, thus inaugurating a form that all the later films using *Shoah* outtakes would assume.[6] As we will see, this form also casts the filmmaker in a new role.

A Visitor from the Living draws on the 2-1/4-hour interview that Lanzmann conducted in 1979 with Rossel, who had worked for the ICRC in Berlin from April 12, 1944, to January 1, 1945, when he was twenty-seven years old. During this eight-month period, he quickly became a "specialist" in visiting internment camps in Germany, the Sudetenland, and southwestern Poland—primarily prisoner-of-war camps, as Rossel is at pains to specify, but also several "civilian" concentration camps.[7] The film focuses on two of these visits: an unannounced and unaccompanied visit he made to the territory of Auschwitz on September 29, 1944, and a long-negotiated and

5. Lanzmann, "Seminar with Claude Lanzmann 11 April 1990," in "Literature and the Ethical Question," ed. Claire Nouvet, *Yale French Studies* 79 (1991), 82.

6. Yehuda Lerner in *Sobibor, October 14, 1943, 4 p.m.* (2001); Jan Karski in *The Karski Report* (2010); Benjamin Murmelstein in *The Last of the Unjust* (2013); and Ruth Elias, Ada Lichtman, Paula Biren, and Hanna Marton in the four films, each with its own title, that make up Lanzmann's last work, *Four Sisters* (2018).

7. Sébastian Farré and Yan Schubert, "L'illusion de l'objectif: Le delégué du CIRC [Comité international de la Croix-Rouge] Maurice Rossel et les photographies de Theresienstadt," *Le mouvement social* 227/2 (2009): 73. The dates of Rossel's mission in Berlin are drawn from his personnel file in the ICRC archive, as reported by Farré and Schubert. It is unclear why Rossel, in his interview with Lanzmann, states that his work in Berlin began in 1942.

carefully-orchestrated tour of the Theresienstadt ghetto (the Czech Terezín) three months earlier, on June 23, 1944.[8] In the vast militarized zone of Auschwitz, Rossel does not seem to have reached Auschwitz I or the Auschwitz-Birkenau death camp. He did have a meeting with an SS officer he describes as the camp commandant, but, as he expected, he was not permitted to inspect any parts of the camp that held prisoners.[9] The meticulously planned guided visit of Theresienstadt was another matter. There, accompanied by two Danish consular officials, he was flanked by a representative of the German Red Cross (under Nazi control) and six SS officers. Their scripted and carefully monitored tour guide was Paul Eppstein, the leader of the Judenrat (the Jewish Council, charged by the SS to administer certain aspects of existence in the ghetto) at the time. Rossel was shown, among other sights, a firefighters' drill, children at play and in school, an orchestral performance of Verdi's *Requiem*, and a soccer match.[10] He was permitted as well to take photographs. Following the visit, he submitted what Lanzmann calls a "rosy" report, one that for the most part reproduces what he heard from his German hosts and from Eppstein. A Theresienstadt survivor later recalled that Eppstein "was sure, as he told us, that the members of the commission would realize the bluff the Nazis were putting up."[11] But Rossel did not realize the bluff. Rather than a place ruled by terror, what he saw and reported was, to quote the report he submitted to the ICRC, "a town living an almost normal life."[12]

8. In his interview with Lanzmann, Rossel has difficulty recalling the date of his visit to Auschwitz. Lanzmann supplies the year 1943, which Rossel accepts. The published transcript of the film, subtitled "Auschwitz 1943 – Theresienstadt 1944," repeats this apparent error. The official report appears as "Visite au Commandant du camp d'Auschwitz d'un délégué du CICR (septembre 1944)," in *Revue internationale de la Croix-Rouge*, 28th year, 328 (April 1946): 281-82.

9. The precise details of Rossel's visit to Auschwitz remain uncertain, particularly as to the questions of whom exactly he met and where in the Auschwitz territory this meeting took place. For a careful consideration of the available historical evidence, as well as of later allusions to and rumors concerning this visit, see Fabrice Cahen, "Le comité international de la Croix-Rouge (CICR) et les visites de camps: Étude d'une controverse," *Revue d'histoire de la Shoah* 172 (2001/2): 43-56.

10. Farré and Schubert, "L'illusion de l'objectif," 77-79.

11. Max E. Mannheimer, "From Theresienstadt to Auschwitz," in *Jewish Survivors Report: Documents of Nazi Guilt* no. 3. Qtd. in Cahen, "Le CICR et les visites de camps," 29n.4

12. For an illuminating discussion of Rossel's photographs, see Farré and Schubert, "L'illusion de l'objectif."

Lanzmann's questions zero in on a series of spectacular failures. We hear repeatedly how at Auschwitz Rossel saw nothing:

Claude Lanzmann: And what did you see of the camp?
Maurice Rossel: Nothing. Of the camp, I saw barracks.

CL: Of Birkenau, you suspected nothing?
MR: No.
CL: The Birkenau death camp is one kilometer from the main camp.
MR: Exactly. Nothing.

CL: . . . you are there and you see nothing.
MR: And you see nothing. Yes, that's what I mean, to bring back nothing. No information that is valuable.

MR: I saw neither the glow of flames nor smoke.
CL: Nothing?
MR: Nothing.[13]

The visit to Theresienstadt is similarly structured around a failure to see. Rossel knows it is a "staged visit," "like a theatrical performance," "a farce," "a setup (*mise en décor*)." He realizes that he was shown "a Potemkin camp, a fake camp." Yet he repeatedly maintains that there was nothing to see beyond the façade:

A man who spends months, as a profession, visiting prisoner camps, is used to being winked at to draw his attention to something. It happened often. But here, nothing, nothing.

You expect a wink, a suggestion, something. But I got nothing. I mean nothing. Nothing is nothing. Nothing is nothing. (*Rien, c'est rien.*)

As we hear Rossel's repeated insistence that at Auschwitz and Theresienstadt he saw nothing, and that there was nothing to see, that "nothing is nothing," these nothings find an echo in Lanzmann's later description of the raw footage of the interview as "nothing" ("I had nothing, I had absolutely no material"). To see "nothing" in the raw footage is also, then, to recognize that the question of how and why Rossel sees nothing lies at the heart of the film. To make this nothing into a film, in turn, means to see Rossel's nothing in a different way from Rossel himself. For Rossel, nothing means an absence of apparent evidence. The film, by contrast, brings nothing into the

---

13. Throughout, unbracketed ellipses indicate ellipses in the original (interruptions or pauses in speech), while bracketed ellipses indicate my omissions.

field of vision. Rather than seeing blindly, it attempts to see the blindness. Nothing is not nothing: it is precisely what must be seen.

THE BANALITY OF VISION

How and why, then, does Rossel see nothing? Intervening in and contributing to a historical debate concerning Rossel's missions as well as the broader wartime role of the ICRC—and by extension, of the international community—*A Visitor from the Living* exposes two overlapping sources of blindness. First, there are the limitations of the professional gaze, and particularly of the strategies it employs to maintain a claim to neutrality and objectivity. "That's what I was shown. I have nothing to add. I couldn't invent things I didn't see," Rossel maintains, echoing his description of institutional conventions in portions of the interview not included in the film: that "no personal interpretation" and "no sentiments should be included."[14] Along with this professional protocol, the ICRC adhered to a legalism and to a policy of political neutrality and nonintervention that prevented it from acting more forcefully to investigate and call attention to the genocide of the Jews, despite information dating at least to late 1942.[15] Fabrice Cahen argues that these conventions are what primarily explain Rossel's misapprehension of the reality of Theresienstadt: "What we can take away from the example of Maurice Rossel is the suppression of the individual conscience of an employee who, during certain of his activities, proved to be too respectful of the instructions sent down from above and who, above all, tended to think of himself as a function more than as a subject."[16] Echoing Hannah Arendt's analysis of Adolph Eichmann as a man wholly absorbed by his function, this understanding of Rossel's blindness attributes it to what we might call a banality of vision. Seeing becomes a bureaucratic function. The claim to neutrality, to objective vision, thus obstructs rather than enables the ability to "see beyond." Rossel and the ICRC consequently become instrumentalized by and complicit with the Germans.

---

14. Claude Lanzmann Shoah Collection, United States Holocaust Memorial Museum.

15. Jean-Claude Favez, *The Red Cross and the Holocaust*, ed. and trans. John and Beryl Fletcher (Cambridge, UK: Cambridge University Press, 1999), esp. 21-52.

16. Cahen, "Le CICR et les visites de camps," 60.

This banality of vision becomes apparent first in Rossel's account of his visit to Auschwitz. His account of groups of emaciated prisoners along his route in the camp territory comes in response to Lanzmann's observation that even well after the war, "one is gripped by a feeling of horror" at Auschwitz. Rossel replies:

> MR: Yes, the sensation of horror, you know, you would have had it even more if, upon entering, you had crossed paths with lines of prisoners, right? In groups of thirty or forty, skinny skeletons.
> CL: Yes?
> MR: Yes. When you cross paths with them like that, I don't know, four or five hundred on the route you are taking . . .
> CL: Seeing those people, did you feel these were people who were suffering greatly, in fact who were dying or condemned to death?
> MR: That's what it was. They were truly walking skeletons, because they weren't fed, were they?
> CL: Yes.
> MR: Only their eyes still lived.
> CL: Only their eyes still lived, yes.
> MR: Yes.
> CL: Those were the ones they call *Muselmann*. They have a very intense gaze.
> MR: Yes, very intense, very intense, those people observing you with an incredible intensity, right? As if to say, "Oh, here is one now . . . a visitor from the living. (*En voilà un qui vient . . . un vivant qui passe.*)"

Despite having encountered these "walking skeletons," and despite having just heard from a British prisoner of war of the rumored existence of a gas chamber at Auschwitz,[17] Rossel recalls his meeting with the SS officer that same day as a matter of routine, where he was received "very politely," where they spoke about "this and that," and where it was "totally out of the question" to ask about the treatment of the Jews. Lanzmann suggests that "this is after all, quite an astonishing thing, to talk in a kind of intimate way with these people." But Rossel likens his meeting to an ordinary conversation, in fact to the very conversation he is having with Lanzmann: "It seems unbelievable, but we spoke like I'm speaking to you. [. . .] It was a piece of

---

17. Rossel does not mention this detail in his interview with Lanzmann, but he writes about having heard this rumor in his report on his visit to Auschwitz. "Visite au Commandant du camp d'Auschwitz," 282.

theater that we played. That's all, that's all." To Rossel, the theatricality of this encounter renders it inconsequential. It is little more than a game. This same sense of indifference resonates as well in the phrase that provides the title to the film. As Ophir Levy suggests, "this 'vivant qui passe' designates nothing more [. . .] than the terrible lightness of the passerby, of the tourist."[18]

Perhaps even more striking in Rossel's account of this encounter with the *Muselmänner* is the disavowal of the first-person that takes place when he casts his encounter with them as something *you* would have seen had you been there, as he speaks of them "observing *you*." I will return at the end of this essay to this scene, and to how Lanzmann and the film might imagine and hear a different form of address in these eyes that speak in a very particular way. For Rossel, however, it would seem that whatever they convey is suppressed in the service of maintaining a certain distance, of not seeing himself as their addressee. The meeting he then conducts with the SS officer can conform to routine and result in what he blithely calls his "little report"—"little" due to a banal vision that circumscribes what seems to him worth seeing and asking about and reporting, what to him counts as "information": "And you see nothing. Yes, that's what I want to say, take back nothing. No information that is valuable."

This banality of vision also characterizes the account of his visit to Theresienstadt. He can only report what he saw, even if everything he saw was "a farce": "It was a visit planned by the SS, about which one could only say, 'I saw that, I saw this, I photographed this thing.'" The absence of a wink, of a clandestine note slipped into his pocket, of someone taking it upon themselves to say, "I'm going to scream. I'll speak up"—the absence of what his experience at prisoner-of-war camps had led him to expect—blinds him to the "complete terror," as Lanzmann will describe it, that ruled the ghetto and that precluded any unscripted gestures. The Jews, he says, echoing his account of his meeting with the SS officer in Auschwitz, are "actors" in a "piece of theater." But when they do not break out of their roles and reveal a backstage reality, he assumes that their performance is all there is. If Rossel does not suspect that the very absence of the usual winks and clandestine notes is itself the clue—the clue left, as it were, out in the open—this is because what does not conform to a preconceived

18. Ophir Levy, "La forteresse et l'aveu: À propos d'*Un vivant qui passe* de Claude Lanzmann," *Témoigner: Entre histoire et mémoire* 107 (April-June 2010): 56.

idea of what would be "beyond" remains invisible to him, as his hosts cannily anticipated. As Lanzmann notes ironically, "that you were duped was no surprise, because they wanted to dupe you."

AN "IMPRESSION"

A second and overlapping source of blindness that the film troublingly brings to light is the knot of antisemitic stereotypes warping Rossel's vision and memory. As opposed to his vivid recollection of the SS officer he met with at Auschwitz—"He was a young man, a very elegant young man, with blue eyes, very distinguished, very friendly"—Lanzmann underscores the way Paul Eppstein, the leader of the Theresienstadt Judenrat with whom Rossel spent at least several hours, remained somehow invisible to him. "What did he look like, physically?" "I don't see him. I see an elderly man, I see . . . but no, I would be . . . no, I don't see him. I can't say that I see him, and I can't describe him to you." This sense becomes more pointed in Rossel's "impression" of the Jews of Theresienstadt:

> I believed, and I still do, that I was shown a camp for notable Jews, for the privileged. That's the impression it left on me. I never put it in writing, in black and white. I found the behavior of the people there quite unpleasant, the attitude of the Jews in that city. The behavior of the people was also such that . . . it was . . . very antipathetic. The attitude of the Jews in this . . . this city. . . . I had the impression that there were really Jews there— and I still think the same—who, using dollars from their Portuguese bank accounts, bought a better situation for themselves and stayed alive.

To Rossel, the Jews of Theresienstadt are the "privileged," the "*Prominenten*," who he believes are culpable of buying their security at the expense of other Jews and participating willingly in the Nazi charade in order to survive. As Swiss historians Jean Farré and Yan Schubert observe, this vision is "nourished by antisemitic stereotypes associating the Jews with a social elite and with wealth, very common in Swiss society during the war [. . .]. These explain perhaps the susceptibility of the delegate to the mise-en-scène proposed by the SS."[19]

The stereotypes that the historians note were common in Europe during the war surface as well several decades after the war as Lanzmann interviews Rossel. Consider in this regard the following three

19. Farré and Schubert, "L'illusion de l'objectif," 83.

statements, the first couched in the past, the other two in the present. Describing the sense of physical revulsion he felt at Jewish passivity, Rossel reports: "Well, what I have seen beyond was this subservience and this passivity, which is something I couldn't stomach (*que je n'avais pas digéré*)."

Returning again to this sense of revulsion, he now shifts to the present:

> But here, nothing, nothing. A docility, a passivity which was to me . . . that still creates the worst malaise.

> I've never myself had a gun to my back, but finally this passivity is really something very difficult to swallow.

The shift in tenses suggests the resurfacing of something irrepressible, "something very difficult to swallow," welling up again in the moment of speaking. Swiss film critic Alain Freudiger notes that Rossel frequently seems ill at ease during the interview. When he shifts in his seat and leans towards the ashtray with his cigarillo, as if trying to escape the frame, this brings into view, Freudiger argues, the ways that the film upsets the claims to neutrality that Rossel makes as a delegate of the ICRC and as Swiss. Rather than remaining in the comfortable role of one who reports on others' testimony, "he is disgusted at becoming the center of his testimony. He wants to be neutral."[20] The physical malaise created by his impression of the behavior of the Jews adds another dimension to this analysis. What may disgust Rossel is not only a challenge to his neutrality. It is also an exposure (conscious or not) to *his own* passivity. This passivity, the film suggests, belongs not to the Jews but to Rossel himself, who projects it onto the Jews, in the form of a disavowed fear that Sartre described as the very mechanism of antisemitism.[21] "You should have gone into the huts,

20. Alain Freudiger, "La place de l'Helvète: Considérations sur *Un vivant qui passe*," *Décadrages* 12 (2008): 81.

21. "We are now in a position to understand the anti-Semite. He is a man who is afraid. Not of the Jews, to be sure, but of himself, of his own consciousness, of his liberty, of his instincts, of his responsibilities, of solitariness, of change, of society, and of the world." Jean-Paul Sartre, *Anti-Semite and Jew* (1944), trans. George J. Becker (New York: Schocken, 1976), 38. In his autobiography, Lanzmann discusses the impact of this text on him: "When, four years later, after the war, I read his *Réflexions sur la question juive* (*Anti-Semite and Jew*), I first devoured the chapter 'The Portrait of the Anti-Semite,' and with every line I felt alive again or, to be more precise, I felt I had been given permission to live." *The Patagonian Hare*, trans. Frank Wynne (New York: Farrar, Straus and Giroux, 2012), 78.

the barracks, where the people lived just like in Auschwitz," Lanzmann insists. "They had prepared for you a Potemkin ghetto, completely [. . .] Did you sense it at that time?" And when Rossel protests that "I couldn't invent things I didn't see," Lanzmann replies: "But you could have. . ." As *A Visitor from the Living* exposes Jewish passivity as the fantasized lens through which Rossel sees—and fails to see—Theresienstadt, it does this, then, by opposing to it a vision of Rossel's own passivity. While Rossel claims to see nothing, the film makes this nothing visible.

But in order to do this, it cannot simply rely on Rossel. Still seemingly entrapped by the banality of vision and by a specular antisemitism that projects culpability onto the Jews, he defends the report he submitted:

> MR: I made a report that I stand by and maintain as entirely valid.
> CL: Do you regret your report today?
> MR: I couldn't have made any other. I'd sign it again.
> CL: Knowing everything I've told you?
> MR: Yes, of course.

The inconsistencies, evasions, and denials that Lanzmann's questions elicit, as Rossel fails to see his blindness even thirty years later and holds to the validity of his report, erode his credibility as a witness. He becomes, as Levy observes, "the incarnation of a failure of testimony, of a negation of testimony."[22]

LANZMANN'S COUNTER-REPORT

One might imagine that if the form of the film were different, if it were simply an appendix to or extension of *Shoah*, that it might counter Rossel's testimony through the patient and painstaking juxtaposition of other eyewitness testimonies. One might recall, for instance, the juxtaposition of Simon Srebnik's testimony with that of Frau Michelson in the opening sequences of *Shoah*. "Nobody meets anyone in *Shoah* . . . but there is a corroboration in spite of this," Lanzmann states.[23] But this material calls upon Lanzmann to invent a different way of confronting Rossel's prevarications, evasions, and blind spots. Now, Lanzmann himself assumes responsibility for providing an alternative account. The text that scrolls up a black screen

22. Levy, "La forteresse et l'aveu," 55-56.
23. Lanzmann, "Seminar with Claude Lanzmann 11 April 1990," 84.

and that Lanzmann recites at the opening of *A Visitor from the Living* explains that the interview with Rossel was omitted from *Shoah* "for reasons of length and architecture." Yet we might suspect that it is also the foregrounded, excessively visible role that Lanzmann plays in this interview that made it incompatible with the form of *Shoah* and that required it become a film of its own. Thus, in contrast and in response to Rossel's vague and contradictory recollections of what he knew of Auschwitz at the time of his visit, it is Lanzmann who insists that Rossel, without acknowledging it, was at the heart of an extermination camp, and that anything he thought he learned from the SS officer with whom he met were the statements of a "master liar." And where Rossel is taken in by the masquerade of "almost normal life" performed for him in the Theresienstadt ghetto, it is Lanzmann who supplies the real: that the ghetto had undergone a massive "beautification action" to fool the ICRC delegation, and that soon after the visit the fake synagogue, the music pavilion, the nursery and playground and more were dismantled; that the number of calories given to the Jews was half what Rossel was told and reported; that the mortality rate in the ghetto was more than ten times what Rossel believed; that in order to mitigate the appearance of overpopulation, five thousand Jews had been sent to Auschwitz in preparation for the visit;[24] and that, far from being an *Endlager* or "final destination" whose inhabitants might be able to survive the war, for nearly 100,000 Jews it was instead a transit camp from which the majority were sent to be killed at Treblinka or Auschwitz.[25]

As these facts accumulate, the film does more than merely interrogate Rossel's version of history. It also launches an interrogation into the authority of the visible, exposing the ways that Rossel's blindness is tied to his "stubborn confusion of vision and knowledge."[26] He believes, for instance, that the photographs he was invited to take in Theresienstadt "say even more than ten thousand words, isn't it so?"

24. This is the number Lanzmann cites. 7,503 Jews from Theresienstadt were sent to Auschwitz in three transports, on May 15, May 16, and May 18, 1944, in preparation for the ICRC visit in June. United States Holocaust Memorial Museum, *Holocaust Encyclopedia*, https://encyclopedia.ushmm.org/content/en/article/theresienstadt-concentrationtransit-camp-for-german-and-austrian-jews.

25. This is the number Lanzmann gives. According the *Holocaust Encyclopedia*, of the 141,184 persons who were at one time or another interned in Theresienstadt, approximately 85,000 were deported and died in other locations, while more than 35,000 died while interned in the ghetto itself. Ibid.

26. Levy, "La forteresse et l'aveu," 56.

But where Rossel believes his photos speak truth, they were, as historian Jean-Claude Favez notes, "no more truthful than movie stills."[27] As Lanzmann observes, the photographs had no way of seeing beyond the deception because they were an integral part of it: "precisely, they hoped you would take those photos."

In place of Rossel's captive and complicit vision, Lanzmann, then, is called upon to present a report of his own, a counter-report, that sees through and beyond the deceptive power of the Nazi-generated images. What underwrites this counter-report is not merely hindsight. It is also a critical view of images themselves. This question acquires particular urgency in light of the ways that Rossel's blinded and false images themselves carried deadly force. Lanzmann underscores the complicity of Rossel's report with murder in evoking the ways that the "beautification action" in Theresienstadt spelled the deaths of thousands. When Rossel refers to the Jews as "actors," Lanzmann counters that that "the directors (metteurs en scène) were the Germans." What takes place in preparation for the ICRC visit to the ghetto is thus the construction of an image, a mise-en-scène, a work of editing, that is literally murderous. In reproducing and accepting as factual the directorial vision of his German hosts, Rossel's report and his photographs become the accomplices of this vision, particularly as they serve the purposes of Nazis propaganda.[28] Where Rossel falls back on the cliché that a picture speaks a thousand words, Lanzmann underscores the potential of the image to silence and to kill.

This interrogation of the image culminates in the last moments of the film, where Lanzmann reads aloud a translation into French of the last speech that Eppstein, the leader of the Judenrat, gave to his fellow Jews, three months after Rossel's visit. After reading this speech and relating Eppstein's execution by the SS three days later,

27. Favez, The Red Cross and the Holocaust, 44.

28. As Lanzmann notes in an omitted part of the interview, the report "helped them to make others believe that, in the end, Theresienstadt . . . was not bad, was not so bad." Claude Lanzmann Shoah Collection. A copy of the report along with several photographs were sent to Eberhard von Thadden, head of the Jewish desk of the German Foreign Ministry. Foreign correspondents in Berlin were presented with Rossel's report in the month following the inspection, and von Thadden, as he wrote in a letter to Rossel thanking him for the report, would produce Rossel's photographs "on occasions when foreigners turn[ed] to him again concerning alleged horrors in Theresienstadt." Qtd. In Nicholas Stargardt, Witnesses of War: Children's Lives under the Nazis (New York: Knopf, 2006), 55.

Figure 1. 01:07:25

Lanzmann concludes: "It's heartbreaking, this text. (*C'est déchirant comme texte*)." A film focused on the problem of seeing thus ends on the word "text" and on an image of Lanzmann slowly replacing this text into his binder and setting it on a table off-screen (Fig.1).

A Visitor from the Living is thus not only about Rossel. It is also about the ways that images can produce a catastrophically selective vision. As such, Rossel and the Nazi *metteurs en scène* provide a dark reflection of Lanzmann's own work as a film director. As has often been observed, Lanzmann was particularly attuned to the potential violence associated with making films; he would compare both shooting and editing film to acts of killing.[29] This association surfaces as well in the ways that *A Visitor from the Living* can be seen

29. Lanzmann's association of film shooting with killing, as Judith Kasper and Michael Levine demonstrate, assumes signal importance in *The Last of the Unjust*. "The Persistence of the Witness," *Critical Inquiry* 46 (Winter 2020): 386-87. On film editing as killing, see Lanzmann, "Seminar with Claude Lanzmann 11 April 1990," 82-83, and Cazenave, *The Archive of the Catastrophe*, 47-50.

as a counter-report not only to Rossel, but also to Steven Spielberg's widely acclaimed and enormously popular *Schindler's List*, released in 1993, four years before *A Visitor from the Living*. Viewed in light of Lanzmann's frequently-voiced criticisms of Spielberg's film, *A Visitor from the Living* constitutes, as Cazenave argues, a "refutation of the 'quite rosy' depiction of rescue staged in *Schindler's List*."[30]

But to Cazenave's observation that *A Visitor from the Living* makes a *historical* argument contra Spielberg, I would add an essentially *cinematographic* one. For Lanzmann's critique of *Schindler's List* does not merely or even primarily concern the inaccuracy of foregrounding a story of rescue. "I feel he has made an illustrated version of *Shoah*, he has supplied images where there were none in *Shoah*," Lanzmann writes in 1994. "Images kill the imagination and make it possible for people to identify with Schindler, who is a highly debatable 'hero.' [. . .] My fundamental criticism of Spielberg is that he shows the Holocaust through the eyes of a German."[31] Lanzmann's criticism of Spielberg thus coincides with the case against Rossel: the Swiss envoy also sees Theresienstadt through the eyes of the Germans. But this annihilating perspective is not only due to the historical positionality of Schindler or of Rossel. It is also, Lanzmann suggests, a question of cinematic form. What produces a falsified vision, what circumscribes Spielberg's and his viewer's perspective and routes it fatally through the eyes of a German, is the image itself. To "illustrate" is literally to light up, to clear up, to elucidate. It is to produce an image that claims to reveal and to explain. If images that illustrate kill the imagination, this is because they constitutively cannot account for what cannot be explained, for what remains obscure, unseen, invisible. They leave nothing to the imagination—which is also to say that what they cannot see is *nothing*.

THE PERFORMANCE OF TRANSPARENCY

Understood as a film that continues and even radicalizes the critique of cinematic illustration already at work in *Shoah*, *A Visitor from the Living* stands out for the seeming transparency of its filmic strategies. In contrast to *Shoah*'s epic length, its contrapuntal form, multiple

30. Cazenave, *The Archive of the Catastrophe*, 220.

31. Claude Lanzmann, "Why Spielberg Has Distorted the Truth," *Guardian Weekly* (Manchester), April 3, 1994. Originally published as Claude Lanzmann, "Holocauste, la representation impossible," *Le monde*, March 3, 1994, Arts et spectacles, vii.

locations, and extended cast of characters, *A Visitor from the Living* takes place almost entirely in a single room in Rossel's home—his living room or study. After the scrolling text that Lanzmann recites at the beginning, in the remaining 62 minutes of the film, the camera focuses on Rossel for all but six minutes. Due to its minimal editing and limited use of montage, the film appears as an almost transparent, unmediated document.[32] Whereas Lanzmann, after the making of *Shoah*, consistently emphasized the importance of his use of mise en scène in eliciting testimonies of extraordinary power—staging Abraham Bomba's testimony in a barber shop, to cite only the most famous example—*A Visitor from the Living* seems deliberately to eschew such strategies. Here we have nothing but the filmmaker and his subject, sitting in a room and talking. It is a film almost without style, an anti-film.

And yet this seeming transparency, I would suggest, serves not to leave the image behind but rather to redirect our attention to the ways the film confronts, and transgresses, the limits of its own perspective. This occurs because the near-total elimination of obvious signs of style is so explicit, so blatant, that it becomes itself a radical style. Rather than fight with the "nothing" of the raw material, the film foregrounds that nothing and discovers in that nothing what makes it into a film. What this also means is that those few moments when something does unsettle the focus of the interview become even more powerful, more potentially significant. In these moments, rather than exercising selective vision and producing exclusions and silences, the film opens up perspectives that cannot be fully grasped either by Rossel or by Lanzmann.

This takes place, for one, in a strategy the film employs that continues the methods of *Shoah*, namely the three moments in the film when location shots of Terezín replace the image of Rossel's study even as we continue to hear the interview unfold, now as voice-over. As the camera scans the near-empty streets of the former ghetto site, sometimes from an upper story or rooftop, at other times at street level from a moving vehicle, Terezín appears in ways similar to the landscapes in *Shoah*. It is what Lanzmann calls a "non-site of memory," a place that "no longer resembles what it had been" and thus shows us

---

32. See Brad Prager's distinction between document and documentary in *After the Fact: Holocaust Documentary in the Twenty-First Century* (New York: Bloomsbury, 2015), 13-14.

not what happened there but rather an absence of traces.[33] To viewers
familiar with Lanzmann's earlier films, these moments can appear as
the signature of the style of an *auteur* and as the imposition by Lanzmann of his particular perspective. And yet the very opacity of these
location shots instead suspends the power of any definitive authorita-
tive perspective. All they show is that there is nothing to see.

At other moments, however, the film dislodges the perspective of
the filmmaker using strategies absent from *Shoah*. The first involves
what appears to be an accident. When a child is heard coughing in
the background, Rossel calls for a cut: "Excuse me. I think we have
to stop filming and then get rid of this child. [calling to someone off-
screen:] 'Take him out!' Excuse me, we can't have him coughing in
here."[34] Anticipating the ways the film will critique Rossel's selective
vision, the film keeps this moment intact, contravening his orders
and his idea of what ought to be part of the film and of what we
should see. However accidental the child's cough may be, Lanzmann
understands it as a crucial moment in his encounter with Rossel.[35]
"In fact," Lanzmann suggests, "it's a Freudian gesture (*acte manqué*).
The one he really wanted to throw out was me."[36] As Lanzmann acts
against Rossel's principle of selection by *not* editing out this moment,
he also introduces a perspective that he identifies with—the child's—
but that also remains outside the frame—a perspective that we can
only imagine. In a later discussion of the film, Lanzmann recalls the
circumstances of the interview in terms that resonate here: "I was
afraid the entire time that he would stand up and say, 'That's enough.
Stop. I refuse to speak further.' That's why I was extremely prudent
with my questions."[37] During the interview, then, Rossel did have
the power to declare a "cut," to usurp the role of the director and to
silence the story Lanzmann wanted to tease out. Lanzmann in turn
must act as if what is unfolding is a normal conversation between
host and guest, reserved and decorous. But in preserving the child's

33. Marc Chevrie and Hervé Le Roux, "Site and Speech: An Interview with Claude
Lanzmann about *Shoah*," trans. Stuart Liebman, in *Claude Lanzmann's* Shoah: *Key
Essays*, ed. Liebman (Oxford: Oxford University Press, 2007), 39.

34. It is interesting to note that these words are omitted from the published transcript of the film. See Lanzmann, *Vivant*, 18.

35. In his essay on *Four Sisters* in this volume, Stuart Liebman notes the importance of another seeming accident, dogs barking in the background, in the *The Hippocratic Oath*.

36. "Deux enfants de *Shoah*."

37. Ibid.

cough, he at the same time identifies a different dynamic at work in the encounter, one in which he is not only an inquisitive and polite guest, but also a figure whom Rossel sends into exile, whom he expels. What appears on the one hand as an accident, even a mere instantiation of the reality effect, also opens up the perspective of this invisible off-screen figure, of someone who coughs as if he were experiencing something difficult to swallow.

Just as the coughing child dislodges the centrality and authority of the filmmaker's perspective, a similar effect occurs, however counterintuitively, precisely at the moments when the camera focuses on the filmmaker himself. *Shoah* noticeably rejected the inclusion of reverse or reaction shots, of the filmmaker as interviewer or listener, as part of a larger rejection of the cinematic gestures of conventional documentary. In *Shoah*, the filmmaker only appears on screen when he is in the same frame with others—for instance, in the opening sequence, walking with Simon Srebnik through a field in Chelmno—or in establishing shots, as when we glimpse Lanzmann's eyes in the rearview mirror as he drives into the town of Treblinka. In this light, the three reverse shots that appear in *A Visitor from the Living* could appear as a reversion to such conventional techniques. But they do more than meets the eye.

These reverse shots, as an examination of the raw footage confirms, are non-synchronous with the interview itself. Filmed using one camera, they are spliced in from footage taken after the interview was concluded, where Lanzmann spends five minutes in various poses of silent listening. In the first reverse shot, approximately twelve minutes into the film, Lanzmann appears very briefly in the role of silent listener, for just two seconds. This occurs just after Rossel, as part of a preliminary discussion of his role with the ICRC, describes negotiations he conducted in German prisoner of war camps, where he would use Allied POW camps holding German soldiers as leverage:

> MR: It's the only way to talk, and absolutely horrible when a man's life is at stake, but at last, there's no other . . . It was bargaining through and through, and it worked.
> CL: And it worked?
> MR: It worked very well.

At this moment, in a brief transition before the discussion moves to Rossel's life in Berlin, we see the filmmaker for the first time, listening in silence.

Figure 2. 00:16:26

The second reverse shot appears four minutes later, for just six seconds. Here, we see Lanzmann's face as Rossel, now off-screen, discusses the pressure put on the ICRC by the American Joint Distribution Committee to obtain information about Jewish victims. Sixteen minutes into the film, this is in fact the first mention of Jews, when the word *"Juive"* appears in an on-screen gloss of "Joint" superimposed on the image of Lanzmann (Fig. 2).

What might appear as rather randomly placed reverse shots work instead to place the filmmaker as a phantasmatic surrogate for an absent other. In the first reverse shot, his silence stands in for the prisoner of war whose life is negotiable. In the second, he becomes the figure, the representative, of the Jew.

These two earlier reverse shots allow us to see the final shot of the film, where we see Lanzmann reading Eppstein's speech to the off-screen Rossel, also as a phantasmatic double image. For as the film cuts away from Rossel to Lanzmann, in the midst of the reading of the speech, it does so just as Eppstein invokes hope for the new year: "Let us enter the new year with seriousness and confidence and with the firm wish to hold out and do our duty." These last forty-five seconds are drawn from footage filmed after the interview is over and where Lanzmann reads through Eppstein's speech again, and then, visibly dissatisfied with his performance, reads it aloud a third time. This is a self-conscious performance, in other words, a theatrical moment where Lanzmann plays himself as interviewer and filmmaker, and at the same time assumes the role of Eppstein. In performing this speech, he thus opens a space between the present—a point in time when Eppstein's execution is irremediable—and a past perspective from which there was still hope in the future. Suspended between this crushed hope and the fact of Eppstein's execution, it is not only the text that Lanzmann reads that is *"déchirant,"* heartbreaking or, more literally, that tears one apart. It is also the image itself that is "déchirant," that tears Lanzmann apart. As he plays the part of Eppstein, he appears both as himself and as the incarnation of the one who was invisible to Rossel.

AN IMAGINED ADDRESS

Rossel's meeting with the SS officer and his visit to Theresienstadt were, to him, nothing but "pieces of theater." The challenge of the film, I suggested earlier, was to see beyond the performance, beyond the charade. But the final moments of the film, when Lanzmann deliberately assumes the part of an actor embodying Eppstein, suggest that to bear cinematic witness to history means not to substitute fact for fiction, but rather to reimagine what it means to recreate, to perform, the role of the witness. Rather than a limit that circumscribes vision, that dooms it to banality and specularity, the theatricality of his performance, embodied in the roles he plays as both director and actor, exposes his vision to perspectives that it cannot account for, that decenter and exceed it. Whereas to see something as theater meant, for Rossel, to recuse himself of responsibility for what he saw, to contain what he saw within the boundaries of "nothing," Lanzmann activates the power of the theatrical and of the cinematic to cross boundaries—between histories, locations, and incommensurable realities.

In this light, I return to the scene that takes place in the borderland of Auschwitz, on the road. What appeared to Rossel as a moment of "passing by" becomes, as we return to this moment in light of the ending of the film, a scene also of *passing on*, the scene of an astonishing transmission. I suggested before that, in his account of crossing paths with the "walking skeletons" of Auschwitz, Rossel effectively suppresses his own conscience and symptomatically dissociates himself from the gaze of the prisoners by absenting the first-person singular, by talking only of how "you" would see and be seen by them. But as the film reimagines what it means to play the role of the witness, it also invites another look at this moment. For as Lanzmann at the end of the film deliberately and self-consciously takes on the role of Eppstein, becoming his mouthpiece, it opens the possibility that Rossel may also be, though without necessarily knowing it, the vehicle of an address that he was not able to hear and of a gaze that he was not able to see.

The *Muselmann*, Primo Levi writes unforgettably, is at once the "complete witness"—the one who saw the "bottom" that those who survived managed to evade—and, at the same time, the one who, having seen the bottom, does not survive to testify.[38] And yet, astonishingly and seemingly impossibly, Lanzmann suggests that Rossel, however unwittingly and unwillingly, bears the testimony of the *Muselmann*. His speech is haunted by the impossible address of the dead, of eyes that speak across the boundary of death and themselves express their astonishment at the possibility of life: *"En voilà un qui vient . . . un vivant qui passe."* In placing the film under the sign and seal of these words, Lanzmann allows us to hear them in a new way—not only as words designating the "terrible lightness of the passerby, of the tourist," as Ophir Levy suggests, but also as indicating hope in the possibility of life, hope that this gaze and this appeal might be passed on.

Indeed, strikingly, at the moment that Lanzmann imagines that this gaze belongs to the *Muselmann*, he also brings it into the present tense, imagines that he himself sees and is seen by this gaze. "They *have* a very intense gaze," he says, with Rossel following suit: "Yes, very intense, very intense, those people *observing you . . . .*" At this moment, the past crosses paths with the present, and Rossel himself becomes the meeting point and the boundary line between the gaze of the *Muselmann* and "you." He is no longer merely "the eyes" of the professional observer, or of the specular antisemite. The film instead discloses at this moment an abyss within him as he transmits, despite himself, a message that was passed on in silence by the living

38. Primo Levi, *The Drowned and the Saved*, trans. Raymond Rosenthal (New York: Vintage, 1988), 83-84.

eyes of the *Muselmänner,* who are reduced to nothing but eyes, and who therefore also become the eyes. This intense but invisible gaze posits a perspective, a gaze from beyond, that the film transmits but for which it does not and cannot provide an image. Beyond what appears to be nothing, this unfathomable perspective leaves everything to the imagination.

JUDITH KASPER

Revolt as a Study in Precision: *Sobibor, October 14, 1943, 4 p.m.*

How do you tell such an unlikely truth, how do you foster the imagination of the unimaginable, if not by elaborating, by reworking reality,
by putting it in perspective? With a bit of artifice, then![1]

THE SINGULAR MOMENT

How can we wrest singular, unmistakable, memorable moments
from the Holocaust? The voices of individual witnesses are crucial.
They are moments of incarnation, as Claude Lanzmann puts it with
respect to *Shoah*. The multitude of singular and unforgettable voices
in *Shoah* accounts for the unique way in which the viewer experiences time: nine-and-a-half hours are at once an eternity and an in-
stant. Lanzmann made his film *Sobibor, October 14, 1943, 4 p.m.*
twenty-two years after *Shoah*, using one of its many outtakes.[2] It
is a film that once again reflects upon the events of the genocide,
also and in particular as a temporal experience. However, Lanzmann
adopts a markedly different mode of presentation from *Shoah*. One
might even say that *Sobibor, October 14, 1943, 4 p.m.* forms a precise
counterpoint to *Shoah*: it presents not a multitude of witnesses, but a
single witness; it lasts not nine-and-a-half, but a mere one-and-a-half
hours. Like many other survivors, the witness—Israel-based Yehuda
Lerner—gives an account of his persecution by the Nazis, but he also
tells of his escape, of resistance, revolts, and liberation—aspects that
do not feature in *Shoah* in this way. Lerner was one of the instigators
of the uprising. For the meticulous visualization of the revolt in his
film, Lanzmann chooses a construction unusual for him, namely, as
I will show, centering on the Aristotelian unities of character, place,

1. Jorge Semprun, *Literature or Life*, trans. Linda Coverdale (New York: Penguin,
1997), 124.
2. The Polish diacritical mark in the name of Sobibór does not appear in the title
of the film. I follow this practice, using Lanzmann's spelling when referring to the film
and the diacritical mark when referring to the place.

YFS 141, *Lanzmann after "Shoah,"* ed. Levine and Stark, © 2022 by Yale University.

time, and plot. The title of the film states the place and the date, right down to the exact hour: October 14, 1943, 4 p.m.

Using this powerful construction based on the fundamental poetic elements of drama, Lanzmann seeks to wrest a singular moment of interruption from the events of the genocide; in the course of the film, viewers realize that the constructed unities of time and place are made to be broken. It is the heroes of the uprising who bring the place—the Sobibór extermination camp—crashing down. The moment of revolt brings about a unique implosion of time: the hour is broken down into minutes, minutes into seconds, and seconds into split and microseconds. By precisely illuminating each moment of the revolt, this interruption of the annihilation machine—this black out, this crash of the Nazi system—becomes a temporal abyss.

The crash is sensational. But it is also infinitesimally small if we view it on the historical axis of the time and space of the genocide as a whole. The event is in danger of being overwhelmed and overshadowed by the weight of the sheer number of murder victims. Lanzmann knows that it takes a powerful artistic intervention to turn the revolt that transpired here into a true event.[3] By "true event" I mean an event having an impact that is not confined to the past—that is, an event that also makes an unforgettable imprint on listeners/viewers as it is conveyed to them as an auditory and visual event in the present. This means that the event is not by any means universal—for that it is too dependent on the many concrete details from which it cannot be separated. It is highlighted as a singular event and only as such can it be transmitted into the memory of those who come after. Only an act of artistic elaboration is able to accomplish this. This seems to me to be the film's main concern. When we compare it with the raw recording of the interview that Lanzmann conducted with Yehuda Lerner in October 1979 while he was working on *Shoah*, we have to bear in mind the difference between the witness's original statement and Lanzmann's subsequent heavy editing.[4] Research devoted to this film has been sparse to date. Aside from one essay by the

---

3. Although the Nazis destroyed all of the documentation, the Sobibór revolt has been relatively well recorded. The uprising allowed three hundred prisoners to escape, the majority of whom were killed shortly afterward. Lerner was one of the approximately fifty survivors.

4. The outtake is available under the link: https://collections.ushmm.org/search/catalog/irn1004204 (accessed on May 17, 2021); a transcript of the interview can be found here: https://collections.ushmm.org/film_findingaids/RG-60.5030_01_trs_fr.pdf.

German Studies scholar Manual Köppen from 2014, mention must be made of Gary Weissman's recent article of 2020,[5] in which the author is very hard on Lanzmann. Above all, he criticizes the way that Lanzmann distorts Lerner's testimony, his "living word" (as Lanzmann puts it). He argues that the film marginalizes Lerner's testimony and story of survival in order to create an alternative narrative, "with different emphases and effects than the one spoken by Lerner."[6]

The volume in which Weissman's article appears discusses Lanzmann's films against the backdrop of their outtakes and shows in a particularly impressive manner how Lanzmann saw himself: never as a documentary maker, always as an artist and creator. The volume picks up on earlier studies, for example the one by Dominick LaCapra, who stressed early on with respect to *Shoah* that "the role of mise-en-scène in the film is indeed crucial."[7] The editors of the volume even say in their introduction that Lanzmann is a "director" "who wished to retain absolute control over the filmed material's afterlife," and go so far as to add a little later that he "is asserting total control over his film."[8]

This impression is in fact confirmed upon closer analysis of Lanzmann's film *Sobibor, October 14, 1943, 4 p.m.* But by that I mean that it is precisely this film that shows how necessary it is for the director to assume this attitude. It is a result, so to speak, of the attitude adopted by the witness at the center of the film, who attributes the success of the revolt in Sobibór to the military principles of organization, control, and precision.[9]

5. Manuel Köppen, "Searching for Evidence between Generations: Claude Lanzmann's *Sobibór* and Romuald Karmaka's *Land of Annihilation*," *New German Critique* 123, German Memory and the Holocaust: New Films (Fall 2014): 57-73; Gary Weissman: "Yehuda Lerner's Living Words: Translation and Transcription in *Sobibor, October 14, 1943, 4 p.m.*," in *The Construction of Testimony: Claude Lanzmann's Shoah and Its Outtakes*, ed. Erin McGlothlin, Brad Prager, and Markus Zisselsberger (Detroit: Wayne State University Press, 2020), 175-205.

6. McGlothlin and Prager, "Introduction," in McGlothlin, Prager, and Zisselsberger, *The Construction of Testimony*, 19.

7. Dominick LaCapra, "Lanzmann's *Shoah*: 'Here There Is No Why,'" *Critical Inquiry* 23/ 2 (1997): 232.

8. McGlothlin and Prager, "Introduction," 6, 10.

9. It must be added in this context that the preparations for the revolt in Sobibór were made by a secret collective led by the Russian-Jewish officer Alexander Petchersky who had been deported to Sobibór. Petchersky had the necessary military know-how to plan such a complex revolt right down to the last detail. Petchersky survived and testified at the Sobibór trial held in Kiev on August 1, 1961, and elsewhere. His

In the following, I will concentrate on Lanzmann's filmic approach, which I will critically appraise as an artistic adaptation of the testimony of Yehuda Lerner, arguing that it is precisely this adaptation that allows us to see the Sobibór revolt as a paradigmatic moment of resistance and uprising in the first place.

THE OPENING OF THE FILM

What is striking but not atypical of Lanzmann's filmic practice is, firstly, the complicated way in which he frames his film. Several thresholds precede the actual interview with Lerner, forming a series of metafilmic moments that reflect upon different modes of approaching the Holocaust.

The film begins with a black and white photograph, an archival image from the museum in Sobibór, in which stalwart SS officers can be made out standing in a circle; one of them has his arm raised in a Nazi salute. It is unclear around what exactly they are standing. The camera spends twenty-three seconds on this silent photo. A caption explains: "SS officers giving the Nazi salute by the coffins of comrades killed during the Sobibór uprising. (Sobibór Museum)." Cut. It is directly followed by a close-up in color—a prolepsis—of the man who will play the main role in this film. After a few seconds, we hear a question off-camera in the voice of Claude Lanzmann: "Had Mr. Lerner killed before?"[10] This is followed by a Hebrew translation in a female voice (that of Francine Kaufmann) and then Lerner's swift response—first in Hebrew, then translated into French: no, he had never killed anybody before. The camera spends a few more seconds on Lerner's face. We see a nervous tick in the left corner of his mouth. Forty-six seconds of the film have passed. Cut. This is followed directly by an aerial color image of dense autumnal forests (in Poland and Belarus), similar to the

statement (in Yiddish) is held at the Central Archives in Ludwigsburg (file BArch, B 162/4437, Blätter 2671 - 2678). See Ayse Sila Çehreli and Tobias Herrmann, "La Zentrale Stelle de Ludwigsburg, entre archives et mémoire," in *Vingtième Siècle. Revue d'histoire* 111 (2011/3): 159-69, here 163. Moreover, Petchersky himself, severely wounded in a military hospital, compiled a report on the uprising very early on, which was first published in the Soviet Union in 1945 and was reissued in 2013. I had access to the report in German translation: Aleksandr Petscherski, *Bericht über den Aufstand in Sobibor*, ed. and trans. Ingrid Damerow (Berlin: Metropol, 2018). Lanzmann pays respect to the memory of Petchersky at the beginning of his film (04:24-05:47).

10. The English subtitles are quoted from this edition: *Sobibor, October 14, 1943, 4 p.m.* (*Sobibor, 14 octobre 1943, 16 heures*) (France 2 Cinéma, Les Films Aleph, Why Not Productions, 2001), DVD, 95 min.

many takes we see in *Shoah*. We hear the twittering of birds while the credits run over the forested background image. A dedication ends the sequence: "For my friend Gilberte Steg, in memory of her sister Hedy Nissim, gassed at Sobibor in March 1943" (01:17-01:23). Cut. It is only now that an opening moment typical of Lanzmann's films takes place: a five-minute prologue composed of vertically scrolling white text against a black background, which we hear in Lanzmann's voice.

Let us spend a few moments on the incipit. By showing an archival photo from the museum in Sobibór, which is explained in an image caption, Lanzmann makes use of a stylistic device that he had always previously rejected. *Sobibor, October 14, 1943, 4 p.m.* was released in 2001, at a time when Lanzmann was embroiled in a heated debate with Georges Didi-Huberman and other French intellectuals about the status of the archival image within the context of Holocaust representations. Is this opening a confession or more a polemical gesture of defense? Probably the latter. For in powerful—but symmetrical—contrast, it is followed by the first color close-up of Yehuda Lerner. Whereas the archival photo is blurry and does not allow us to make out any faces, just the stereotypical Nazi salute and the just as stereotypical black uniforms, in the close-up we can even see Lerner's facial features. Without a caption, the archival photo would remain silent, just as silent as it is when initially displayed. The close-up, however, marks the beginning of speech, which starts with a question: the question of killing. Compared with the understandably predominant historical imaginary, the roles here have been reversed: SS officers are shown as victims and mourners and as the dead; the Jewish Pole-by-birth Yehuda Lerner, now an Israeli, is shown as the one who is alive and who has killed—the one who is alive because he has killed. Is he a perpetrator? Certainly not. The SS are mass murderers; Lerner is an insurgent who carried out an ethically responsible, heroic act of killing at a specific, historically necessary moment in time, whose act would be categorized by the courts as an act of defense or as tyrannicide.

Moving from threshold to threshold, the film begins again shortly thereafter, this time with a prologue/monologue, read by Lanzmann. The text briefly describes the conditions under which the film was shot. Upon closer examination, we realize that Lanzmann has been arguing on the level of film aesthetics from the outset. He thus begins not only by situating the film within the context of *Shoah* but by introducing Yehuda Lerner as the "emblematic hero" of the revolt (02:25). Moreover, the film presents a historico-philosophical argument that connects *Sobibor* with *Tsahal*, his 1994 film about the Israeli military: "It [the revolt] is a paradigmatic example of what I've elsewhere referred to as the reappropriation of power and violence by the Jews" (02:50-03:00).[11] According to this argument, the origins of Israel's military preparedness can be found in the Jewish records of the resistance and revolts that took place in German concentration and extermination camps.[12] The film thus explicitly sets itself the task of debunking "the two-part myth" (*"double légende"*) (03:19), according to which Jews allowed themselves to be led into the gas chambers and did not mount any resistance against their oppressors.

Lanzmann's return to the 1979 interview more than twenty years later leads him to follow in the footsteps of Lerner—"to go where Yehuda Lerner had been" (*"suivre les traces de Yehuda Lerner"*) (05:52), which for him means traveling once more to Sobibór. There were a number of other options available to him to deal with the recorded material, such as calling upon Lerner again in Israel, where he lives to this day. He also could have made contact with other surviving witnesses. Lanzmann did none of this. His own journey to Sobibór is influenced by the montage of visual material that underlines Lerner's words. Upon his return to Sobibór, Lanzmann notes the changes that have taken place, acknowledging the "small and touching red-roofed museum" (06:34) that has been built, before, however, closing his speech with an apodictic statement that clearly puts in question the archival image that was shown at the beginning: "But museums and monuments instill forgetfulness as well as remembrance. Now we'll listen to Yehuda Lerner's living words" (6:53-7:04).

FAITHFUL REENACTMENT AND TRANSFORMATIVE INTERVENTION

Lanzmann's journey takes him to Minsk and Sobibór via Warsaw. For long stretches, the film seems like a sheer illustration of the words

11. Film critics discussed the film's Zionist mission early on, for example Laurence Giavarini, "Sur les héros de Sobibór: Le dernier film de Claude Lanzmann et la représentation de la Shoah," *Cahiers du Cinéma* 565 (Feb 2002): 46-47.

12. Lanzmann expressly commented on this connection between *Tsahal* and *Sobibor* in a long 2001 interview given upon the release of the film to the *Cahiers du Cinéma*. See Lanzmann, "Sur le courage," interview with Claude Lanzmann conducted by Patrice Blouin, Franck Nouchi, and Charles Tesson, in *Cahiers du Cinéma* 561(October 2001): 46-57. Köppen analyzes this connection in more detail, especially on 63-65.

and sentences of Lerner's testimony, something to which Lanzmann, on other occasions, was decidedly opposed. Here, however, in an almost mimetic way, the images filmed on Lanzmann's journey cleave to Lerner's testimony, virtually merging with it. More than a mere illustration, we could speak of a kind of visual reenactment. In fact, together, words and images burn themselves into the skin of the film-strip (the proximity to skin persists in the French *pellicule*).

When Lerner, for instance, recounts how he escaped from a camp and survived by eating the roots he found in the fields, the camera ranges at length over harvested fields. When Lerner tells the story of how he was once again captured after an attempted escape and then transported to another camp in a truck, the viewer travels with him through a camera that is directed at a truck: we experience sensory impressions of a journey over a bumpy forest road, while the dark edges of the forest jerk across the screen.

The extreme, nearly literal conformity of the cinematic, visual reenactment to Lerner's words, on the one hand, contrasts with Lanzmann's powerfully transformative interventions, on the other. The tension between cinematic reenactment, which follows from Lanzmann's fidelity to Lerner's account, and the sovereignty of his directing, evident in the editorial control he exerts over the interview, is pushed to the limit in the scene with the geese (39:51-41:18), one of the most impressive points in the film in terms of image and sound. Lerner tells the story of a flock of geese that had been bred by the Nazis. The geese would be startled during gassing operations so that their honking would drown out the screams of the prisoners being murdered in the gas chambers. This in itself grotesque, shocking detail in Lerner's account is accentuated filmically by a flock of geese that marches in rank and file, turning in a circle. Their honking gets louder and louder, and even drowns out the presence of the interview and Lerner's own speech for a few seconds. Then the sound is slowly turned down and the image disappears. This powerful filmic intervention does not just connect the historical account with the geese that still honk in present-day Sobibór; Lanzmann also suggests that a certain honking still threatens to mute the testimony of the survivors.[13] However, he also portrays himself as the one who, like a *deus*

13. Lanzmann comments on this risky montage in the interview he gave to *Cahiers du Cinéma*: "There are geese in *Shoah*, at Treblinka and in the surrounding villages. I saw many geese in Poland. But there, it was a gigantic troop of eight hundred

ex machina, can end the honking of the geese and will once again allow the testimony to be heard in an even stronger sense.

Gary Weissman criticizes Lanzmann's interventions for heavily
editing Lerner's "living word," to which I would respond that Lerner's statement is brought to life by the ways it is edited, crafted, and
dramatized. It is treated in a way that intensifies its aesthetic impact.

DRAMATIZATION OF TESTIMONY

In order for a revolt against the well-organized, systematic, punctual
Nazi logistics of extermination to succeed, it had to work with the
same means. This is one of Lerner's central statements. It is difficult
to overlook his own fascination with punctuality and precision. It is
also difficult to overlook Lanzmann's embrace of the two cinematographic principles of editing and montage that are at the heart of the
precision work he carries out on the recorded material. In Lanzmann's
dramatic editing, Lerner's account becomes a kind of clockwork or
"machine infernale" (Jean Cocteau), which brings the infernal system of extermination crashing down in a veritable *coup de théâtre*.
Lerner's account heads straight toward the climax of the dramatic
arc—the splitting of an SS officer's skull with an ax.

The slightly simplified argument that I would like to make on
the basis of this observation (to which I will return at the end of the
essay) is that Lanzmann forms Lerner's account into a classic, pyramidal drama, divided into five acts and based on the classical unities
of time, place, and action: Act One, exposition: Lerner's removal from
the Warsaw ghetto, the beginning of his deportation at the *Umschlag-
platz* (holding area); Act Two, rising action: imprisonment in various
camps, repeated escape, deportation to Sobibór; Act Three, climax in
resistance and revolt: first blow of the ax; Act Four, falling action: second blow of the ax, escape; Act Five: collapse, sleep—and termination
of the interview by Lanzmann.

---

geese. Filming that was just stupefying. When they turned in a circle, forming an im-
maculate white disc, they did that all on their own. I didn't stage that, I didn't tell
them, 'Do that.' [. . .] It seemed to me impossible to use that footage, which, I thought,
could only appear obscene. It was everything I detest: it has nothing to do with the
question of representation, but rather with *illustration*. [. . .] I told myself: 'The geese
cover up the cries of the people being murdered' and then I had the idea, I was quite
proud of it, believe me, to have Lerner's voice fight against the geese." ("Sur le courage," 53, trans. Jared Stark)

What is the motivation behind this kind of dramatization? Let us go back to the prologue once more. Here, Lanzmann already speaks in poetic and literary terms:[14] he describes Lerner as an "emblematic hero," a "surprising figure." That he is "emblematic" means he is stylized in the form of an allegory. That he is a "figure" means he is presented as a character or protagonist in a drama or film. Lanzmann also speaks of the "the two-part myth" of the helpless and passive Jew, that is, of a narrative that we must decidedly work against by reading it (in the literal sense of the *légende* or legend: that which can be read)—reading it against the grain, and creating a counter-myth. It takes powerful aesthetic means to construct such a counter-myth. Lanzmann finds these means in Aristotelian poetics, which is almost unavoidable but for Lanzmann in every sense astonishing—*unavoidable* because Aristotle's poetics have shaped the Occidental construction of drama up to the modern age, even in firm rejections of it. French classical drama took these poetics to their highest precision. The Aristotelian influence is astonishing because Lanzmann's film aesthetics have always rebelled against these kinds of classical narrative forms and dramatizations of the Holocaust. They are more a thing of Hollywood cinema—and there is nothing more removed from Lanzmann's approach to film than Hollywood. Finally, of course, *Sobibor, October 14, 1943, 4 p.m.* cannot be mistaken for a melodramatic heroic narrative like *Schindler's List*.[15] And yet, I maintain that Lanzmann here subversively appropriates elements of classical drama and expropriates them from Holocaust kitsch in order to utilize them in his construction of a counter-myth: the new myth of the Jewish fighter, the myth of the birth of the Israeli actively defending himself in National Socialist camps.

14. *Shoah* also begins, as Francine Kaufmann rightly puts it *in nuce*, in the mode of fiction: "Like a work of fiction, *Shoah* begins with the written words: 'The story begins in the present at Chelmno, on the Narew River, in Poland.'" She mentions Lanzmann stating that he wanted to get his interviewees to "perform" their testimonies as "actors" and as "characters." See Francine Kaufmann, "The Ambiguous Task of the Interpreter in Lanzmann's Films *Shoah* and *Sobibor*: Between the Director and Survivors of the Camps and Ghettos," in *Interpreting in Nazi Concentration Camps*, ed. Michael Wold (New York: Bloomsbury, 2016), 162.

15. Köppen mentions other film portrayals of the Sobibór uprising, in particular Jack Gold's box-office hit *Escape from Sobibor* (1987). This film is based on the book by Richard Rashke, *Escape from Sobibor* (1982), in which Rashke interviews twenty survivors of the uprising, including Lerner. (For references, see Köppen, 62-63.) Köppen describes the film as an "exciting and dramatic narrative of resistance," "with effective fictionalizing strategies," similar to the TV series *Holocaust* (63).

The way that Lanzmann artistically intervenes in Lerner's testimony becomes quite obvious and aggressive at the end, when he terminates Lerner's account at an extremely precise moment. Lerner is in the midst of describing how, after completing the act of revolt—the climax of his drama, to which I will return in more detail shortly—he escaped, collapsed in the forest out of exhaustion, and fell asleep. Lanzmann's off-camera voice terminates the interview at this point with the following metadiegetic intervention: "We'll stop here. It's so beautiful when he collapses in the forest. The rest is an adventure of freedom. The extermination devices and gas chambers were demolished by the Germans immediately after the uprising. No more convoys arrived at Sobibór station. There, at least, the extermination had been stopped" (1:32:03-1:32:32).

"It's so (*trop*) beautiful . . . ": At this point, Lanzmann lifts Lerner's faithful, historical account of uprising and escape into the realm of the "beautiful" for a short moment and reflects upon it according to aesthetic criteria. Lanzmann has left his role as an interviewer; he speaks as a theater director and then, shortly thereafter goes even further, usurping the place of his character. Now, he speaks *about* him and summarizes the events that follow in the most concise manner.[16] Why this sudden shift of roles and rhythms? It is almost as though Lanzmann were himself completing his blow of the ax here, as if the only way that he could avoid letting go of the moment of interruption—which is what this revolt in the midst of a genocide was—the only way to hold on to it for eternity, is by making this hard cut.

THE LOGIC OF THE "I'D RATHER" (*PLUTÔT*) AS A TRANSITION TO ACTIVITY

The division of Lanzmann's film into dramatic acts that I have somewhat exaggerated and that has never been explicitly described as such by Lanzmann himself is complicated by other forces. For one of the fundamental questions posed by Lerner's testimony is how a person who has been persecuted and who is physically extremely debilitated is able to find his way out of the abuse he has suffered and take ac-

---

16. In his article about Lanzmann's late film *Napalm*, Michael G. Levine points out how, at a crucial point in his film, Lanzmann describes his role as film director as a role that he plays, thereby falling out of his role.

tion in the form of revolt. This transformation is not to be understood from the telos of the revolt but is born of an energy that is the subject above all of the first half of the film. It would be too simple to describe this energy as a positive will to live. Lerner escaped from eight camps within the space of six months. Lanzmann asks almost incredulously: "Why such determination (*rage*) to escape? Or was it simply easy?" (20:09-20:11). Lerner describes this "*rage de l'évasion*," as Lanzmann puts it, as a negative energy within the realm of total negation and annihilation. The drive comes from what Francine Kaufmann translates repeatedly with the adverb *plutôt*: "I'd rather [French: *plutôt*] be shot or hung than starve like this" (19:02). Shortly afterward: "I have nothing to lose. I'd rather attempt anything than live this nonlife" (20:45-47). And a little later: "Only death awaited a Jew. But I'd rather take a bullet than go back there" (22:13-22:19).

"I'd rather" expresses a philosophical attitude and a guiding principle. Close to death, in an absolute lack of freedom, it creates a tiny space for maneuver. In this tiny space, fortunate coincidence befalls Lerner time and again. "Luck" and "chance" are other keywords in Lerner's account: they are elements that stand in the way of the strict tragic necessity of a drama that takes place according to the principle of clockwork.

The French word *plutôt*, which sets the tone in the original version of the film, then, also expresses the precision of temporal preemption, the successful anticipation that will ultimately prove itself to be crucial to the success of the revolt.

We see here how the pyramidal form of dramatic progression is altered by a circular movement driven by a relativistic *plutôt*, which "luck" will prove right time and again: the hero destined for death avoids his fate on this circular path; he revolts, that is, he pivots and turns against his tragic trajectory.

BLOWS OF THE AX

In Act Three—the act of revolt—his repeated luck ("*chance*") becomes "our only chance was to kill the German" (48:20). It is only possible "to kill the Germans" with "précision" (incredible punctuality) (49:57). And in fact, the climax of the dramatic account is the precise implementation of a meticulous plan that includes a temporal consideration: namely, that the Germans are always on time. This time, punctuality, the foundation of the Germans' power, will prove to be their weakness, because punctuality makes them predictable.

On October 14, at exactly 1600 hours, the sixteen SS officers dwelling in the camp were called into the various workshops. Lanzmann asks, underlining the temporal precision: "À quatre heures précises?" ("At 4:00 p.m. sharp?") (01:06) Lerner responds, underlining the precision of the moment in hand gestures: "Exact comme une montre!" ("just like clockwork") (1:06:56): "In fact, our whole plan was based on that. We knew the Germans were very punctual. We only succeeded because Germans are so punctual" (1:07:04-1:07:16).

Lerner stood by with another prisoner in the tailor's workshop—both armed with axes that had been pilfered from the woodworking shop. At exactly 4 p.m., SS Officer Greischütz showed up for his appointment to have an overcoat tailored. As Greischütz, whom Lerner describes as a giant monster (1:08:42-1:09:41), bent forward, Lerner produced his ax and split Greischütz's skull in two.

In Lerner's words, translated by Francine Kaufmann, the scene is visualized as follows:

> J'ai pris la hache, j'ai fait un tout petit pas vers lui et tout a duré peut-être un millième de seconde . . . C'était même . . . tellement rapide que je peux même pas vous . . . Imaginez, c'était un quart de millième de millième de seconde et tout s'est fini [. . .] La hache est entrée exactement au milieu de son crâne [. . .]. je peux dire que je lui ai coupé le crâne en deux, exactement . . ."
> (English subtitles: "I gripped the ax and took a tiny step towards him. It all took a 1/1000th of a second. It was even . . . so rapid that I can't even say—it was over in a quarter of a millionth of a second. [. . .] In one blow, the whole ax went into his head. [. . .] The ax went right into the middle of his skull.") (1:13:35–1:14:26)[17]

---

17. Gary Weissman examines this passage precisely and illustrates the differences between Lerner's choice of words in Hebrew and Kaufmann's translation. Of interest for my purposes, Lerner speaks twice of a "fraction," once of a "fraction of a thousandth of a second," then of a "fraction of a second" (Weissman, 192). This word does not appear in Kaufmann's translation; however, this illustrates the idea of the division of time even more clearly. In this context, I would like to note that Weissman is certainly right in criticizing Lanzmann for obviously not being interested in retrospectively providing Lerner's original statements with subtitles. Kaufmann relied on consecutive interpretation without the opportunity to take notes (see Kaufmann, "The Ambiguous Task"). The film is thus, like *Shoah*, a film that is conceived in French.

The precise, complete splitting of the skull coincides with the splitting of time into microunits that are no longer perceptible. Lerner's rhetoric is testament, on the one hand, to the obsessive precision, within which all power and violence seem to be embedded, that is unleashed in this fraction of a second. On the other hand, what he says touches upon temporal dimensions that cannot be registered by any consciousness and that—speaking psychoanalytically—violate perception and consciousness, leaving behind permanent traces in another system, the unconscious, as shock or trauma. It is no longer a moment in time, but a splitting of time, the splitting of an atom that unleashes powerful energies that crush the Nazi system but also leave lasting marks on the testifying subject. I will come back to this later on. "[U]nimaginable"—"incredible" (1:17:45)—something that blows our powers of imagination to pieces—is what this act is. It is just as "incredible" that, after this precise blow of the ax, exactly five minutes later, the next SS officer was due to appear to try something on in the tailor's workshop. It is unimaginable that they were able to remove the body including the blood stains within five minutes so that the next officer would not suspect anything. Lerner (in Kaufmann's translation, translated into English): "Yes, it seems impossible, but everything depended on German punctuality and our own rapidity. The Germans were punctual and our plan worked like clockwork" (1:18:05-1:18:11).

Act Four, the extension of the climax, which delays it and slows it down, begins with the entry of the second officer at exactly 1605 hours. He steps on the arm of the body of his colleague, which inadvertently juts out from a pile of coats. "So the German started shouting, Was ist das? Was ist das? What is it?" (1:20:05-1:20:13).

This moment of reaction becomes the moment in which the next blow falls: "Immediately, my comrade leapt forward and struck him. The German collapsed from the blow, and I quickly gave him a second blow. I think I'll always remember—the ax struck his teeth and made a sort of spark" (1:20:16-1:20:56).

The drama of the moment is grounded in the matter itself. It is intensified by the spark struck from the violent splitting of the skull. The spark ignited by the blow is reflected in the sparkling eyes of the hero recounting this moment thirty-six years later. And when we see the film forty-two years after the interview, it is still as if this powerful blow had just fallen. The spark struck by the revolt illuminates the night in a flash—the night that fell early on October 14, 1943, the night of the history of the oppressed, which continues to this day.[18]

Lanzmann insists that Lerner be precise in his description of the act of killing. Lerner goes into more and more detail; his otherwise seemingly calm and sovereign body begins to speak with him, he imitates the gesture once again on camera, and the collapse is expressed onomatopoetically (a loud "wrah!") (1:14:02). Köppen draws the following conclusion from this moment: "*Sobibor* seeks to stage a cinematic monument: the Israel Defense Forces and modern Israeli identity find a point of origin in the swing of Lerner's ax."[19] And Weissman interprets it similarly: "The skull-splitting moment captures what Lanzmann, in the film's introductory scroll, calls 'the reappropriation of power and violence by the Jews.'"[20]

Without a doubt: mythically speaking, it is David who triumphs over Goliath here, and Lanzmann has set us up for this interpretation. The ax as an archaic instrument is not just a weapon but also a tool for cutting and splitting that can be used to build something new.

But Lanzmann's insistence on the detailed performance of skull splitting seems to me to indicate that there is also another obsession at play. Lanzmann's autobiography begins with his repeated haunting by the guillotine as an instrument of killing; in *Shoah*, Lanzmann has Polish farmers repeat the gesture of "off with his head" again and again, the silent and cynical gesture that announces death in the camps to the deported Jews peeking out through the narrow windows of the railroad cars, a gesture that—as many surviving witnesses emphasize—was not understood. Lanzmann's third-to-last film (*The Last of the Unjust*, 2013) about Benjamin Murmelstein, the Jewish Council leader in Theresienstadt, is predominantly about the shots that the Nazis fired into the back of the necks of the members of the *Judenrat* to murder them. In all of these manners of death, the focus

18. The Austrian poet Ilse Aichinger, who wrote a brief film critique of *Sobibor* upon its release, notes aptly: "Yehuda Lerner erzählt seine Geschichte mit der Axt, wie Geschichten von Dostojewskij erzählt sind, auch in ihrer Exzentrizität." (Yehuda Lerner tells his story with the ax in the way that Dostoyevsky tells stories, in their eccentricity as well.) *Der Standard*, Oktober 27/28, 200, https://www.derstandard .at/story/757976/16-jahre-alt-ist-jehuda-lerner-als-er-im-konzentrationslager-sobibor -einen-deutschen-bewacher-mit-einer-axt-den-schaedel-spaltet (accessed on May 17, 2001).

19. Köppen, 67.

20. Weissman, 194.

is on the neck, that which connects head and torso, that which is destroyed by horizontal cuts and shots. But here, in *Sobibor*, it is about an act of skull splitting imagined vertically, a Jewish act of revenge on the Nazis, which stands in marked contrast to the other techniques of killing. One might even go so far as to say that this vertical act of symbolic splitting strikes through the other ways of killing in order to usher in a fundamentally different course of history. The blow of the ax also strikes through time—in the sense of chronologically measurable, historical time. It is at precisely this point that history reaches beyond itself into an a-historical, mythical realm extending far beyond the previously noted connection to the Israeli army and its readiness to defend itself.

Act Five, the final act—Lerner's escape from the camp and his collapse and exhaustion in the forest near the camp—is told quickly. For it is Lanzmann, as I noted above, who swings the ax here. He cuts off Lerner so that he can be the one to speak in his place at the moment of his collapse. The film ends with an epilogue, in which Lanzmann reads aloud a text that appears as a black rolling title with white letters (as at the beginning). While his hero sleeps, Lanzmann holds a wake, spending eight minutes reading the dates of all of the transports to Sobibór. Intoned in his deep and unmistakable voice, the recitation has the sound and significance of a kaddish. The last transport arrived from Treblinka on October 20, 1943, with one hundred prisoners onboard. In the end, the dead numbered over 250,000.

PHYSICAL SYMPTOMS

Although it once more proclaims the end of camp terror, this ending actually highlights the fact that the Holocaust does not have a narrative, only statistics, as the historian Dan Diner once observed.[21] The ending also refutes the argument that I made at the beginning about *Sobibor* being based on a classical dramatic structure. At most, this structure is used to lend Lerner's account a dramatic quality in the middle part of the film, ensuring that it will remain seared into the viewer's memory.

---

21. Dan Diner, "Gestaute Zeit. Massenvernichtung und jüdische Erzählstruktur," in Diner, *Kreisläufe. Nationalsozialismus und Gedächtnis* (Berlin: Berlin Verlag 1995), 125-39.

The film almost incidentally records the fact that Lerner's drama does not have an end, without addressing it. We do not learn anything about how he lives in Israel. A sturdy fifty-year-old man sits before the camera with distinctive furrows in his brow and lively eyes. He seems self-possessed and self-confident. His emotional state is only addressed once, when Lanzmann observes that Lerner turns pale when he recounts how he killed the SS officer with the ax. Lerner's response seems a little like a stuttered denial:

> Of course I'm pale. When you recall things like that—the joy of succeeding—when you recall things like that, you can't help but feel something bubbling up inside. It's a feeling of joy at having succeeded, but you have tears in your eyes because so many died there. It's the satisfaction of succeeding in avenging those who died and the feeling of having done the right thing. [. . .] An experience like this happens once in a lifetime. It's the experience of life and death. (1:22:12–1:23:59)

When the interview moves on to the subject of his feelings, Lerner no longer speaks in the first person, trying instead to translate his speech into a general "one" (*on*). He wants there to be an umbrella term for what he has recounted and remembered in detail, a term that does not exist. It remains "a thing like that" ("*une chose comme ça*")—something unnamable. What the collision between the triumphant feeling of revenge and the simultaneous awareness that 250,000 people were killed in Sobibór does to someone remains unnamable and unsayable. Its only traces are barely noticeable symptoms.

I would like to conclude by dwelling on these symptoms. There is the sudden total exhaustion of which Lerner speaks that makes him collapse and fall asleep once he has barely escaped, while he is still near the camp and therefore in extreme danger. In Lanzmann's film *Tsahal*, an Israeli soldier speaks of a similar experience: during the Six-Day War, the nervous tension among the members of the tank crew was so high that they repeatedly fell asleep for a matter of seconds between one shelling and the next.

But there is also the nervous twitch at the left-hand corner of Lerner's mouth, which speaks along with him, unsolicited and silent. This is not a place for psychological speculation. But on the formal level of the film, it is striking that the fracturing of the seconds, the breaking through of time that Lerner speaks of, becomes visible on the film's surface as a tic.

Lanzmann's kaddish at the end of the film is based on a calendar that can state when the killings in Sobibór ended.

Time stands still in Yehuda Lerner's face; the hand keeps ticking and ticking in him as in a broken clock, always stuck at the same place.

—Translated by Lydia J. White

ALEXANDER GARCÍA DÜTTMANN

"I was a report": *The Karski Report*

It is impossible to move and even to breathe. The slightest distraction would prove deadly. All eyes and all cameras are on me. I must sit up with my back straight. I must appear resolute, unflustered and in command, which is not the same as haughty. No sweat must form on my forehead. It is all highly demanding and also effortless. It is an artificial state in which everything comes naturally because nothing is left except what counts. I understand the requirements. My eyes are a transparent blue, perhaps slightly greyish.

This is the place of precision. Precision mortifies me and turns me into a machine. Only as a machine, or an automaton, can I deliver the information I keep within myself without anything external interfering with my report, making it approximate, vague, unspecific, singular, unrepeatable, and finally self-defeating. I must report precisely what I saw and what I know without superfluous conjectures and digressions, without doubts and fictions that fill the voids, without relishing or cursing my privilege, without mannerisms, idiosyncrasies and trademarks, without the distorting effects of self-centeredness tampering with perception, awareness, cognition, and recollection. What I saw and what I know I must make suitable for storage and exhibition, for the archives of history and humanity and their consultation, as if I had seen it with an unflinching eye and known it with an equanimous mind. The exactitude of objectivity at which precision aims is a sharpening subtraction, a clarifying cutting away, a healing mutilation. My self, on whose capacity to see and to know, to focus and to comprehend everything seems to hinge, must cease to be peculiar and characteristic and become generic and abstract. It has to free itself from itself. It has to purify itself. Because I must be precise, I am more focused than ever, more centered, and I entirely rely on my self

YFS 141, *Lanzmann after "Shoah,"* ed. Levine and Stark, © 2022 by Yale University.

to achieve such focusing, such stability and security. Yet at the same time I no longer feel myself, having entered an objective realm, the realm of an indistinguishability of life and death, time and timelessness, history with a lower-case h and History with a capital letter, in which my I or my self appear to have shrunk to a purely formal, or logical, entity that holds together whatever information it must convey. My I or my self ensures the unity, identity, and identifiability of this information, its smoothness and transmissibility, its compactness and fluidity because their own identity remains unassailable, is not altered by the information. The personal pronoun "my"—"my report"—indicates the fact that there is someone there who cannot be replaced. Yet it does not qualify this presence any further. Only I have the information to be conveyed and only I am capable of the highest possible precision. One follows from the other, but they can also be separate. In the first case, precision will depend on what I can achieve when trying to convey it. In the second case, I happen to be especially good at attaining precision and the information that needs to be conveyed happens to be mine.

When walking the dog with the ambassador and sharing an undisturbed intimacy into which not even his wife was allowed, a moment of concentration, confidence, frankness, and transparency, he reminded me of my verbosity, my propensity to talk too much. My report still lacked precision and concision. I had to keep rehearsing. He would not be able to assist me when presenting my report.

However, the one who is there and to whom the personal pronoun points—"my report"—has also assumed the responsibility of erasing himself completely so as not to relinquish the precision of which he alone is capable, whether he is particularly talented and accomplished as a precise witness or not. I am both a very important man, even a hero, with everything at my disposal, and I am no one, forever anonymous, untraceable and entirely replaceable. My hyperbolic self-importance verges on nothingness.

The place of precision could not be any narrower. It forms an almost imperceptible gap between impenetrable and unsurmountable walls. In this gap, the exigency, the claim, or the demand is engendered and proves intractable. Its address—"be precise!"—confines me to a solitude irredeemably mine. Never did the personal pronoun make more sense, never was it more meaningless. I must submit to the discipline of precision. Following the injunction that resonates silently in my hollow body means intuiting the might and sensing the weight of the walls. I am both crushed and elated, annihilated and carried beyond myself. On one side—but can I still orient myself and distinguish between one wall and the other?—there is the unprecedented. No one has ever seen the unprecedented before, no one has ever known about it. This is why it is unclear what seeing and knowing it, reporting about it as a witness, could possibly mean. There is no point of comparison for such horror, nothing that could uphold and sustain me, nothing to which I could cling. When faced with the unprecedented, my only chance is to acknowledge that I cannot experience it, that I must eliminate experience, run away and become a recording machine that registers and reproduces it impassively. I must not see anything, not know anything, so as to record it all. Hence the difficulty of establishing an origin for the precision required of me. Must the machine of precision, the care that abandons my own needs altogether, rest on the unprecedented if it is to function properly? Does precision originate in the challenge posed to any attempt to repeat and to reduplicate the unprecedented, to any attempt to report it? Does precision call for the unprecedented in order to feed on it and prove itself? Does the unprecedented originate in precision as the object best suited to it? Is precision an invention of the unprecedented? Or is the unprecedented an invention of precision? Is precision the folly of the unprecedented, which must lack measure, standards, and criteria, and render assimilation, alignment, adequation, and adjustment impossible? Or is the unprecedented the folly of precision? Does precision therefore justify the unprecedented? Does the unprecedented justify precision?

The effort to achieve precision when reporting is not merely a manner of transporting what is supposed to be reported. It is already a comportment toward it, toward the unprecedented, a way of handling it and creating a precedent, no matter how invisible and unobtrusive the manipulation. It attenuates the impact of a traumatic incomprehensibility and unfathomability. A report that succeeds in being precise, in bringing back its object unchanged, as if one came across this object for the first time and without mediation, or as if one touched upon the letter[1] that defines the ahistoricity or the truth of history,

---

1. "It is this literality and its insistent return which thus constitutes trauma and points towards its enigmatic core: the delay or incompletion in knowing, or even in seeing, an overwhelming occurrence that then remains, in its insistent return, absolutely *true* to the event. It is indeed this truth of traumatic experience that forms the

still historicizes the unprecedented, strips it of its constitutively ahistorical quality, exposes it to development and debasement while itself stiffening into something incomprehensible and unfathomable that petrifies its hopeless audience.

I come from hell and I return to hell. This is how I find myself in the place of precision, trapped between the wall of the unprecedented and, on the other side, the wall of power. The former drives me almost mad, the latter humbles me. Precision is my torment but also my respite and my haven. Although I have been granted an appointment with power, it is unthinkable for me to address it. All I can do is present my report to it and answer the questions it may address to me with the same precision with which I will have prepared my report. This is something that power has in common with the unprecedented, for I have not been able to address the unprecedented either. I have had to pretend that it addressed itself—not to me, specifically, but to the agent of an unheard-of and quasi-automatic precision. Power and the unprecedented both annul any form of initiative, of daring and relating, to which addressing belongs. They do not allow themselves to be addressed, though they must still address themselves to a witness. The unprecedented needs a witness to ensure that it leaves a trace rather than disappearing unnoticed. Power needs a witness to supply the information and the precision necessary for it to manage, preserve, renew, and extend its resources. Power—the power overwhelmingly embodied and unambiguously held by an American president who is a world leader and perhaps even the leader of the world, of the human race—looks at the present and the future, at history and destiny from high above. This power pronounces itself in universal terms—"this will be the war to end all wars"—using capital letters. If it does not occur to the witness to insist on a precise element of his report—the element of the unprecedented—rather than even-handedly displaying this element among the report's other elements, this is because, from the start, he is well aware of how inappropriate it would be to disturb the reclusiveness that defines power and that stems from its vast and far-reaching outlook. This outlook must be super- or supra-human, it must be the outlook of a hardened heart if it is not to lose sight

---

center of its pathology or symptoms; it is not a pathology, that is, of falsehood or displacement of meaning, but of history itself." Cathy Caruth, "Trauma and Experience: Introduction," in *Trauma and Experience*, ed. and with introductions by Cathy Caruth (Baltimore: Johns Hopkins University Press, 1995), 5.

of humanity. Or does a super- or supra-human outlook suffer more rather than less and have a deeper insight into mankind?

Power is pressed for time because it is preoccupied with broad and global visions that must remain intact. The constraints that precision puts on the freedom of saying it all, down to the most insignificant aspect and the most minute item, are also the temporal constraints of power. Power must rely on a division of labor, on allocated jurisdictions, and cannot be interested in details, regardless of the urgency of certain "problems." Problems are solvable in the short or the long run. Power must consider them petty affairs, as atrocious and abominable as they may be, as much as the Jews in Poland may need immediate help if they are not to perish in an unprecedented act of extermination. Is not "the Jewish problem"—an expression the witness uses or mentions often since it is widely employed in the sphere of power—a term designed to downplay the unprecedented and to produce a smoke screen? Is it not even a term that partakes in the antisemitism that the leader of the world has pledged to fight? Yet to the extent that power indulges in broad visions and disregards details, or "problems," it is prone to lapsing into dumbness. At any given moment it can fall prey to the most unexpected of particulars and reveal its own blindness. The leader of the world does not want to hear about the "Jewish problem," just as Poland is not his major worry. He does not grant the witness, who is so much in awe that he has no expectations and directs his undiminished attention to giving precise answers, the freedom of an exhaustive report. But he asks him only whether the horses that the German army needed for its campaign against the Soviet Union had been requisitioned from Polish peasants. Was Poland not mainly an agricultural country before the war?

Power, which exists only for as long as its servants know their place and do not overstep the boundaries assigned to them, is charged with a historic mission. It delegates "problems" and entrusts them to its representatives, to the ones who are its minor embodiments. When the very concept of a problem no longer suffices to contain what appears to be more than simply problematic, the representatives of power deal with "problems" by denying their existence. They acknowledge tacitly the existence of the unprecedented, as can be seen from Karski's account of the bodily transformation undergone by a Jewish member of the Supreme Court whom he describes as physically small and yet as an imposing emanation of brilliance. At the president's request, or in response to a gesture of goodwill that could be regarded as a manifestation of benevolence inseparable from the shrewdness and dumbness of the self-preservation that power must seek, Justice Frankfurter listens to the report of the extermination of his people in Poland, of the witness's clandestine visit to the Warsaw ghetto and of his sojourn, disguised as a guard, in a so-called transit camp. (The witness recollects the encounter as posterior to his meeting with the president, though a biographer claims that it actually preceded it.) As Justice Frankfurter listens, he averts his gaze and his body begins, in the eyes of the reporting witness, to shrink, as if it could not bear the weight that the report carries. However, his mind comes to the rescue and introduces a distinction between what it can recognize, understand, and believe, and what it cannot, at least if it does not want to give up on intelligibility and the possibility of universalization, on the accountability of human motives, actions, and historical deeds. To remain unscathed and not to be drawn fatally into the same movement of disintegration to which the body cannot but succumb, the mind, on the one hand, avoids calling the witness an outright liar and his report an incredible and horrendous fabrication, while, on the other hand, it reaffirms its own limits and limitations, the rights of its rationality, the principles or the fundamental beliefs on which this rationality relies, and the perception and the knowledge informed by it. The mind succeeds in occupying a position of hypocrisy where the body fails to do so, where the body is too clumsy despite its own lightness and ephemerality, and where its sudden reaction, its almost accidental contact with the report and the unprecedented, threatens to taint the spirituality into which it dissolves, the indisputable and impressive authority of a superior judge of man, an expert of humanity and confidant of power, someone with whom one does not argue.

Located between the unprecedented and power, the place of precision, the place where it emerges, is the place of a twofold determination. Precision emerges when it is impossible to put an event or a series of events—"problems" that are incommensurable with "problems"—into perspective on the basis of their recognizability, their identifiability, and their assimilability, and when a witness must be sent out into absolute darkness—a deadly darkness and a darkness worse than death—so as to report back. At the same time, precision is the aim of an activity that must falter when it lacks an established frame of perceptual and intellectual, cognitive and evaluative operations that would provide guidance and sustain a reasonable order—an order in which the principle of reason holds sway, an order into which even the reasons of the heart can be admitted, as a complement or as an exception, and an order that is always also an order of power since something unprecedented may constantly challenge it, something that must be contained. Is it surprising then if the witness slips, if he behaves erratically, if he seems to hover undecidably and in an elusive and ultimately ungraspable manner between functioning like a machine and putting on an act, between the precision of a faithfulness to objectivity—this is how things really are, this is what really happened—and the exaggeration of a subjective, transgressive, substitutive, imprecise intervention? "I am a report" means: I turn into a machine, but also: I am an actor, another kind of machine.

It is perhaps this trouble with the witness that shows in Claude Lanzmann's film *The Karski Report*. A supplement to *Shoah* (1985), it was first screened in 2010. The preceding remarks about precision are based upon it. In the long preface that Lanzmann adds to his film, a written text that scrolls over the screen and that its author reads out with a powerful voice, the exclusion of part of the conversation with Jan Karski, the witness, from *Shoah* is justified by an appeal to the constraints artistic creation, or construction, impose upon the filmmaker. "Dramatic tension"[2] had to be preserved, Lanzmann claims. Without it, it would seem, the coherence of *Shoah* as a film would have been endangered. It would have been an overly long film.

Lanzmann compares his work to the work of an archaeologist. Everything he was looking for when making *Shoah*, an entire world with its victims, its witnesses, and its torturers, appeared to have been destroyed. It was no longer part of the present, had dissipated in a world in which the Holocaust, left in the hands of specialists, had been hushed up. He tells how "each time" he found a survivor, it felt like "a shattering exhumation, just as when archaeologists come across that rare thing, a cornerstone, after several long months of digging patiently and in the dark." Lanzmann warns against the "retrospective illusion" that is forgetful of the "complexity, the heaviness, the opaqueness" of a historical period, aligning the archaeologist's task with a dismantling of this illusion. He asserts that the "majority of Jews could not be rescued" once Hitler had launched "his

---

2. From here on, and if not indicated otherwise, all the quotations are from the text with which *The Karski Report* begins. I have retranslated them from French where necessary rather than relying on the existing English translation.

war against them" and thereby exonerates the people in positions of power to whom Karski had presented his report. His point, though, is ambiguous because it is not clear whether the "true configuration of the impossible" of which he speaks in this context refers to history in general, to the necessity of history producing a "retrospective illusion," or whether it refers to the period in which the Holocaust took place. *Shoah*, the result of the filmmaker's archaeological venture, should be seen, according to Lanzmann, as a labor of "resuscitation" that "inscribed" a witness such as Karski, still alive and willing to report about his reporting, within "History" and "Objective Spirit." In the text, Lanzmann capitalizes history. The striking capital letter indicates perhaps more a resistance to silence than a complicity with power. The Hegelian notion of "Objective Spirit," however, denotes an idealism difficult to reconcile with this silence, as if in the end the filmmaker's archaeology sought an acknowledgment of the Holocaust—or "what was called Holocaust" and he calls "Shoah"—by its integration into History and into the reality of society and the state, whose ultimate accomplishment is itself historical, or, to be precise, "world-historical."

So why the supplement, why the decision to render the material excised from *Shoah*, the film, visible? Because Lanzmann deems it "absolutely necessary to re-establish the truth," not only in relation to a questionable fictionalization of Karski's report but more crucially to fulfill his archaeological task and reinscribe the Holocaust or the Shoah in History or in World-History, from which it had been banned. But how, exactly, does *The Karski Report* contribute to the truth being brought to light—that is, to an acknowledgment, a resuscitation, and a reinscription? *The Karski Report* makes us face the "seriousness" of a "central question," namely "what is knowledge?"—the very question of Socrates or of philosophy, it could be added. It makes us face the question of knowledge in the guise of another question, a question both historical and ahistorical, the question of the unprecedented: "What can information about a literally unheard-of horror mean to the human brain, which is not prepared to receive it since what is at stake here is a crime without precedent in the history of mankind?"

Lanzmann deems it "absolutely necessary to re-establish the truth" and supplement *Shoah* with *The Karski Report*, with material excluded from the main film for artistic reasons. Yet he also mentions another reason for the exclusion, one that remains more puzzling. The artist merely alludes to it and does not explain in what it actually consists. He observes that, on the second day of shooting, Karski, a "capital witness," "behaved very differently" from the way he had behaved on the first day. This statement invites a close analysis that compares the extracts from the conversation included in *Shoah* with the extracts that went into *The Karski Report*. Perhaps a remark Lanzmann made in 2015 as a participant in a question-and-answer session following the screening of *The Karski Report* that took place in Jerusalem, may also prove helpful here. Underlining the difference between his two films, *Shoah* and *The Karski Report*, Lanzmann dwells on the question of tone. The events Karski reports in *Shoah* are "tragic,"[3] he says, and hence the tone is also "tragic," while the events Karski reports in *The Karski Report*—the meetings with President Roosevelt and other US dignitaries—are not "tragic" and hence the tone cannot be "tragic" either. Is it involuntarily comic? In the programmatic notes that introduce *The Karski Report*, Lanzmann defines what is "tragic" about "History" as the impossibility of it taking another course. Surely, this tragic dimension, along with the urge to resist the silencing of historical events of an unprecedented nature, prompts him to write history with a capital letter. The difference in tone then translates into a difference of behavior. On the first day of shooting, or in the material included in *Shoah*, Karski breaks down in front of the camera at the very beginning of his attempt to go back thirty-five years and return to the Warsaw Ghetto. His voice is suffocated by tears. The memories—the report—and the machine are too much for his mind and his body. They undo the discipline he tries to impose upon himself. Having to adopt another tone, a non-tragic tone, when relating his encounter with Roosevelt on the following day, Karski begins to act, to show off, to become self-aware and play a role as the camera rolls on and tracks him around the room where Lanzmann is interviewing him. Now his demeanor is the demeanor of a ham, not exactly a model of precision. It is *cabotin* (theatrical), as Lanzmann puts it in French after the Jerusalem screening.[4] The witness does not turn into a machine anymore but into the agent of a rather crude, uninhibited, and somewhat shameless re-enactment, though perhaps this is merely a

3. See: http://www.alliedpowersholocaust.org/2015-conference-archive/video-archive/
4. Ibid.

different way of turning into a machine and even into a machine of precision.[5]

The reason—or one of the reasons—for there being at least two films with Karski, *Shoah* and *The Karski Report*, must be sought in the trouble with the witness, whose behavior or demeanor is also irreproachable when measured against the contents of his report. The trouble with the witness, however, springs from the fact that he is a witness and, as such, in pursuit of precision. For a witness finds himself cornered by the unprecedented and by power, by that which transforms reporting into a difficult and demanding task and by that which countersigns the report and confers authority upon it. The witness finds himself torn between the tragic and the comic. In the end, he brings the comic to the tragic, contaminates one with the other, because, as a witness, he records, reproduces, or reduplicates the unprecedented and cannot avoid supporting "retrospective illusions." Hence it is not as if there *could* be a supplement to *Shoah*. Rather, there *has* to be such a supplement. Regardless of how accurate its construction may be, there is a gap in *Shoah* that only *The Karski Report* can supplement without ever filling it. Between *Shoah* and *The Karski Report*, this gap, or the blind spot of precision and witnessing, is incessantly displaced. Perhaps it is at this dynamic juncture, or in this "true configuration of the impossible" that defies knowledge as much as belief, that *Shoah* and *The Karski Report* come into their uncertain existence and that history's capital letter begins to fade.

---

5. Of course, the distinction to be made in a discussion of *Shoah* and the films that supplement it is not a distinction between a witness who acts and one who does not, as witnessing and acting may be perfectly inseparable. Acting is a form of being a witness, one on which "authenticity" depends, as Lanzmann demonstrates: "It is crucial for Lanzmann's film that he encourage a certain margin for play." Gertrud Koch, "The Aesthetic Transformation of the Image of the Unimaginable: Notes on Claude Lanzmann's *Shoah*," *October* 102 (Spring 1989): 20. The distinction to be made is a distinction between tonalities or styles—or non-styles—of acting: between being a ham and not being a ham. Does Lanzmann appreciate it when, in *The Karski Report*, the witness resembles a ham? When, exactly, does acting sabotage the "authenticity" of witnessing? Shoshana Felman construes an analogy between Lanzmann and Karski that makes such questions all the more virulent: "I would now suggest that Lanzmann's own trip is evocative of that of Karski: that Lanzmann, in his turn, takes us on a *journey* whose aim precisely is to *cross the boundary*, first from the outside world to the inside of the Holocaust, and then back from the inside of the Holocaust to the outside world." Shoshana Felman, "The Return of the Voice," in Shoshana Felman and Dori Laub, *Testimony: Crises of Witnessing in Literature, Psychoanalysis, and History* (New York: Routledge, 1992), 238.

SARA GUYER

Testimony beyond Justice:
The Last of the Unjust

Claude Lanzmann's 2013 film *The Last of the Unjust* is a testament to confusion. The film dramatizes the disturbances brought about by life-sustaining acts of compromise that are also murderous acts of violence. Like *Shoah*, it bears witness to experiences of extremity, but it also is composed of material that *Shoah* could not hold within its frame. This is literally the case, insofar as it centers around a week-long interview with Benjamin Murmelstein, the clever Viennese rabbi and head of the Jewish Council in Theresienstadt, that Lanzmann could not find a way to incorporate into his earlier film and that haunted him for nearly four decades. But it is conceptually the case too. In bringing these interviews belatedly to light, Lanzmann reflects on the place of interpretation and judgment in testimony. The film leaves entirely unclear what should be done with Murmelstein. Put another way, I wish to suggest that Lanzmann's acknowledgment that the Murmelstein interviews could not be made to fit within the framework of *Shoah* and the practices of testimony that it defines reflects—but is not identical with—the moral framework that has distinguished the response to Murmelstein, from Hannah Arendt and Gershom Scholem to our present. Murmelstein is a risk to testimonial and moral practices, to witnessing and judgment. Testimony and judgment here overlap, while remaining distinct concepts—and problems—that *The Last of the Unjust* navigates, as much as it navigates Murmelstein's own unsettling testimony. The film, in this sense, is not about a crisis of judgment, but rather a crisis of testimony that operates within the scene of justice. The relation between justice and testimony, witnessing and judgment, is neither coherent nor supportive. It is an ongoing interpretive challenge—one that Lanzmann, through this film, undertakes to dramatize and reveal.

YFS 141, *Lanzmann after "Shoah,"* ed. Levine and Stark, © 2022 by Yale University.

Murmelstein was a survivor and a witness, a bystander, and a perpetrator. As a result, he could not fit in *Shoah*'s architecture. But more than this, his testimony threatens the project of witnessing that *Shoah* inaugurates. Deeply educated in religious and secular texts, erudite, and aware of the power of literary analysis, analogy, and allegory, Murmelstein, in his conversations with Lanzmann, scrambles the frameworks of sense when he glides between a firsthand account of his experience as a member of the Judenrat and literary references belonging to another order of representation, that of myth (Orpheus and Eurydice) or epic (One Thousand-and-One Nights). Throughout, there are interruptions, whether in the turn to literary and mythic texts, or when his speech seems to break off, as in the following brief exchange in which they speak about whether Murmelstein was—and implicitly *how* he could become—the only leader of the Jewish Council to survive. In the passage below, the ellipses do not indicate missing text, but the interrupted and hesitant pace of this exchange:

> Claude Lanzmann: Many people told me that Murmelstein is dead, Murmelstein has to be very old.
> Benjamin Murmelstein: I am that. I am that.
> CL: No.
> BM: I want to tell you something. I have to support those who said that to you. According to the Talmud there is an ancient saying which says: A poor person is just like a dead one. Thus, if you understand it in this manner, you were not wrong.
> CL: Well, this is not exactly . . . not exactly so. You are . . . . You are the last of the Jewish Elders.
> BM: No, I am the only one who survived, the last one, you might say. How you look at this, if you regard it qualitatively or chronologically . . . it does not matter.
> CL: Yes, you are the last one, there are no others.
> BM: No.
> CL: . . . on earth, in all the earth, isn't that so?
> BM: No, it . . . I would not know, I would not know. I am the last one. I was . . . this is also a funny matter, to be the last one.[1]

1. All quotations from the film are from Claude Lanzmann, dir., *Le dernier des injustes* (*The Last of the Unjust*) (2013). Translations follow the subtitles. There is one part of this exchange that appears in the rushes for *Shoah*, but that Lanzmann cuts from *The Last of the Unjust*. Just before Murmelstein says to Lanzmann, "I want to tell you something," the two men at the same time say, "Me too." The reference—to age? to hearing the same message?—is unclear even as the shared identity is vividly established (and ultimately cut). https://collections.ushmm.org/search/catalog/irn1003918.

In this twisting and interrupted exchange, both *death* and *the last* seem untethered from their conventional references and meanings. It is unclear whether these are philosophical reflections on definition, strategic evasions, or symptoms of persistent trauma. It is this coagulation of reflection, evasion, and interruption that the film observes but cannot resolve.

Murmelstein negates Lanzmann's statements, turning statements of fact into shimmering uncertainties. First, Murmelstein goes nearly so far as to announce that he is dead, placing his words in the frame of impossibility or fiction, and in any case, in a wildly contradictory logic. He is both old and dead. He is not the last, yet he is also the only survivor. Murmelstein lives in the language of the Final Solution and the destruction of language that poets like Paul Celan and writers like Theodor Adorno and Maurice Blanchot sought to witness. This early scene shows how Lanzmann's late film moves from testimony as a challenge of narrative integration to testimony as a challenge to interpretation and meaning (not as significance, but as coherence). From this very early scene through to Murmelstein's reflections toward the end of the film on sense and nonsense, we discover that the demand of *The Last of the Unjust* is to give place in the world of testimony for this violence against sense. It acknowledges rather than resolves the unstable meaning of words like "last" or "unjust," upon which we rely for sociality and action and which form the ground for our interventions and interpretations. The film reveals how this violence suspends the orientation that terms like "last" and "unjust" offer; it reveals that there is no last interpretation, just as there is no one who rests clearly on the side of justice—or its opposite. This disorientation is core to the film's reflection.

The *facts* of Murmelstein's case, and not only his account of them, also reflect the ambiguity of his position: he was imprisoned in part by choice, exonerated by a Czech court, prevented from participating in Eichmann's trial due to his "unreliability," excluded from visiting Israel, and ultimately lived out his days in exile in Rome, where he died in 1989. He accepts everything and nothing. He does not deny the facts of his situation, but challenges their interpretation and meaning. He is proud of his accomplishments, dismisses Arendt's understanding of Eichmann (whom he believes was viciously brilliant), and implies that no one could know, see, or do what he alone accomplished in his role leading the Judenrat. He scandalized Scholem and, although he was himself a rabbi, the Rabbi of Rome refused to officiate at his funeral. He is immense and ambitious, yet small-minded and petty. It is not only that these *interviews* do not fit the architecture of *Shoah*; it is that Murmelstein does not fit into a world in which we can live. This is a world of pervasive indirection in which even the deceptions of the Nazi genocide make more sense, in their undeniable violence, than the testimony of Rabbi Murmelstein, which pushes to the limit the role of testimony as unstable and unreliable speech.

While testimony in *Shoah* exposed a gap in the source of knowledge and visibility of evidence, here testimony shakes the foundations of judgment and understanding. *The Last of the Unjust* has elements of judgment, giving a platform to the testimony that could not be heard in Eichmann's trial. Yet it is also that which could not be adequately processed in any trial, just as it could find no place in one of the twentieth century's most significant accounts of the Holocaust (*Shoah*). In this way, the film reflects Lanzmann's effort to face the confusion of salvation and murder and the production of a universe in which sensible alliances collapsed in the name of survival. Lanzmann's discomfort with this indeterminacy, far from resolved by devoting an entire film to Murmelstein, is on full display. The film does not resolve this duplicity in judgment or deny it by establishing an alternative history. Instead, the film produces an experience of it, one that, if taken seriously, matters as much for our own present as for the past that it undertakes to access.

FIRST OPENING

The film begins with Lanzmann's need to process Murmelstein's story and make it known. It opens without an image or a voice—the two affordances of cinema—but rather with an introductory note that silently scrolls the screen. Opening in this way, by evoking the decades of silence between the moment of the initial interview with Murmelstein and the present of the film's release, *The Last of the Unjust* begins by resisting its own cinematic power (the capacity to integrate material that had no clear place) and uses its power only minimally. The moving text is the remnant of cinema's capacity to see and to move, but it withholds anything more. In opening with this silent text, the film forms its addressee not as a viewer or witness, but as a reader.

The note with which Lanzmann introduces the film, although written in black and white, is far from clarifying. It is an example of what Jonathan Rosenblum has called a "dialectical palimpsest."[2] While Lanzmann uses this moment to explain the film's origins and provide background on its key figure, he does so not in the mode of historical objectivity, but in a signed, first-person narrative in which he has become witness to a knowledge that is both burdensome and unsettling. He writes:

> Rabbi Benjamin Murmelstein was the last Chairman of the There-sienstadt Judenrat (Jewish Council). I filmed him during a whole week in Rome in 1975. In my eyes, the case of Theresienstadt was capital, both lateral and central, in the genesis and process [*déroulement*] of the Final Solution. These long hours of interviews, rich in first-hand revelations, have continued to dwell in my mind and haunt me.

Introduced in this way, the film reflects Lanzmann's vision: not simply as what he sees, but what he understands. "In my eyes" ("dans mes yeux") for Lanzmann means reading, interpretation, and judgment, rather than vision. Here the screen is black; Terezín is not what is seen. It is the "model camp" designed to obscure vision. It is what must be un-seen. Lanzmann recognizes this physical scene of deception as "capital"—or key to—the Final Solution. In the book that he published after the release of the film, Lanzmann also refers to Murmelstein in these same terms as a "témoin capital" (a key or essential witness), implicitly suggesting that Murmelstein is not just an instance, but that he too is "both lateral and central" to our understanding, not (or not only) of the Final Solution, but of testimony itself.[3]

Capital in English does not have the clear sense of centrality that it does in French. Nevertheless, it evokes another significant reference: the capital punishment that Murmelstein evaded, leaving him to remain the last of the Jewish Elders, whether or not he accepts this position. Further, *capital* is etymologically related to head, and evokes Murmelstein's own position as the "cap," "*chef*," or "head" of the Council. The question that burdens Lanzmann is what we do with the head—and, in this case, the head that alone survives and survives alone. Once seeing is narrated but not experienced, once cinema gives nothing to see and only material to read, interpret, and judge, once it becomes this set of eyes that do not see, we come to be aware

2. Jonathan Rosenblum, "Claude Lanzmann's *The Last of the Unjust*," *Artforum* 52/6 (February 2014), https://www.artforum.com/print/201402/claude-lanzmann-s-the-last-of-the-unjust-45001.

3. Claude Lanzmann, *Les derniers des injustes* (Paris: Gallimard, 2015).

of the sheer confusion that the film documents. *The Last of the Unjust* reflects Lanzmann's effort to come to terms with Murmelstein, not as a man, but as a significant, even devastating risk to testimony and its instabilities of meaning. The film is not an achievement, but a lonely, lingering compulsion. It is not a success, but an experience of confusion and acknowledgement of risk.

Murmelstein and his account are, to evoke the name of Lanzmann's own production company, a *synecdoche* of testimony, he is a part that stands in for the whole. Yet, in this way, he also reveals the darkest side of figure, providing a testimony that depends upon sheer substitutability and ungrounded meaning in the almost infinite possibility of reference. This mobility of reference is a source of fascination and disturbance. It is the film's point of departure and its limit. Murmelstein thus seems to reflect both the kind of person who can survive under these conditions, and the profound relationship between figuration, indeterminacy, and survival. It is as if the capacity to reframe, analogize, or undo reference are intimately related to the capacity to navigate the Nazi regime and live through it. By turning his experience into one that can be perpetually reinterpreted and by revealing his seduction with the comparisons of literature and life, he also makes his own story elusive and a site of unfinished interpretation, rather than definitive understanding. It is so mobile and so capable of being reframed and reinterpreted that its meaning becomes obscure.

One framework for making sense of Murmelstein appears in the extensive account presented in *Choices under Duress of the Holocaust*, in which Leonard H. Ehrlich and Edith Ehrlich implicitly respond to the set of questions posed by Murmelstein's life.[4] Is he the worst of the worst or someone whose affectless calculus allowed him to make decisions others carefully avoided? Was he a victim? A savior? A criminal? Can we know him—and can he know himself? Unlike the Ehrlichs' extensive profile, Lanzmann's film frames another set of questions: can testimony (and testimonial cinema) endure Murmelstein? Is Murmelstein not only *The Last of the Unjust* but also the truth and destruction of testimony? I read Lanzmann's return to the Murmelstein interview as an effort to face these questions. As

---

4. Leonard H. Ehrlich and Edith Ehrlich, *Choices under Duress of the Holocaust: Benjamin Murmelstein and the Fate of Viennese Jewry*. Volume 1: Vienna, ed. Carl S. Ehrlich (Lubbock, TX: Texas Tech University Press, 2018).

he explains, "I knew that I was the custodian of something unique but backed away from the difficulties of constructing such a film. It took me a long time to accept the fact that I had no right to keep it to myself."[5] This obligation to the public and to the future led Lanzmann back to Murmelstein; it also led him to reflect on his own responsibility—and implicitly on a testimonial form that sets out from an acknowledgment that there is no ground for a clear verdict.

The opening silence of the scrolling text gives way to a film that is virtually all voices. The 1975 exchange between Murmelstein and Lanzmann (and sometimes a translator) that did not appear in *Shoah* is framed by new footage taken when Lanzmann returns to make a film centered around Murmelstein. In these newer sections, Lanzmann appears not as a disembodied voice, but as a still robust, yet aging body that resembles, but is not identical with, the man who had interviewed Murmelstein decades earlier. In these contemporary scenes, shot on location, Lanzmann stands in the place of the deported and dead without any conjuring power beyond that of his voice. This appears equally as a substitution of the living for the dead and as a means of demonstrating unsubstitutability. Lanzmann is apparently alone on screen and fully present to the camera, often reading a text, which is only sometimes his own. The film also is punctuated by the sounds of contemporary Europe and the recitation of ancient Hebrew liturgy. These images, while understated, nevertheless remain occasions in which interpretation—ultimately, judgment itself—are needed. At the same time, the first exchange with Murmelstein, where life becomes death and lastness becomes a question, throws into disarray the work of interpretation, revealing its relation to duplicity and fiction.

SECOND OPENING

The Last of the Unjust is an act through which Lanzmann avoids backing away from what might be the most significant challenge to his own project: Murmelstein's testimony. The first image of the

5. Lanzmann uses a slightly different formulation in the introduction to the 2015 book *Le dernier des injustes*; he does not insist upon rights and obligations, but rather upon necessity. Further, see Judith Kasper and Michael G. Levine on the various figures of the back in the film, evoked here in the act of "backing away from" rather than "facing" a significant challenge to film and to sense. "The Persistence of the Witness," *Critical Inquiry* 46 (Winter 2020): 6-7.

film is of *Lanzmann*, facing us and walking toward us. He stands on a platform beneath a sign that reads "Bohusovice." There is a train shelter behind him and train tracks on either side. It is 2013, the year of the film's release, and Lanzmann begins with a halting question: *Qui . . . aujourd'hui . . . dans le monde . . . connait le nom du Bohusovice et de la gare?* (Who . . . today . . . in the world . . . knows the name and the station of Buhosovice?) On the one hand, everyone watching the film now knows this name because they see and hear it. But what do they know? What kind of knowledge is this? When I search *Bohusovice* today, Wikipedia gives it three short sentences suggesting location, population, geographic features. Further down, I have a weather report, a COVID-19 report, a list of hotels and restaurants. The accounts are spare, and for all of their information they affirm that no one today (seven years after the film's release) knows anything of the station. Only *Tripadvisor* associates Bohusovice with the more familiar name Terezín. Who in the world today knows this station? The answer is that those who know it cannot any longer know.

Lanzmann then moves from his position underneath the sign for Bohusovice to the track it marks. He stands there, speaking to the camera in a second instance of introduction that replaces the disembodied, voiceless text with the fullness of a living body and the voice of a European Jew standing where others once arrived. He explains that this is a stop on the route between Prague and Berlin and, as he speaks, the trains begin to pass. There is a cut, and he turns from facing the camera to facing the trains. We see him not head-on or from the back but at a lateral view, in between the two positions he had marked out. His face is turned away from us to watch the trains—loud, rumbling, cutting through the cloudy air. At that moment, we come to see that sitting on the bench, waiting, are three people engaged in conversation, almost invisible to us even as their movement synchronizes with Lanzmann's when he turns to follow the passing train. The train is long, missing many containers, allowing a second train, passing alongside it on the opposite track, to become visible. Lanzmann turns his head back and forth toward the oncoming train and then, following it, toward the camera. His grey hair and papers blow in the force of a wind that seems not natural, but rather an effect of the train's powerful motion—a violent force. Each time he goes to speak, another train passes by, and he begins to grow exasperated, shrugging his shoulders, gesturing, throwing up his hands as if to ask when will this end, but also moving his hand, up and down, as if to measure time, as one does when reading a poem or keeping the beat in a song. The empty trains, loud and rumbling, keep going, first in one direction then in the other. The station's clock, just above his head, marks the minutes and registers that we are losing time. Lanzmann's frustration grows—the trains are interrupting his speech, delaying the film, even if only by a minute. Is his impatience with the trains merely the performance of a mundane annoyance that is wholly inadequate to the history that these tracks bear but do not reflect? Has Lanzmann inadvertently become someone who wants the trains to hurry up as he stands overlooking the tracks that once carried so many to their deaths? Or is it not death and the question of what one would do were they in a position of unsettling responsibility but rather the interruption of testimony and speech that is the film's subject?

Looking out in the distance, Lanzmann's glance meets with another passing train that now becomes the camera's only object. He continues, in words equally strange in their reference, addressed in part to his team: *Nous ne pouvons pas contrôler le trafic.* The camera now pivots to follow in the direction of the train—we don't know whether it is headed toward Prague or Berlin—bringing the station's sign, this place, in lieu of the clock marking the time, again into view as the train moves away from us. Our gaze, like that of Lanzmann, follows the train. On its cars, we read: Maesk, HanJin, K Line. The global shipping industry rushes past, indifferent to this film. Behind the trains we catch a glimpse of a single human figure watching the train, standing barely visible across the track. The camera pivots again, revealing the absence of any human figures— lingering over buildings with peeling paint, faltering stucco, and exposed stonework—perhaps some houses, it is unclear—a parked car. There is something and nothing, someone and no one to see. Lanzmann speaks over the panorama of the scene from the platform, reinscribing with his words this station not only as the place about which no one knows, but the place about which almost all those who did know have been murdered. This was the platform on which 140,000 Jews "were disembarked" upon arrival *en route* to Terezín.

From here, Lanzmann ironically cites the twisted language of the Nazis, reminding us in French and then in German and then in French again, that Terezín was called "The Führer's gift to the Jews." "*Quel cadeau!*" (What a gift!) As he says this, as he continues to speak, he turns again, walking back toward where he began, looking not at the camera—which he had addressed before—but toward the tracks. The scene ends and the camera turns back on the sign for the Bohusovice station. There is no one in the shot, neither Lanzmann nor the bystanders, but it has begun to rain. With no one left on the scene, Lanzmann begins to read from Murmelstein's anatomy of Terezín.[6] The book describes Terezín as a spa town with hotels, yet we continue to see only the train tracks for as far as the eye—or camera—can see. This does not mean that there aren't windows and structures overlooking the endless series of electrified tracks, only that there is no one there. The disjunction between the description in the text and the image before us continues a repeated theme in Holocaust film at least since *Night and Fog*. One does not see. Film's task, after Auschwitz, is to allow us to see not *what* we do not see, but *that* we do not (did not, cannot) see. Rather than stopping here, however, *The Last of the Unjust* does not allow this negative knowledge to be any consolation in the face of absence.

The film cuts again to Lanzmann, who now is standing on the other side of the tracks, where he continues to read aloud from a French translation of Murmelstein's book printed out on A4 paper. The papers fly up and almost blow away as the trains pass by; Murmelstein's account, and Lanzmann's translation of it, is almost lost at the station, even before we face him. But Lanzmann persists. He continues to read as we notice that more people have gathered at the terminal, awaiting the train. We see the train arriving. A second-class car; people get on and off. A crew member walks out of one door, onto the platform, and returns following the quotidian gestures of their task. As the train "today" pulls out of the station and the porter descends, Lanzmann continues to read Murmelstein, describing the scene as Murmelstein once witnessed it. He recalls the lies and chaos of the "model" camp designed to obscure the Nazi project in its actuality:

> When the train pulled into the station at Bohusovice, the journey was over and the illusions too. The welcome committee was made up of SS militiamen, anxious young Jews, and a few Czech gendarmes. Flowers were missing.

6. Benjamin Murmelstein, *Terezin: Il ghetto-modello di Eichmann* (Milan: La Scuola, 2013). The book was first published by Cappelli in 1961, but reissued to coincide with Lanzmann's film.

From the carriage windows hoary heads peered out looking for a porter. Their expressions soon shift from curiosity to doubt and then terror.

To screamed orders the elderly try to climb down from the train in their best clothes to make a good impression in the boarding houses where they have booked rooms with views of the lake from the panoramic terrace. No one holds out a hand to the newcomers: some of them fall, bowler hats roll over the ground, shoving, slapping, beating, screams, women's sobs, a tangle of bodies, crutches, and suitcases. An apocalyptic vision.

The image today is not "apocalyptic," but empty and quotidian. The clock remains in the background marking our present. It now appears to be several hours since the first shots, even if only minutes have passed in the film. The camera turns to follow the train out of the station, and the color image of the station in the present is replaced by silence and an old photograph of the crowded scene that Murmelstein describes. The photograph is the break between two moments in Lanzmann's film—his 2013 return to the Czech Republic to witness the absence about which he speaks and his 1975 meeting with Benjamin Murmelstein in Rome to elicit his testimony.

These two moments of introduction in *The Last of the Unjust*—the signed opening text in which Lanzmann describes the film's origins and the opening address in which he stands on the platform reading Murmelstein's book aloud—reflect two modes of cinematic address in which testimony and reading are entangled. They show how the effort to return to an enigmatic figure and face duplicity also suffers from it and they register the difficulty of maintaining distance. Murmelstein's experience and our understanding of it cannot be resolved in a singular frame, but generate reading, interpretation, and judgment. In this way, the film suggests that ethical questions and questions of culpability are indissociable from questions of testimony.

Facing us, at last, Lanzmann is cut off by the trains that interrupt and delay him. But he is here not only to provide a unique testimony but to bring Murmelstein's testimony to light. The constant disruptions with which the film opens and the questions that it poses—*Is seeing interpretation? Is "who" "no one"?*—reveal an uncertainty that carries into the present. What appears to be as black and white as the opening text is in fact murky. In this way, the film stages the question of how to read and think together the demand of witnessing, the inevitable possibility of substitutions and deceptions, and the lingering, untimely, and unfinished work of judgment.

Lanzmann acknowledges, further, that testimony is not the only way of indexing loss. The film also includes static commemorations in plaques, preserved buildings, and public inscriptions. These plaques, including memorial inscriptions of thousands of names of the dead that he films, are irreplaceable. These are lists without stories: the singularity of a name that indicates the absence of testimony.[7] In a later scene, Lanzmann stands in front of the gallows of Terezín, frustrated that, just as he could not control the traffic at the station, he cannot make these names or these places come to life, or make any sense, even through cinema. He cannot make meaning of deaths that were both mass in their scale and individual in their effects. While there is no one left to stand with him at the camp, the living nevertheless continue to show up throughout the film. Uncannily, in these places of death, absence, and commemoration, other people appear, whether they are accidental passers-by or active commemorators. They include the security guard who stands watch outside the synagogue; the man on the street merely walking by; the group of vigilant citizens, holding signs, who march along the pathway of memory paying tribute to those killed in the Holocaust; the cantor reciting kaddish; as well as those commuters on the train platforms. Whether they are preserving or merely inhabiting the *lieux de mémoire*, they show that the living are no more managed or scripted in the film than are those Lanzmann cannot bring back to life. The living, including Murmelstein, it turns out, demonstrate how memory and forgetting remain outside of cinema's power.

Through Murmelstein, Lanzmann discovers that testimony can become the archive of intimate deception. It can leave us not more knowledgeable, but merely responsible for a narrative that has no place and might have no truth. This burden, which evidently troubled Lanzmann for decades and which he ultimately represents for us here, becomes our burden. It is relevant not only for the light it sheds

---

7. Geoffrey Hartman and Paul de Man both have acknowledged the way in which the commemorative name, like that on a grave or on these walls, also operates as a figure that animates. I discuss this structure in *Romanticism after Auschwitz* (Stanford: Stanford University Press, 2007) and "Rwanda's Bones," *boundary 2*, 36 (2009): 155-75. See also Sarah Kofman's account of discovering her father's name in the list of those deported in *Smothered Words*, trans. Madeline Dobie (Evanston: Northwestern University Press, 1998).

on the past and on the destruction of Europe's Jews, but for the light it sheds on our present.

TESTIMONY, TODAY

I want to conclude with a reflection on testimony today. *The Last of the Unjust* compels us to ask, with Lanzmann, whether we have a concept of testimony that is adequate to the case of Murmelstein. This would need to be a concept of testimony that not only supplements the absence of what Primo Levi identified as the drowned with testimonial accounts of the saved, but a concept of testimony that admits interpretation.

When Lanzmann brought his reflections on Murmelstein to the twenty-first century, it was on the cusp of Donald Trump's run for President in the United States. The film appeared in the final moments of naïveté, in which it was still unthinkable that a country that valued democracy would support white supremacist and fascist leadership. After Trump, the confusion that Lanzmann recognized in Murmelstein's testimony, the confusion between salvation and destruction, between interpretation and truth, has become newly resonant. We now need to ask whether we have a concept of testimony that is adequate to post-truth. Can testimony survive as a resource when its documented relationship to fiction protects deception rather than a finally inaccessible truth?

To address this situation, we need to move, as Lanzmann does, from the accounts of testimony that emerged in the 1970s and 1980s—the time when the collection and theorization of testimony coincided with post-structuralist accounts of history and epistemology—to the 2010s and 2020s, when the "deconstruction of truth"—no longer a means of deconstructing the hegemonic power of colonialism and the Enlightenment in order to reveal the construction of exclusionary knowledge—came to be used to *affirm* white supremacy, antisemitism, and patriarchy. This uncanny reversal, powerfully documented by Andrew Marantz, who has profiled how alt-right activists appropriated post-structuralist theory for the purposes of dissimulation and destruction, resonates with Murmelstein, who turns to philosophy, Greek mythology, and European literature to frame his position.[8]

8. See Andrew Marantz on alt-right influencer Mike Cernovic: "His survey courses in philosophy also covered postmodernists like Foucault and Lacan and Derrida. A lot

"The Humanities of Testimony" is the title of a 2006 special issue of *Poetics Today* edited by Geoffrey Hartman as well as his opening essay in it. It is a curious title. How, for example, should we hear the genitive "of"? What does *humanities* signify in a context where the human—as both a capacity for survival and speech and for evil and destruction—is on full display? Does *testimony* emerge here as a field of knowledge? A method? A genre? An act? A configuration of disciplinary or ideological approaches? In the context of the journal *Poetics Today*, is "testimony" a synonym of "poetics"? More than this, it could be taken even further to signify not just poetics, but poetics *today*.

In his opening essay, Hartman describes a transformation of "disciplines of knowledge"—history, literature, aesthetics, philosophy—through oral testimony, new media (video), archival activism, new protocols for dialogue, and the recognition of another set of voices, genres, media, and methods. Yet, by the end of the essay, he also worries that this transformation within academic, cultural, and archival universes has had virtually no effect. He worries that testimony—and the attendant transformations of knowledge, of what and how we know—have not prevented the recurrence of genocidal violence around the globe, and that the testimonial turn offers neither "sparks of hope [n]or effective moral and political lessons." So, what is the point? Classrooms, technologies, frames of recognition have opened to testimonial voices, but Hartman worries: what, if anything, has changed? I would suggest that *today*, fifteen years after Hartman's essay, the problem itself has changed. It is true that hope and lessons are in short supply. However, something more serious has emerged. The relation to truth that makes testimony a resource for awareness of that which cannot simply be corroborated or established as empirical data is also what has allowed it to be used a tool of destruction. This unhappy insight is one that Lanzmann grasped with Murmelstein and sought to make visible.

---

of what they wrote struck him as faux-intellectual bullshit, but he boiled it down until it made sense to him. The postmodernists seemed to be arguing that there was no single, absolute truth—that everything was just a narrative, a socially contingent power struggle, which implied that even history and current events were subject to personal interpretation the way that novels and movies were. Mike didn't know whether this was objectively true, but it was an interesting way to look at the world." Marantz, *Anti-Social: Online Extremists, Techno-Utopians, and the Hijacking of the American Conversation* (New York: Viking, 2019), 137-38.

Just as disciplinary knowledge and critical methods have been transformed by this opening to testimony, testimony, as is evident in *The Last of the Unjust*, also has introduced a risk that has become increasingly palpable today. In recent years, in response to a global pandemic and climate change, which have become ideological rather than epistemological conditions, there has been a resounding call for truth, a demand for scientific knowledge that dismisses the value of testimony—with its incomplete witnesses, crises of certainty, analogies, and necessary projections. This leads us, with Lanzmann, to wonder, what has happened *today* to testimony? What happens to testimony, figuration, and hermeneutics in the world in which living can be called death and chronology can be reinterpreted (Murmelstein); in which climate change, the history of slave ownership, and rates of viral infection are not points of agreement, but of reversal, contestation, and deniability (our own). Murmelstein exposed testimony's risk, just as our more recent experience of "post-truth" left many longing for a form of evidence more certain than slippery.

In 2013, *The Last of the Unjust* does not replace lying and indifference with fact or counter-narratives; it does not recover cinema from the testimonial turn. Rather, it positions its audience as readers. Further, Lanzmann locates himself, standing in the place of the absent witness as one who can only read, rather than see or remember, as one who has no other power than to make the difficulty visible, to recognize rather than ignore it. Lanzmann's approach is relevant not only to our understanding of the Nazi genocide, but to our ability to recognize the importance of the humanities even when the "post-fact" or "post-truth" cultures of deception unsettle them and us. Far from irrelevant in a moment when we are desperately in need of rational and factual truths in order to live, the humanities, like testimony, are what prepare us to be readers in a world like the one to which Murmelstein testifies. This is "The Humanities of Testimony," and it is not, or not only, as Hartman worried, the powerlessness of testimony to prevent genocide—or other forms of violence—but the urgency of reading a testimony whose value might not be its truth. It is the task of the humanities today to face these questions and to explore anew the array of forms through which inquiry, disposition, futurity, and the possibility of non-fascist freedom can be instantiated and preserved institutionally.

Two decades ago, Derrida imagined the university as this institutional space, in part because of its relation to testimony. Derrida's vision of the university evokes the path that we have been following in Lanzmann's cinema:

> Here then is what I will call the unconditional university or the university without condition: the principal of the right to say everything, whether it be under the heading of fiction and the experimentation of knowledge, and the right to say it publicly, to publish it. This reference to public space will remain the link that affiliates the new Humanities to the Age of Enlightenment. It distinguishes the university institution from other institutions founded on the right or the duty to say everything, for example religious confession and even psychoanalytic "free association." But it is also what fundamentally links the university, and above all the Humanities, to what is called literature, in the European and modern sense of the term, as the right to say everything publicly or to keep it secret, if only in the form of fiction. I allude to confession, which is very close to the profession of faith, because I would like to connect my remarks to the analysis of what is happening today, on the worldwide scene, that resembles a universal process of confession, avowal, repentance, expiation, and asked for forgiveness [sic]. One could cite innumerable examples, day after day. But whether we are talking about very ancient crimes or yesterday's crimes, about slavery, the Shoah, apartheid, or even acts of violence of the Inquisition . . . repentance is always carried out with reference to the very recent juridical concept of "crime against humanity."[9]

How, today, can we maintain a relation to the past and future, testimony and the subjunctive, without ceding to the opposition between fact and lie, without ceding interpretation and reading? How can we establish a culture that resists the fascism of post-fact and the austerity of evidence without imagination or interpretation? How can we avoid trying to counteract the perversion of the freedom to say anything, the regime of post-fact, by putting in its place a newly dangerous culture of hyper-restraint? How can we see restraint as a condition of future survival, without foreclosing the poetic, the unconscious, or the imaginative?

Perhaps we should imagine freedom, independence, and exposure not as freedom from fact, but rather as an opening that allows us to live—survive—within the conditions that haunt us, from the past or

---

9. Jacques Derrida, "The future of the profession or the university without condition (thanks to the 'Humanities,' what *could take place* tomorrow)," in *Jacques Derrida and the Humanities: A Critical Reader*, ed. Tom Cohen (Cambridge: Cambridge University Press), 26-27.

toward a future that seems to be already written, or not. Murmelstein's testimony—in its confusion and disarray, in its avoidance of humiliation and in its acts of self-defense, whether conscious or unconscious, strategic or habitual—exposes the risk of testimony. Testimony is not without these risks—the risk of deception, of irresolution, and of deferred judgments. More than *Shoah*, then, *The Last of the Unjust* is the film in which Lanzmann exposes the meaning, the necessity, and the risk of testimony today.

STUART LIEBMAN

Four Sisters and Claude Lanzmann's Holocaust Film Project

The 237-minute-long *Les quatre soeurs* (*Four Sisters*), the last work that Claude Lanzmann carved out of the hundreds of hours of interviews he recorded to prepare his widely celebrated major achievement, *Shoah*, received its United States premiere at the New York Film Festival in October 2017. Its European broadcast on the Arte channel followed in January 2018 and the film finally reached French movie screens on July 4, 2018, just one day before the director's death. The work is unusual in that it presents the stories of four Jewish women survivors, a dimension long missing from his ongoing Holocaust project, and in an anthology format—a suite of four individually titled films—that he had never used before.

Critics overwhelmingly responded positively to Lanzmann's valedictory contribution to the canon of Holocaust cinema. Yet underlying some of the respectful critical praise one can detect a subtle undercurrent of reservations suggesting that *Four Sisters* was somehow a lesser work.

Writing for Rogerebert.com, Matt Zoller Seitz noted:

> Some viewers of Lanzmann's work, including staunch admirers, have wondered if what he's doing in these movies is really "filmmaking" as we traditionally understand it, or something more along the lines of skillful interviewing that happens to be recorded. . . . The story is shaped in the process of recording it, rather than being excessively manipulated after the fact.

Lawrence Garcia made similar comments in his review for avclub.com:

> To offer these stories in such an unadorned manner is itself a kind of integrity, and no reasonable person could object to presenting them

YFS 141, *Lanzmann after "Shoah,"* ed. Levine and Stark, © 2022 by Yale University.

to a wider audience. That said, it's fair to wonder whether the final shape Lanzmann arrives at here yields much more value than, say, the individually archived clips themselves. There's a lingering impression that he has fashioned more of a document—a pure oral history—than anything else.

Even Jennifer Cazenave in her excellent book about the outtakes not used in *Shoah* concludes that Lanzmann neither frames the women's stories in a historical context nor does he make their accounts into part of a larger argument about the Shoah as he does in his other Holocaust-related films. What is more: *Four Sisters'* sustained focus on the interviewees, with only occasional reverse or medium shots of the filmmaker/interviewer, closely tracks the procedures in "talking heads" documentaries and audiovisual testimonies. She therefore deems Lanzmann's *Four Sisters* to be more a document than a documentary.[1]

Four Sisters is certainly more modest formally than *Shoah*. The interviews recorded for *Shoah* included a much larger number of witnesses. It offered panoramic coverage of extermination sites from which nearly all traces of the crimes have been erased—what Lanzmann calls the *non-lieux de mémoire* (non-sites of memory).[2] The fragmented, circular shape of *Shoah*'s narrative, moreover, is also far more complex than the simpler, essentially chronological accounts offered in *Four Sisters*. As a result, the careful construction of the sound and image tracks—in short, the effects of editing—are not as conspicuously present in Lanzmann's last Holocaust-related work.

Lanzmann did, however, carry over some strategies from *Shoah*. He continues to focus on his subjects' voices, facial expressions, and gestures as they tell their stories because he believes these bodily responses "incarnate" the truth of their experience. He continues to use props to provoke memories by his witnesses. As in *Le dernier des injustes* (*The Last of the Unjust*), *Four Sisters* adds brief cutaways to

---

1. Jennifer Cazenave, *An Archive of the Catastrophe: The Unused Footage of Claude Lanzmann's* Shoah (Albany: State University of New York Press, 2019), 227–29. She borrows the distinction of document/documentary from Brad Prager, *After the Fact: Holocaust Documentary in the Twenty-First Century* (New York: Bloomsbury, 2015), 13-14.

2. See Lanzmann's explanation of the term in Marc Chevrie and Hervé Le Roux, "Site and Speech: An Interview with Claude Lanzmann about *Shoah*" (1985), trans. Stuart Liebman, in *Claude Lanzmann's* Shoah: *Key Essays*, ed. Stuart Liebman (New York: Oxford University Press, 2007), 39.

archival images of various kinds, which Lanzmann had foresworn in *Shoah*. Lanzmann also devotes more concerted attention to a much greater range and depth of biographical details in his discussions. Perhaps most interesting is the manner in which Lanzmann conducts the interviews as well as his self-presentation in *Four Sisters* because they raise questions about some of his most vigorously asserted rhetorical positions concerning his goals and methods. Such questions in turn throw into relief and suggest reconsideration of some of the more accepted critical interpretations of the motivations behind his engagement with traumatized Holocaust survivors.

I would argue that invidious formal comparisons obscure much that is of interest in *Four Sisters*. The film provides insights into a broader conception of Lanzmann's Holocaust project, and may even be said to serve as a capstone of a project that from its start was not conceived as a single film. His conception evolved over several decades, constantly expanding into an extraordinary, if ultimately incomplete, multiform work that aimed to create a historical "Gestalt" encompassing the largest comprehensive, if not an impossibly total, representation of the Shoah. *Shoah*, of course, lies at the project's center; the post-*Shoah* films all build around it in various formal ways while adding new content perspectives as well.

An analogy might be useful to clarify what I mean. Lanzmann's Holocaust project might be likened to a Renaissance polyptych altarpiece, albeit one developing over time. *Shoah* embodies Lanzmann's understanding of the central historical experience of the Holocaust and functions as the secular equivalent of the key iconic image—a crucifixion, say, or pietà—of such an altarpiece. Below the central image of such an altarpiece are a number of predella panels that tell related stories that enhance the imposing physical and narrative dimensions of the whole. Conceived in this way, Lanzmann's later Holocaust-related films, such as *Un vivant qui passe* (*A Visitor from the Living*) and The *Karski Report*, similarly enlarge the scale and scope of his project. Finally, flanking side panels generally feature martyrs, saints, or pious donors who bear witness to the iconic scene, thereby affirming their presence as atemporal witnesses of its truth. As this analogy suggests, *Four Sisters* may be said to present secular equivalents of those suffering figures who testify to, amplify, and supplement the truth of the central scene. Each film is a whole differing in form and content from the others, but is set within and engages with a larger architectural whole.

As I have already suggested, the most obvious dimension of *Four Sisters* that should be celebrated is its in-depth focus on Jewish women who survived the Holocaust. As such, *Four Sisters* constitutes an importantly compensatory gesture for *Shoah*'s earlier silence about the experiences of women. As is now well-known, Lanzmann decided to focus *Shoah* on the Nazi machinery of mass death by gassing which remained, for him, the central defining event of the Holocaust. He consequently chose men who had served in the *Sonderkommando* squads at death camps such as Chelmno, Treblinka, and Auschwitz as what he referred to as his principal "characters." Only these individuals, Lanzmann maintained, could offer detailed, emotionally wrenching, first-hand accounts of how millions of Jewish men, women, and children had been exterminated in such an unprecedented way. That no women had participated so intimately in this ultimate stage of the "final solution" provided him with an implicit rationale for including so little of the testimonies of the women he had, in fact, interviewed in the 1970s. There was, he would subsequently argue, no obvious place for their expansive accounts within *Shoah*'s thematic and cinematic architecture. The few, brief excerpts of their remarks that he did include—and, indeed, this point is more generally true of most of the approximately forty individuals who assumed what might be considered secondary roles in *Shoah*—were used primarily to provide crucial historical facts or contextual frameworks for the testimonies of *Shoah*'s major witnesses.

The marginalization of women's experience was apparent soon after *Shoah*'s April 1985 premiere, in part because a scholarly interest in how women suffered during the Holocaust had recently emerged. Some years later, after *Shoah* had become the most celebrated film about the Nazi genocide of European Jewry, Marianne Hirsch and Leo Spitzer mounted a powerful, searching critique of how the film ignored women's unique, searing accounts of their personal experiences. Women had suffered different, but equally awful, terrors as men, and they had faced them with comparable courage. Lanzmann had not accorded them enough time to describe the multiple ways women had been traumatized by the perpetrators: sexual humiliation and rape; the loss of their menstrual cycle and their fears of sterility; the medical experiments they were subjected to; the extreme risks of immediate gassing that pregnant women faced when they entered the camps; and for those who made it through the selections, the necessity of aborting or killing their own or other's babies. He also failed to underline women's solidarity in helping each other endure unspeakable brutalities. By effectively ignoring the role gender played in the Holocaust, they argued, Lanzmann had implicitly adopted the Nazis' dehumanizing attitudes toward their victims, both female and male. Finally, they asserted, in the conceptual economy of *Shoah*, women were presented as midwives of Orphic male creation; they functioned as symbols of passivity and resignation, or embodied potential mortifying threats to the men's resolve to survive and testify. Such metamorphoses blurred and ultimately denatured women survivors' authentic historical and, indeed, bodily experiences.[3]

Thanks to film archivists at the United States Holocaust Memorial Museum (hereafter USHMM) who reconstructed, restored, digitized, catalogued, and made available online most of the outtakes as well as many documents from *Shoah*'s production, we can now better assess the charges Hirsch and Spitzer made. We know that as Lanzmann embarked on what would become his nearly twelve-year journey to complete *Shoah*, he had cast his net very wide. He would spend years researching the Holocaust in order to respond to Alouph Hareven's charge to make a work that would "take in what happened in all its magnitude" and, furthermore, would tell the story "from our point of view, the viewpoint of the Jews."[4] In addition to consuming a great swath of the existing historical literature, Lanzmann embarked on a quest to find those who could testify to a host of issues, including the Jewish Councils' administration of the ghettos; the efforts of rescuers; the attitudes of bystanders; the motivations and procedures of those who perpetrated the exterminations as well as those who revolted, among other topics. None of these topics, however, received sufficient attention in *Shoah*, largely for reasons of length and the limitations Lanzmann ultimately settled on for the film.[5]

---

3. Marianne Hirsch and Leo Spitzer, "Gendered Translations: Claude Lanzmann's *Shoah*," in *Gendering War Talk*, ed. Miriam G. Cooke and Angela Woollacott (Princeton: Princeton University Press, 1993), 3-19. Reprinted in Liebman, ed., *Claude Lanzmann's* Shoah, 175-90. For a brief bibliography of feminist writings about the Holocaust, see Notes 4 and 5 to Hirsch and Spitzer's article.

4. In 1973, Hareven served as Director-General of the Israeli Ministry of Foreign Affairs. Lanzmann remembers his challenge to embark on such a huge project in his autobiography, *Le lièvre de Patagonie* (Paris: Éditions Gallimard, 2009), 429. In Frank Wynne's English translation, *The Patagonian Hare* (New York: Farrar, Straus and Giroux, 2012), 411.

5. *Shoah* could not encompass all these topics. Lanzmann was thwarted from addressing the "Holocaust by bullets" in the Soviet Union, among other East European

During the period when he conducted the vast bulk of his interviews, moreover, Lanzmann also filmed interviews with at least eleven women. Two were non-Jewish bystanders—Martha Michelson and Helena Pietyra—who witnessed from their homes, respectively at Chelmno and Oświęcim, the deportation and mass murder of Jews. They were chosen largely because both singularly exemplified obtuse, indifferent onlookers of the murders of thousands at their doorsteps. Lanzmann, however, also filmed immensely moving accounts with at least nine Jewish women survivors.[6] Six had suffered in ghettos and camps (Paula Biren, Ruth Elias, Malka Goldberg, Ada Lichtman, Lore Oppenheimer, and Gertrude Schneider). Inge Deutschkron reported how she survived the war hiding in Berlin. Finally, the Hungarians Hansi Brand and Hanna Marton, whose testimonies were among the last Lanzmann collected, shared the unique fate of having been among the 1670 Jews who survived on the "Kasztner train" that carried them to safety in Switzerland.[7] Only four of these survivors—Biren, Deutschkron, Elias and, in a singing role, Schneider (accompanied by her mother and sister)—appeared in *Shoah*. Their screen time was, moreover, uniformly short; Lanzmann used only small fractions of the hours of detailed testimony he recorded.[8] It is understandable that Hirsch and Spitzer, who at the time they wrote their article could only focus on *Shoah* and had no access to the outtakes, argued so pointedly against what seemed Lanzmann's indifference to the experience of women.

Even though he was certainly aware of Hirsch and Spitzer's critique,[9] Lanzmann made no effort to respond to their arguments,

---

locales, by *Einsatzgruppen* members, and did not vigorously pursue the collaboration of occupied European governments, including France, with Hitler. *Shoah* did not attempt to offer a comprehensive history of the Holocaust, as is sometimes claimed.

6. A complete, documented list compiled by Lindsay Zarwell and Jennifer Cazenave is published in *The Construction of Testimony: Claude Lanzmann's* Shoah *and Its Outtakes*, ed. Erin McGlothlin, Brad Prager, and Markus Zisselsberger (Detroit: Wayne State University Press, 2020), 421-55. Gertrude Schneider's mother, Lotte Hirschhorn, and her sister, Rita Wassermann, also appear in *Shoah*. They make some remarks, but were not interviewed in depth. Israeli-born Hannah Zaidel, the daughter of Motke Zaidel, a male survivor from Vilna, also briefly appears but was not interviewed in depth.

7. The train departed Budapest on June 30, 1944 with 1684 Jewish passengers. There were some births and deaths, and several on the train were detained in Bergen-Belsen, where the passengers were held for up to several months.

8. Elias had been interviewed for 3.4 hours; Biren for 2.7 hours; Deutschkron for 3.8 hours; Schneider for 2.3 hours.

9. He knew that I included it in my anthology about *Shoah*. See Note 2.

nor did he address more widely expressed concerns about the absence of women's voices in his films for many years.[10] Over the three decades after 1985, in fact, he excavated four new films from the corpus of *Shoah*'s unused footage; none touched upon the particular experiences of women during the Holocaust.[11] Even in his 2009 memoir, *Le lièvre de Patagonie* (*The Patagonian Hare*), while Lanzmann offered protracted accounts of his personal engagement with male *Sonderkommando* survivors such as Srebnik, Bomba, or Müller, briefly acknowledged several female collaborators, and provided details about his many personal romances, he never mentioned any of the Jewish female survivors he had interviewed in 1978-79.[12]

It was only very belatedly in 2017 that he turned his attention to the testimonies of the Jewish women survivors he had filmed nearly forty years earlier. His delay in making this effort, however, does not mean that *Four Sisters* should be characterized merely as an afterthought. In remarks made during his interview with Gauthier Jurgenson less than a month before his death, one can easily discern Lanzmann's defensiveness about this delay, but also more than a hint of remorse for how long he had failed to devote a film to the subject of women's experiences.

> [It] was very difficult for me to go back there, to all these past events. I do not know how to explain this. I did not know what to do with these interviews [with women survivors]. Each of these deserved a film of its own. I met these women, and I found each capable of providing testimonies that were unique and extraordinary. To have put them in *Shoah* would not have made any sense.[13]

10. In a public interview on July 1, 2019, Regina Longo, a former USHMM film archivist who had begun work on the outtakes in the late 1990s, commented that Lanzmann told her that, whatever their terrible experiences, he did not consider the women survivors whose conversations he recorded as central eyewitnesses to the ultimate stage of the Nazis' "final solution to the Jewish question." She never got a clear answer about whether he ever really intended to include their voices in *Shoah*. https//www.youtube.com/wtch?v=Pmnl71en8 (accessed December 8, 2020).

11. *A Visitor from the Living* (1997); *Sobibor, October 14, 1943, 4 P.M.* (2001); *The Karski Report* (2010); and *The Last of the Unjust* (2013). In *Shoah*, Jan Karski commented on the degradation women experienced in the Warsaw Ghetto. These remarks were not included in *The Karski Report*.

12. Lanzmann mentions his production assistant, Corinna Coulmas, several female translators, and Sabine Mamou the sound recordist. Oddly, he does not cite the crucial contributions of Ziva Postec, the principal editor of *Shoah*.

13. The interview was conducted on June 12, 2018 and published on July 4, 2018 in *Allociné*. http://www.allocine.fr/article/fichearticle_gen_carticle=18674031.html. It was published in English in the Arte Press Notes for the broadcast release.

And he is also to be believed when he commented in the press notes for *Four Sisters* that

> the more I thought about these four women, the more the necessity to bring the spotlight on these female faces of the Shoah seemed important. Each of them deals with a little-known chapter of the Holocaust, each from a unique point of view. . . . The incredible strength in each of them exists in its own right, and yet the exceptional quality they all share also had to come through—that searingly sharp, almost physical intelligence and an irrepressible survival instinct which could not be extinguished, despite an apparently certain death awaiting them.

However belatedly, *Four Sisters* was conceived to bring these four women's "incredible strength" and "searingly sharp, almost physical intelligence" to light. Lanzmann exclusively focuses on one of the women's unique experience in each of the four films that composes *Four Sisters*, and he emphasizes their distinctiveness by entitling each film with a phrase that emerged in their conversations. *The Hippocratic Oath*, the first chapter, features Ruth Elias from Moravska Ostrava, Czechoslovakia, who was betrayed as she hid in the countryside with her family; all were soon deported to Theresienstadt before finally being sent to Auschwitz, where she listened as the Germans gassed the first group of her compatriots in the "Czech Family Camp" and later was subjected to one of Mengele's "medical experiments."[14] The three women featured in the other films suffered in different ways in different places at different times. *The Merry Flea* offers Ada Lichtman's testimony of her travails in Poland culminating in her work at and escape from the Sobibór death camp after the prisoner revolt in 1943.[15] Paula Biren, also Polish, recounts her young adulthood and short service as a Jewish policewoman in *Bałuty*, the site of

---

14. In *Shoah*, Rudolf Vrba establishes the background for this massacre and Filip Müller recounts how the Czech women sang "Hatikvah" in the gas chambers. An online interview with Elias in German elaborates on her account: https://www.deutschland funkkultur.de/wann-reden-wann-schweigen-pdf.media.a2925eea9610ee531948f 599aed60584.pdf. A decade after her interview with Lanzmann, Elias published an autobiographical memoir in German, *Die Hoffnung erhielt mich am Leben* (Munich: R. Piper Verlag, 1988), translated by Margaret Bettauer Dembo as *Triumph of Hope: From Theresienstadt and Auschwitz to Israel* (New York: Wiley, 1999).

15. Lichtman had testified at the Eichmann trial and her testimony is accessible online: https://collections.ushmm.org/search/catalog/irn1001078. Lanzmann alluded to Lichtman in the scrolling prologue to *Sobibor* and stated that her story deserved a separate film. She did not appear in the film.

the Jewish ghetto in Łódź.[16] The last film, *Noah's Ark*, concludes with Hanna Marton's account of her escape from Cluj, Romania, through Bergen-Belsen to Switzerland in the Kasztner train, renamed "Noah's Ark" by the passengers as it carried them to safety.

These women are not sisters in a biological sense. None of their lives ever crossed. They also cannot be said to represent all the varieties of humiliation, brutalization, and terror that women were subjected to during the Holocaust. Elias, Biren, Lichtman, and Marton, however, are sisters in an important metaphorical sense. Each woman tells a singular tale of suffering, courage, and luck in which a common moral theme emerges that is applicable to the experiences of many other victims. Powerless, each was forced to make what the American scholar of Holocaust literature, Lawrence L. Langer, has termed a "choiceless choice";[17] each had to make a life-or-death decision in which the alternatives were equally horrible. Elias was subjected to one of Mengele's medical experiments and forced to kill her child in order to survive. Biren could join the Jewish police force in Łódź or, by refusing, risk deportation and death. In Sobibór, Lichtman entered a gray zone when she had to repair dolls taken from murdered Jewish children so that they could be given to German girls. Marton chose to save herself by boarding "Noah's Ark" even though its organizer, Kasztner, a Jewish community leader, had struck a deal with Eichmann to remain silent about the imminent dire fate awaiting Hungarian Jewry. Though she claimed ignorance of these conditions at the time, Marton's demeanor as she spoke with Lanzmann makes clear that her decision at least retrospectively cast a moral and psychological pall over her life. As a result of the choices each made—that is, were forced to make—to survive, these sisters in misery share what Langer has called "tainted memories" of actions stained by their moral self-condemnation even though they later came to an anguished acceptance of their necessary, if not always admirable, conduct.[18]

16. Joan Ringelheim, working with the USHMM, recorded an extensive oral history with Biren in 2005. It can be accessed online: https://collections.ushmm.org/oh_findingaids/RG-50.030.0500_trs_en.pdf.

17. See Lawrence L. Langer, *Versions of Survival* (Albany, NY: SUNY Press, 1982) and his essay collection, *Admitting the Holocaust* (New York: Oxford University Press, 1995).

18. Langer, *Holocaust Testimonies: The Ruins of Memory* (New Haven: Yale University Press, 1991), 122. Their painful judgment of themselves is augmented by their acute sense of having been the sole survivors from their families. They also shared a keen sense of betrayal at the hands of their fellow citizens: the Czech peasants who

Lanzmann, however, profiles these four women not as abject victims but as individuals whose psychological strength and physical endurance allowed them to become agents of their own survival. Unlike the protagonists in *Shoah*, Elias and the other women present extended accounts of their lives from before and continuing through their ongoing post-war lives. Again, in marked contrast to his practice in *Shoah*, Lanzmann edited their accounts of suffering and survival so that their stories are generally presented in chronological order. In part, this reflects the order in which he asked questions in the unedited version of the interviews. The edited results also reflect Elias's and Biren's strong determination at times to take control of the flow of their life stories to create a more readily followed, linear trajectory for their narratives. The result is that each woman emerges as an independent individual in ways quite different from the fragmented and incomplete personal accounts in the fractured narratives of *Shoah*.

That is not to say, however, that the four films are mere recordings of their testimonies. Lanzmann edited down each interview substantially. As Sue Vice has pointed out, shortening, displacing, and reducing overall length is an essential part of the editing and centering process.[19] The percentage of footage Lanzmann used varies from a minimum of 32.1% for Biren to a maximum of nearly 43% for Marton. The moments chosen do make their stories more straightforward and comprehensible without in any way simply harmonizing away the traumas they experienced.

The conversations, moreover, take place in settings that distinctly recall some of Lanzmann's attempts to create symbolic mise en scènes in *Shoah*. These efforts are admittedly more modest in *Four Sisters*; Lanzmann did not bring any of the women to sites where they had lived through the traumatic events, as he famously had done, for example, with Simon Srebnik. Nor did he set up artificial situations such as the barbershop scene in *Shoah* in which Bomba simulated the motions of cutting hair in Treblinka and then broke down so pitifully.

---

informed on Elias and her family; the Poles who pushed Biren out of bread lines and who did not welcome her when she returned to Łódź from Auschwitz; Marton's Hungarian Christian friends who offered no help. It is perhaps no coincidence that all four eventually left their native countries and emigrated either to Israel or the United States, where they found a renewed sense of security and community.

19. Sue Vice, "*Shoah* and the Archive," in McGlothlin, Prager, and Zisselsberger, *The Construction of Testimony*, 79.

Rather, Elias, Lichtman, and Marton were filmed in their familiar domestic environments in Israel.[20]

When he could, however, Lanzmann did introduce resonant props to provoke their memories. Dolls lie on a table in front of Ada Lichtman to bring back echoes of her past work at Sobibór and she even sews some of their clothes as she speaks. He often cuts into closeups of Hanna Marton's hands as she tightly clutches her late husband's diary to anchor, and perhaps to justify, her now codified and perhaps defended memories throughout the interview.[21] Elias enthusiastically plays an accordion and sings songs she played for other inmates in the kitchens of Theresienstadt. And during the shooting of his interview with Elias, Lanzmann evidently was delighted to include the unanticipated barking of the neighborhood dogs in the background while her own German Shepherd—the preferred type that SS guards used to terrify victims in the camps—sits beside her. Both are ominous, freighted reminders of life in the camps.

As in *Shoah*, Lanzmann actively attempts to excavate and probe his subjects' traumatic memories to get them to express in the present what they experienced in the past in as much vivid physical detail as possible. At key moments, the camera often zooms into tight closeups of their faces, seen frontally or in profile, to highlight gestures and the expressions of their eyes. Such movements, however small, are a form of editing, what film scholars call a *plan séquence*, a sequence shot. The witness's recorded tone of voice, punctuated by moments of silent struggle, also plays a role as it changes when an emotionally challenging memory emerges. Elias tears up as she recounts how she killed her baby. Biren's resistance to answering certain questions about the role of Jewish policemen in Łódź is registered in the set of her lips or her eyes. Beyond this silent refusal, she explicitly debars Lanzmann from pursuing the matter further. Marton is clearly uncomfortable throughout the interview and grips her husband's diary in order to hold back and, for a while, to deny the tears that well up

20. Note that many of his interviews in *Shoah*, including those with Müller and Karski, as well as with Rossel, Murmelstein, and Lerner in his later films, also take place in their homes. The interview with Biren was conducted for purely pragmatic reasons on a beach and in a hotel room in Florida where she was staying for a medical conference.

21. See Primo Levi's comments on the way a survivor's memory "expressed in the form of a story tends to become fixed in a stereotype." *The Drowned and the Saved*, trans. Raymond Rosenthal (New York: Summit Books, 1986), 24.

in her eyes. Lanzmann remarks that in physical reactions like these, "everything became true and personified again. These women bear in themselves their history and that of the extermination of the Jewish people."[22] Their ability to relive these moments, their physical "incarnation" of long repressed events in their bodies' reactions, are for him precious moments that enable the transmission of the palpable truth of their anguished pasts to contemporary viewers. Lanzmann admired these women because they not only possessed the strength to survive but also had the courage to engage with him in exploring painful moments of their life histories.

Some critics of Lanzmann's interview procedures have cast them in quite an ambiguous, even sinister, light. Bomba's breakdown as he recounts the horrible memory of shearing women's hair in the gas chamber at Treblinka has often been characterized as bullying and cruel or worse. Dominick LaCapra, a prominent and probing critic of Lanzmann's work, describes Lanzmann's professed goal of getting survivors to act out their traumas as an effort to re-traumatize them. "One may argue that it is dubious to try to induce the survivor to relive trauma," he writes in *Writing History, Writing Trauma*,

> and in a sense be revictimized before the camera even if one's motive is to empathize or even to identify fully with the victim to transmit the experience to the viewer. (Such an attempt to take the survivor back—figuratively and at times even literally—to the scene of victimization and traumatization is evident in Claude Lanzmann as interviewer in *Shoah*, and at times it leads to intrusive questioning.)

He further attributes to Lanzmann "the desire to identify fully with, and relive the experience of, the victim in however vicarious a fashion," a process that cannot lead to the kind of "empathetic unsettlement" required to be an "empathetic listener."[23]

Lanzmann's comments championing such practices as a guarantor of a testimony's truth undoubtedly have encouraged these kinds of charges. In *Four Sisters*, however, and indeed in Lanzmann's other

22. "Quatre Soeurs: Interview de Claude Lanzmann avec Serge Toubiana," *frenchtouch2*, January 23, 2018. http://www.frenchtouch2.fr/2018/01/quatre-soeurs -entretien-de-claude.html

23. Dominick LaCapra, *Writing History, Writing Trauma* (Baltimore: Johns Hopkins University Press, 2001), 98-102. The critic Leon Wieseltier makes a similar judgment in his essay, "*Shoah*," reprinted in Liebman, ed. *Claude Lanzmann's "Shoah*," 92-93.

Holocaust-related films, including *Shoah*, LaCapra's concerns seem misplaced. His practice has most often belied the rhetoric of his pronouncements.

In *Shoah*, Lanzmann's tone could be sarcastic or condescending with those he disliked or distrusted. At certain moments, he flagrantly lied to or even bullied those from whom he wanted to obtain answers or vital admissions. The famous interview with Suchomel or with the peasant Borowi are obvious examples of Lanzmann's contempt for them. None of his postures as interviewer at these moments can be described as empathetic. In *Four Sisters*, by contrast, he appears to be a largely unassertive and, yes, an empathetic interlocutor in ways that suggest a reconsideration of his interview technique would be in order. The extended sessions he conducts in *Four Sisters* are exercises in careful questioning and intense listening. He maintains a respectful distance from those he interviews. He probes gently and does not press too hard when the women appear vulnerable; he pulls back when they resist answering a question. His inquiries about small, sometimes seemingly irrelevant details attempt to get the survivors closer to their past experiences to bring them into the present. He does so to encourage his witnesses not to flee from memories, but to acknowledge them. In no sense does he attempt to reproduce their trauma in himself as if by contagion.[24] Rather, his affect throughout is one of concern and care for what he hears as he reacts with what seems to be precisely the kind of "muted trauma" that defines the "empathic unsettlement" that LaCapra recommends. Lanzmann's behavior in no way suggests any imperious need to provoke re-traumatization and induce "acting out" by the witnesses.[25]

His questions do not injure those recalling their pasts as LaCapra and others claim to have been the case with Lanzmann's interactions with Bomba. Indeed, a review of the outtakes from his interviews with Bomba and his account of his preparations with him before he shot the barbershop scene in *Shoah* reveals a very different, intimate relationship between the two men. This is certainly the case in *Four Sisters*. His calm attention to what the women say helps to restore a kind of trust for the survivors because their interlocutor is closely attentive and often his face reveals how moved or amazed he is by

24. Geoffrey Hartman, *The Longest Shadow* (Bloomington: Indiana University Press, 1996), 159-60.
25. LaCapra, *Writing History, Writing Trauma*, 102.

what they say. Ultimately, then, the interactions in *Four Sisters* create what the late Geoffrey Hartman called an "affective community." Lanzmann serves as a kind of midwife of a humanizing and transactive process in which the voice and memory of the survivor is recovered from moments of silence and powerlessness.[26] "Cinema," Lanzmann writes, "can do everything. With very little, it succeeds in completely reviving the past." His formulation, here as elsewhere, is certainly overstated. Nevertheless, what he says does ring true: With very few formal means, *Four Sisters* brings aspects of important and in many ways exemplary individual pasts into the light of the present, even if no past is completely revived or restored. And he is right to conclude of his last work that returned to the immense topic he had undertaken nearly half a century before: "I am very proud of this series, which I consider to be central to everything that I have ever accomplished about the Shoah."[27]

26. I owe these formulations to Hartman, *The Longest Shadow*, 153-55.
27. "Quatre Soeurs: Interview de Claude Lanzmann avec Serge Toubiana."

II. "My homeland is my film"

BRAD PRAGER

Israeli Soldiers in the Eyes of the Beholder: *Tsahal*

Claude Lanzmann, in his 2009 memoir *The Patagonian Hare*, only fleetingly mentions *Tsahal* (1994), his five-hour-long documentary about the Israel Defense Forces (IDF), who are known in Hebrew as the *Tsva ha-Hagana le-Yisra'el* (or the "Tsahal," for short). Lanzmann explains that he initially planned to open the film with a depiction of Goya's painting *Duelo a garrotazos* (*Fight with Cudgels*, 1820-23), a work portraying two warriors locked in combat while standing knee deep in what is generally assumed to be mud or sand.[1] The battle's stakes are indeterminate; Goya's painting is an allegory for the intractability of a senseless war. Lanzmann writes that his inclusion of this image, had he decided to use it, would have been "apagogic," or that it was meant to suggest a position that runs counter to the one taken up by the film.[2] The viewer was perhaps meant to assume, upon seeing it, that Israelis and Palestinians are *not* locked in a vain and eternal struggle. Lanzmann then refers to the six major wars that Israel and its neighbors had at that point fought as wars that Israel was "compelled to fight."[3] What is one to make of Lanzmann's assertion? Should it be taken to mean that the Arab-Israeli wars were not wars of choice on the parts of the parties in question, or does he mean that there is hope for an end to these wars—a lasting peace—even if that peace is created by the definitive victory of one party over the other? How, above all, would viewers come to know that the inclusion of the painting is "apagogic"? The hypothetical significance of this excluded image may have been apparent only to Lanzmann himself.

1. Claude Lanzmann, *The Patagonian Hare: A Memoir*, trans. Frank Wynne (New York: Farrar, Straus & Giroux, [2009] 2012), 31.
2. Ibid.
3. Ibid.

YFS 141, *Lanzmann after "Shoah,"* ed. Levine and Stark, © 2022 by Yale University.

Although *Tsahal*, like its later companion film *Lights and Shadows* (2008), touches on Israel's many military conflicts, dating back to the first Arab-Israeli war of 1948, the majority of *Tsahal*'s emphasis falls on the Yom Kippur War of 1973, also known as the October War. Lanzmann's earlier film about Israel, the three-hour *Pourquoi Israël* (1973), had been completed before the Yom Kippur War, and it premiered in the U.S. on October 7, 1973, only a day after that war's outbreak.[4] The film was thus unable to assimilate the conflict's impact. It is possible that Lanzmann revisited this subject twenty years later as a means of picking up where he left off. But even if he only thematized the traumatic impact of the Yom Kippur War for the first time in 1994, he may have been ahead of his time: the impression that that war was uniquely traumatic has been recently highlighted, as though the discussion were entirely new, in the publicity surrounding the Israeli television war drama *Valley of Tears* (2020), a program that dramatizes the anguish associated with the October War's violence.[5]

Lanzmann's 1994 film grapples directly with the grief caused by the October War, but almost entirely from the Israeli side. Following a scrolling title that provides viewers with a nominal amount of historical context, *Tsahal* begins with an audio recording of an attack on Israeli troops in the midst of the Yom Kippur War. The noises of combat, played back on a heavily distorted audiotape, can be heard under the opening scroll. The sounds of war are presented as a lather of male voices. The imperfect audio recording we hear highlights the chaos that Avi Yaffe, the war veteran who is subsequently shown on screen listening to the recording he made, most likely experienced. The impression is all the more chaotic for viewers who do not understand the orders being called out breathlessly in Hebrew. Yaffe then sits in front of Lanzmann's camera recalling the attack. Lanzmann describes the battle's sounds as "terrifying" and calls for the record-

---

4. *Pourquoi Israël* was shown at the New York Film Festival and was reviewed the following day. See Nora Sayre, "Film Fete: *Israel Why*: Lanzmann's Documentary Captures a Country Seething with Complexity," *New York Times*, October 8, 1973.

5. The *New York Times* synopsizes, "the period is so painful that Israeli culture has rarely dared to grapple with it." The series' co-creator explains, "for 47 years, people had the feeling this was a forgotten war and that they would end their lives without anyone knowing their stories." See Isabel Kershner, "An Epic Israeli TV Drama Exposes War Wounds Old and New," *New York Times*, December 12, 2020. https://www.nytimes.com/2020/12/12/world/middleeast/an-epic-israeli-tv-drama-exposes-war-wounds-old-and-new.html.

ing to be turned off. He then asks Yaffe to articulate in his own words his memories of the fear he felt. If it was traumatic for Yaffe to have lived through these events, then Lanzmann now challenges his film's viewers as he, for the sake of *Tsahal*, subjects Yaffe to this wartime recording.

Shortly after this sequence, Lanzmann takes the viewer through an Israeli cemetery: Meir Wiesel, a major in the reserves, points to the graves of fighters who died at ages as young as 19 and 20. After the camera has tracked his movement for a while, we hear another voice, that of the army veteran Yuval Neria, who was decorated for his service in tank combat during the Yom Kippur War. Neria describes the war as having been devastating for members of his generation. Most of his friends, he explains, were killed or heavily wounded over the course of those days in October 1973. He describes the war as "a very big fire which burned the Israeli society," adding, "It is like a hole, not only in my psyche but in the Israeli psyche . . . . It was like a visit in hell, and coming back, coming back to Tel Aviv."[6] Surely Neria and other soldiers are not responsible for their nation's choices. But who, then, according to Lanzmann's film, bears responsibility? Considered in view of Goya's *Fight with Cudgels*, one may wonder who, in his view, it is who has chosen to embroil themselves in this battle. Wars have causes and contexts, and it is unlikely that one can depict a war's horrors without implicitly or explicitly espousing an opinion as to its origins and instigators.

Over the course of his long career, Lanzmann spent a great deal of energy thinking and writing about Israel's policies and about the conflict between Israel and the Palestinians. The director's trilogy of major works—*Pourquoi Israël*, *Shoah* (1985), and *Tsahal*—circle around this topic, and had it not been for the tremendous critical success of *Shoah*, Lanzmann's career would likely have been defined as much by his publications and statements about the Middle East as by his work as a filmmaker. As an editor of *Les temps modernes*, Lanzmann, around the time of the Six-Day War in 1967, was responsible for a 991-page special issue entitled "Le conflit israélo-arabe."[7] The issue was introduced by two essays, one by Lanzmann, the other by Jean-Paul Sartre, and it also featured, in its opening section, a now

6. Ellipses in original (to indicate a pause in speech).
7. See *Les temps modernes* ("Le conflit israélo-arabe") 22/253 (July 1967).

famous essay by the historian Maxime Rodinson entitled "Israël, fait colonial?" in which Rodinson argued that the creation of the state of Israel was aligned with other similar Western colonial projects, the aims of which were to dominate others, politically and economically.[8] The issue was reviewed at length in the pages of *The New York Review of Books* by the American journalist I.F. Stone, who focused on its bifurcated character; it consisted of hundreds of pages of work by Arab writers followed by hundreds of pages of writings by Israelis. Stone mentions Lanzmann's editorial plan for the Israeli and Arab sides each to be able to choose their representative authors in "full sovereignty" with the intention that the issue would achieve a kind of symmetry.[9] Along these lines Stone offers the explanation that one needs a bifocal perspective to even think about Israel, in consideration of that nation's vulnerabilities on the one hand and its unjust occupation policies on the other. Nearly all of Stone's many metaphors point to a dual model: he writes that Lanzmann's issue of *Les temps modernes* is less of a dialogue than a "dual monologue"; that some of its authors suffer from a "moral myopia," which accepts one history and rejects another; and that the conflict has produced a "moral schizophrenia" within the conscience of world Jewry.[10] Stone's review reflects the need for, and the complications that inhere in, adopting a bifocal point of view.

If seeing the Arab-Israeli conflict calls for a bifocal lens, then documentary film may be an apt vehicle for its depiction. Documentary films are generally characterized by double vision: a documentary film's subjects often take turns speaking, each providing testimony or eyewitness accounts and presenting themselves as nonfictional subjects to the audience. However, a film director's voice also makes itself heard through the questions he or she poses and through the editorial decisions that shape a given film. Documentary thus always already incorporates not only bifocality but also *bivocality*. Presenting more than one perspective, it also weaves voices together in a

8. Maxime Rodinson, "Israël, fait colonial?", *Les temps modernes* 22/253 (July 1967): 17-88. Rodinson's lengthy essay was later published in book form as *Israel: A Colonial-Settler State?*, trans. David Thorstad (New York: Monad Press, 1973). In his memoir, Lanzmann wrote that he regretted letting the issue of *Les temps modernes* open with Rodinson's article: "Rodinson's simplifications, though dressed up as 'science,' did much harm" (*The Patagonian Hare*, 400).

9. See I.F. Stone, "Holy War," *New York Review of Books*, August 3, 1967. Reprinted in: I.F. Stone, *The Best of I.F. Stone* (New York: Public Affairs, 2007), 225-44.

10. Ibid., 226, 236, and 237.

composite way. Some filmmakers' works place more emphasis on an individual director's point of view, whereas others focus more on providing a platform for their subjects. The question is always one of degree. Lanzmann's films are just as much about the director's own unique perspective on historical events as they are about the witnesses on whom he relies. *Shoah*, for example, is certainly a compilation of Holocaust testimonies, one in which witnesses speak in their own words, but it is also very much about Lanzmann's own understanding of the Holocaust. *Tsahal* also has multiple standpoints, which makes it hard to grant it a singular, unequivocal meaning. Insofar as Lanzmann's film deals with the Arab-Israeli conflict, the film's distribution of voices raises critical questions about its point of view: whose voice does the film convey most clearly—that of the director or that of his film's subjects? And what are we to make of the paucity of Palestinian witnesses, the many unrepresented subjects whose voices Lanzmann chose not to solicit?

PRESENCES AND ABSENCES IN *TSAHAL*

Tsahal features the voices of numerous traumatized IDF soldiers and their generals. When, for example, Lanzmann, in the course of several sequences dedicated to the might and impenetrability of Israeli-manufactured tanks, interviews Israel Tal, a general best known for his contribution to advancements in strategic tank warfare, Tal describes how each and every Israeli soldier perceives external threats as immanent. The soldiers, Tal says, are on constant alert, never knowing when they are going to be attacked. He adds that this feeling was particularly acute after 1973. Speaking just after the outbreak of the 1973 war, Sartre, who was at that time Lanzmann's co-editor at *Les temps modernes*, underscores this same point of view: "I know only that in this conflict 3 million people are up against 100 million. In Israel every Jew must be trembling for his life, even if he is the bravest, and with him all of the Jews in every country of the earth."[11]

---

11. Jean-Paul Sartre is quoted in Jean Améry's "Antisemitism on the Left," in *Dissent* 29/1 (1982): 41-50; here, 50. Remarks along these same lines are also attributed to Sartre in "La destruction d'Israël, qui se profilait à l'horizon ne pouvait manquer de me préoccuper déclare M. Jean-Paul Sartre," *Le monde*, October 27, 1973. https://www.lemonde.fr/archives/article/1973/10/27/la-destruction-d-israel-qui-se-profilait-a-l-horizon-ne-pouvait-manquer-de-me-preoccuper-declare-m-jean-paul-sartre_3096091_1819218.html.

Sartre's position on Israel's vulnerability was close to Lanzmann's. However, because Sartre knew that there were multiple ways of seeing the Yom Kippur War, he remained open to the idea of double vision. He argues, first, that the invasion of Israel was "absurdly criminal" on Egypt's part and that "the destruction of the Israeli nation by violence is . . . unacceptable. It is unfortunate that Egypt and Syria started this war, causing a massacre in both warring camps."[12] But, similar to Rodinson, he also exhibits awareness that colonialism was fundamental to Israel's creation, claiming, "the heart of the matter is that the Israeli nation, whose first members came from all parts of the world, imposed itself on a territory that the Arabs have ceaselessly declared to be Arab."[13] The Franco-Syrian author Farouk Mardam-Bey, a harsh critic of Israel's military policies, faults Sartre for having labeled the Yom Kippur War an "attack" rather than a Syrian-Egyptian effort to reclaim occupied territories.[14] To be sure, there are a broad range of possible perspectives. But in adopting the position that Syria and Egypt's 1973 invasion of Israel was the source of an Israeli trauma, *Tsahal* admits only a small number of voices who speak directly about Israel's accountability for its conflicts. Unlike his issue of *Les temps modernes*, the film does not strive for symmetry; it does not explicitly address non-Israeli traumas, nor does it recognize that Israel might not have been simply "compelled to fight" each of its wars.

Many viewers concluded that *Tsahal* was largely comprised of unqualified praise for Israel's military, and some even perceived it as an advertisement for the IDF. The film reportedly inspired a politically-motivated gas attack at a theater where it was first shown in Paris in November 1994.[15] In the U.S., some reviewers felt that the film was intended to inspire Israeli youths facing military service, and J. Hoberman described *Tsahal*'s first half as "an almost completely

12. Sartre, *Libération*, October 29, 1973. Reprinted in "Les auteurs de nos 25 ans. 1973. J.P. Sartre. Le philosophe agitateur. Contre la guerre du Kippour." https://www .liberation.fr/france/1998/03/19/les-auteurs-de-nos-25-ans...-jp-sartre-le-philosophe -agitateur-contre-la-guerre-du-kippour_230529.

13. Sartre, *Libération*, October 29, 1973.

14. See Farouk Mardam-Bey, "French Intellectuals and the Palestine Question," *Journal of Palestine Studies*, 43/3 (2014): 26-39; here, 31.

15. Lanzmann mentions the gas attack in *The Patagonian Hare*, 31-32. Janet Maslin fleetingly refers to it in "*Tsahal*: Lanzmann's Meditation on Israel's Defense," *New York Times*, January 27, 1995.

unchallenged celebration" of the IDF.[16] By and large, the film's critics neither complained that Lanzmann had allowed Israeli soldiers
to express themselves, nor did they disagree that the war was traumatic for those soldiers. Instead, they faulted Lanzmann for including too few Arab voices in the film and for avoiding any mention
of Israel's 1982 war with Lebanon. Along these lines, *The Jerusalem
Post*'s standpoint may have been the harshest. It chided Lanzmann
for his near-total failure to mention Lebanon: "It's a war whose messy
morals just don't fit into Lanzmann's own antiquated fantasy view
of the heroic sabra soldier, the ethical generals, the full moon rising
over the desert, all that milk and honey. So he leaves the bothersome
misadventure out."[17] Writing for the *Palestine-Israel Journal*, Amnon
Kapeliouk, an Israeli journalist who covered the conflict in 1982, advanced a similar point of view. *Tsahal*, he wrote,

> is silent about this war, in which the IDF . . . bombed cities, destroyed
> refugee camps in South Lebanon, imposed a terrible blockade on Bei-
> rut and finally took it, enabling Israel's Phalangist allies to perpetrate
> the horrible Sabra and Shatila massacre. Lanzmann simply blots Leba-
> non out of the IDF's history.[18]

Kapeliouk here introduces a comparative perspective, pointing out
that the exclusion of Lebanon renders *Tsahal* akin to "a film about the
French army without Algeria, or the U.S. Army without Vietnam."[19]

Lanzmann was caught off guard by these reactions, each of which
viewed his film as though it had been one-sided. He expressed this
sentiment in an interview with the *New York Times*: "'There were attacks from the extreme left.' To [Lanzmann's] surprise, 'they thought
the film was too positive.'"[20] One wonders, however, why Lanzmann
ever believed his film would be interpreted as critical of the IDF or
of Israel's policies. In that same interview, Lanzmann explains that

16. J. Hoberman, "Never again—*Tsahal* directed by Claude Lanzmann," *The Vil-
lage Voice*, January 31, 1995.

17. Adina Hoffman, "The good, the bad, and the boring," *Jerusalem Post*, January 16, 1995.

18. Amnon Kapeliouk, "*Tsahal* (The Israeli Defense Forces). Directed by Claude
Lanzmann," *Palestine-Israel Journal* 2/1 (1995). https://pij.org/articles/686/tsahal-the
-israeli-defense-forces-directed-by-claude-lanzmann.

19. Ibid.

20. Mel Gussow, "Focusing on History Through Interviews," *New York Times*,
January 25, 1995.

Tsahal is about "the seeming endlessness of conscription, in which generations of the same family are called up to serve in the military."[21] On this point his description is accurate: throughout *Tsahal*, Jewish soldiers explain being drafted into war precisely as their fathers were drafted before them, and the film highlights how these fathers and sons have been mired in their nation's perpetual battles. Yet the policies that put these men (and, in Lanzmann's film, it is almost uniformly men, despite the fact that women, even then, served in many roles in the IDF) in this position are, for the most part, barely called into question. Throughout *Tsahal*'s first half, the interviewees, in particular those in positions of power such as Ehud Barak and Ariel Sharon, are only gently prodded to expand on their opinions. Not one among them is forcefully questioned.

Critical opinions about Israel's policies are eventually voiced by some of Lanzmann's interviewees. We hear from the authors David Grossman and Amos Oz, who speak disapprovingly about Israel's approach. But their positions parallel those of *Shoah*'s expert witnesses Raul Hilberg and Yehuda Bauer: they are scholars or intellectuals, distinct from first-hand witnesses, situated in studies and libraries rather than on the front lines.[22] With reference to the 1987 report of the Landau Commission, which was convened to address the deaths of two Palestinian prisoners who had been held in custody and to study the legality of applying "moderate physical pressure" on detainees during an interrogation, the civil rights lawyer Avigdor Feldman describes the impossibility of acknowledging the use of "physical pressure"—something that may be better described as torture—without "damaging [Israel's] reality," or its sense of national identity. He and other interviewees speak disparagingly of the mild conclusions drawn in the report as well as of the excesses that necessitated its writing. But a critical perspective on such matters is hardly the focus of Lanzmann's film. Had this been Lanzmann's intention, the testimony of someone who had been subjected to such "physical pressure" would have lent the film an essential viewpoint.

21. Gussow, "Focusing on History Through Interviews," C15.
22. Raul Hilberg appeared in the final cut of *Shoah*, but Yehuda Bauer's interview is only contained in the outtakes at the United States Memorial Holocaust Museum (USMHM). On Hilberg and Bauer's roles in *Shoah*, see Noah Shenker, "'The dead are not around': Raul Hilberg as Historical Revenant in *Shoah*," in *The Construction of Testimony: Claude Lanzmann's* Shoah *and its Outtakes*, ed. Erin McGlothlin, Brad Prager, and Markus Zisselsberger (Detroit: Wayne State University Press, 2020), 115-40.

Lanzmann is also averse to making a comparison, as had Kape-liouk, between the occupation of Palestine and the French occupa-tion of Algeria. When *Tsahal* was released in 1994, Lanzmann made this point emphatically: "the Israeli army's role as an occupying force should not be compared to such brutal occupations as that of the French army in Algeria during the 1950s."[23] To this thought—that Israel's occupation is less brutal than the French one was—Lanzmann adds an unprovable, highly subjective, and deeply problematic state-ment: "I don't think that [the Israeli soldiers] . . . have violence in their blood. . . . You can see their faces, you can see that they are soft, they are very tender."[24] Although no one should ever claim to speak with certainty about the violence that may or may not be in some-one's blood, what one sees in soldiers' faces surely depends upon who is encountering them. That perception is in the eye of the beholder. Lanzmann's statement is so willfully naïve about the ambiguities of perception and representation that it only makes sense if one sees it as a deliberate provocation.

Although there were accusations that *Tsahal* was "too positive" about Israel and the IDF, Lanzmann's film is built around an architec-ture that makes a claim about mission creep within the IDF. Lanz-mann famously justified his decisions about what was to remain in the final cut of *Shoah* by referring to its architecture, a structure that makes *Shoah* what it is but also mandates exclusions. That film moved viewers through several stages of extermination, from the gas vans at Chełmno to the chambers at Treblinka and Auschwitz-Birkenau. In this way *Shoah* constructed an argument about the gradual expansion of the killing apparatus and the continual evolution of the Nazi exter-mination policy.[25] *Tsahal* likewise has an architecture—a framework that structures the director's logic of inclusion and exclusion. The film begins by placing its emphasis on warfare—on the trauma of the October War in particular—and then eventually begins to integrate

23. Robert Sklar, "Lanzmann's Latest: After *Shoah*, Jewish Power," *Forward*, Sep-tember 30, 1994.

24. Quoted in Sklar, 10. Lanzmann makes similar remarks in *The Patagonian Hare*, describing the paratroopers' "innocence" and "youth": "in their faces serious-ness vies with tenderness, humanity with asceticism, anxiety with confidence" (*The Patagonian Hare*, 32).

25. On the film's implicit architecture, see Lanzmann's response to Marc Chevrie and Hervé Le Roux, in "Site and Speech: An Interview with Claude Lanzmann about *Shoah*," in *Claude Lanzmann's* Shoah: *Key Essays*, ed. Stuart Liebman (Oxford: Oxford University Press, 2007), 37-49; here, 46-47.

a reflection on some of the disquieting consequences of the occupation. In this regard, it follows a pattern identified by Haim Bresheeth-Zabner, who, in a book that is extremely critical of the IDF, describes how the Israeli military's purpose has transformed over time:

> [T]he main functions of the IDF have continuously morphed from an army fighting state actors toward a force of occupation and settlement. Military force was used for the settlement of Palestine even before 1948. After that war, soldiers were organized in special units of the *Nahal* (Fighting Pioneer Youth), an elite force of the IDF, building military settlements that are later pronounced "civilian."[26]

Although Lanzmann's film mirrors this evolution, anyone who watches *Tsahal* in the hopes of seeing a thoroughgoing reflection on the occupation and its consequences is unlikely to be satisfied by the sequences set in and around the occupied territories, which come quite late in the film. In one such sequence, a Palestinian is shown crossing from Jordan into occupied territory. The man's possessions are searched, which is doubtlessly very unpleasant, yet the scene is hardly comprehensive in its communication of the manifold issues involved. Kapeliouk points out that when he served at that same checkpoint years earlier, he had been "witness to endless acts of brutality and insults meted out daily by some of the soldiers there." He concludes, "nothing of this sort is to be seen in [Lanzmann's] film."[27] As is the case with victims of the IDF's "physical pressure" and with witnesses to the war in Lebanon, *Tsahal* hardly sees or hears from those who live under the occupation.

A MYTH-MAKING TRILOGY

Throughout *Tsahal*, Lanzmann pays little heed to standard positions held by human rights groups or by the majority of the international community, even positions held in 1994, a period of relative calm that followed the Oslo I Accord. Here, as in *Pourquoi Israël* and *Shoah*, Israel is presented as a bulwark against a second Holocaust. In an interview with Robert Sklar, Lanzmann confirmed that all three films were meant to serve as "part of a single subject." Sklar paraphrases: "[*Pourquoi Israël*] concerns civilian life in Israel, the nine-

26. Haim Bresheeth-Zabner, *An Army Like No Other: How the Israel Defense Force Made a Nation* (New York: Verso, 2020), 70.

27. Kapeliouk, "*Tsahal*."

hour *Shoah* documents the Holocaust, and the five-hour *Tsahal*, according to the director, 'shows a reappropriation of force by Jews, by Israeli Jews.'"

Although Zionism is an idea with nineteenth-century origins and Lanzmann's film is surely a multifaceted and polyvalent text, the trilogy structure supports the contention that there is an important causal connection between the attempted extermination of European Jewry and the subsequent establishment and growth of the IDF.[28] National myths regarding the historical foundation of Jewish military heroism have elsewhere been rehearsed along these lines, dating back to the period following Israel's first war in 1948. For her part, Hannah Arendt, who was a vocal advocate for Israel throughout the 1940s and 1950s, was critical of Israel's overreliance on foundational myths, and she questioned the virtue of elevating strength as the central pillar of Israeli identity.[29] In *Eichmann in Jerusalem*, which was written not all that long after the 1956 Suez crisis, Arendt argues that the message of the state-sponsored Eichmann trial was that "the establishment of a Jewish state had enabled Jews to hit back, as Israelis had done in the War of Independence, in the Suez adventure, and in the almost daily incidents on Israel's unhappy borders."[30] Arendt continues, "if the Jews outside Israel had to be shown the difference between Israeli heroism and Jewish submissive meekness, there was a lesson for those inside Israel too."[31] Arendt here objects to what can be treated as one of the central tenets of Lanzmann's trilogy: Israel's *raison d'être* is that it is the realization of the wholly necessary mission of hitting back.

In his memoir Lanzmann reflects on the views he held in 1967 about the unconditional need for Israel, but he maintained that he always attempted to separate that point of view from the idea that Israel's existence owes itself entirely to the Holocaust because he was averse to redemptive Holocaust narratives such as the one

28. In Dominick LaCapra's assessment, such an interpretation "suggest[s] itself strongly on one level." See Dominick LaCapra, "Lanzmann's *Shoah*: 'Here There Is No Why,'" in *Claude Lanzmann's* Shoah: *Key Essays*, ed. Liebman, 191–229; here, 207.

29. See Moshe Zimmermann, "Hannah Arendt, the Early 'Post-Zionist'" in *Hannah Arendt in Jerusalem*, ed. Steven E. Aschheim (Berkeley: University of California Press, 2001), 181-93; here, 190.

30. Hannah Arendt, *Eichmann in Jerusalem. A Report on the Banality of Evil* (New York: Penguin, 2006 [1963]), 10.

31. *Ibid.*, 10.

offered by *Schindler's List* (1993). Lanzmann writes, "Let me be clearly understood: I never considered Israel as the redemption for the Shoah, the idea that six million Jews gave their lives so that Israel might exist; such a teleological argument whether explicit or implicit is absurd and obscene. Political Zionism long pre-dates World War II."[32] Whether or not one understands Lanzmann's trilogy to mean that the tragedy of the Holocaust gave birth to Israel, his films maintain that Israel and the IDF function as a bulwark or a safeguard—Israel is a nation that exists to prevent a reoccurrence of the Holocaust.

To Lanzmann's trilogy of major works, one would also have to add *Sobibor, October 14, 1943, 4 p.m.* (2001), which, seen in the context of the other films, puts forward a closely related argument: it makes an implicit case for the use of force on the part of Yehuda Lerner, a Polish-born Holocaust survivor who is, at the time of filming, a Hebrew-speaking Israeli. In that filmed interview, which was conducted in Jerusalem in 1979 as part of the production of *Shoah*, Lanzmann fixates on the acts of revolutionary violence that took place in the Sobibór extermination camp. Manuel Köppen argues that Lanzmann was, in 1979, already taking steps toward completing the trilogy "with a film that complemented *Shoah*'s central theme of victimization by narrating the reappropriation of power and force."[33] Seeing these films in connection with one another, a standpoint on Israel emerges; Lanzmann's assertion concerns the importance of establishing a state. The logic, particularly the progression from the uprising of prisoners at Sobibór to Israel's contemporary national defense, could not be clearer. Although *Shoah* is a complex text that derives no singular meaning from the Holocaust, and it at no point openly articulates the contention that the redemption of the Holocaust was the creation of Israel, this particular story about atrocities committed against the Jews and about violence in the name of self-defense appears to undergird Israel's foundations. It is part of a tale about the assumption of Jewish military power and guerrilla resistance, seen in acts of defiance in the Warsaw Ghetto and at Sobibór. This storyline

---

32. Lanzmann, *The Patagonian Hare*, 388.
33. See Manuel Köppen, "Searching for Evidence between Generations: Claude Lanzmann's *Sobibor* and Romuald Karmakar's *Land of Annihilation*," *New German Critique* 41/3 (2014): 57–73; here, 63.

thus concludes with *Tsahal*, in which the IDF appears to emerge as the consequence of a long chain of events.

Building on the idea that Lanzmann's major films constitute a myth-making trilogy, Köppen notes that in *Tsahal*, as in *Shoah*, Lanzmann "forsakes expository commentary; he means to define the position taken by the film through its use of montage and its cinematic architecture."[34] The reference to cinematic architecture pertains not only to the time of narrative but also to its deployment of space. The prominent landscapes of *Tsahal* recall the extent to which landscapes were integral to *Shoah*. Régine Mihal Friedman writes about how these two films visually converge in the elliptical formations that characterize Lanzmann's approach. She points to the interview with Yanoush Ben-Gal, a General in the Reserves, who, in *Tsahal*, recalls his family's exile and his flight from the Nazis, from Poland to Siberia. Friedman notes,

> Lanzmann suddenly illustrates this childhood story with snow-covered landscapes that he took from [the filming of] *Shoah*. . . . [T]his child arrives in Iran via India and from there goes to Israel. He then asserts that he was born for the second time in a tank.[35]

Friedman is here noting how *Tsahal* is interwoven with *Shoah*, and how the spaces of Europe interconnect, through the force of Lanzmann's editorial will, with the spaces of Israel, following a trajectory—even if it is not always an absolutely linear one—from Polish exile to the Middle East.

In exploring the continuities between these films, one notes that *Shoah* and *Tsahal* share a common fascination with wide shots or extreme long shots, with empty spaces and the *horror vacui*, as denoted by the presence of diminutive subjects in vast, unpeopled terrains. Throughout his work, Lanzmann alternates between extreme long shots and close-ups. On the one hand, his close-ups of faces, as Béla Balázs observed about close-ups, make us feel that we "have suddenly been left alone with this one face to the exclusion of the rest of the world. . . . [W]hen we look into the eyes in a close-up, we no longer think of that wide space, because the expression and significance

---

34. Köppen, "Searching for Evidence," 63

35. Régine Mihal Friedman, "'Du Wirst Nicht Mehr Töten'—Der Erste von Claude Lanzmann für *Tsahal* vorgesehene Titel," *Frauen Und Film* 61 (2000): 65-83; here, 70.

of that face has no relation to space and no connection with it."[36] There is an unusually large number of close-ups in *Tsahal*, *Shoah*, and throughout Lanzmann's body of work, and these shots are often used to highlight the traces of historical wounds on his witnesses' physiognomies, the worry lines in and around the eyes of Holocaust survivors and military veterans. His extreme long shots, on the other hand, show those same subjects' insignificance and defenselessness in the face of historical forces. In this way, his films are again structured around bifocal sets of associations: as one camera distance enters into dialogue with another, individualized trauma is set against the vastness of landscapes, where subjects are so small that they run the risk of disappearing. The immense landscapes in *Shoah* suggest how the violence of the Holocaust diminishes its victims, while in *Tsahal* the subjects are nowhere to be found in the abyssal desert. Some of the film's long shots may be seen to correspond to the colonial myth that this land was, prior to 1948, more or less uninhabited. Lanzmann's camera seems to sweep across the Israeli landscape, exploring it for signs of life.

COVER STORIES

A seemingly heroic portrait of a Jewish soldier standing in the Suez Canal provides what may be, for some viewers, the most memorable moment in *Tsahal*. Lanzmann and one of his interviewees discuss a photograph taken by Denis Cameron in 1967, which appeared on the cover of *Life* magazine. The photograph features a young IDF fighter in uniform, chest deep in the canal's waters. The soldier is looking up at the sun, smiling, holding an AK-47 in his left hand, just above the water's surface. It emerges that this is Yossi Ben Hanan, winner of the Medal of Courage, who was the operations officer of the 7th Armored Brigade during the Six-Day War. Now, this same soldier appears in *Tsahal*, 25 years later. Lanzmann withholds this salient detail about his identity until after they have begun to discuss the magazine cover, so that the revelation comes as a surprise. The cover brought Ben Hanan widespread recognition, but he is philosophical about its optics. He speaks about the problem of interpreting a single

---

36. Béla Balázs, "The Face of Man," in *Marxism and Art: Essays Classic and Contemporary*, ed. Maynard Solomon (Detroit: Wayne State University Press, 1979), 289-91; here, 290.

static image, noting that one can see many things in it. He asks: does one see a relieved young man, delighted that the fighting has come to an end, or the face of a violent occupier? He takes seriously the notion that some would look at him and see a Jewish conqueror, but the principal feeling, as he recalls it, was that he was overjoyed and thought about how the temple was in Israeli hands and Jerusalem was unified. For some, this image would instantly acquire symbolic overtones and be endowed with national significance. For his part, Ben Hanan foregrounds the ambiguity and bifocality of the image.

That 1967 issue of *Life* magazine contains passages penned by the political journalist and historian Theodore H. White, who, in writing about the war's conclusion, rhapsodizes:

> A flag of Zion floats over Jerusalem for the first time since the Romans leveled the holy city 1,900 years ago. To be a Jew in Jerusalem is to watch the dawn come up through the dark sky and silver the ridge and fortress walls of the Old City in the East—and know that now no threat lurks behind the hills. No muezzin calls from the minarets of the walled city. They will again; the Israelis have promised so. But, for the moment, the beat and pulse of the entire ancient capital lies in Israeli hands. Where legionary and crusader, pasha and commissioner, once made law, Israeli soldiers patrol. Amiably alert, on guard at every crossroad and holy place, in desert battle dress, their Uzi—submachine guns—slung over their shoulders, they pace the streets, check passes and say "Shalom"—Peace.[37]

In White's account, the Israeli soldiers are "amiably alert" and carry messages of peace. He treats the following statement as a universally accepted truth: "Israelis are Jews who have declared that they will not ever again be victims—and their army is an expression of this will."[38] This type of logic would support treating the *Life* magazine cover, featuring a soldier who is notably without an opponent—and who might be seen by some as possessing a soft and gentle face—as an icon with a singular, uncontested meaning. In the interview, Ben Hanan demonstrates his understanding that military iconography can serve as a foundation for national myths. The *Life* magazine image is unlike Goya's allegorical painting, which, because it features two unidentified combatants, knowingly presents its viewers with a surplus

---

37. Theodore H. White, "Wrap up of the War: Final Thrust into Syria," *Life* 62/25 (June 23, 1967), 20–32; here 22 and 24.
38. Ibid., 25.

Figure 1. Two views of Yossi Ben Hanan in Claude Lanzmann's *Tsahal* (1994). DVD capture.

of possible meanings. No one looking at Goya's work would know on which side of the endless conflict he or she is being made to stand.

Tsahal is an unusually lengthy film, and there are many parts of it that center neither on the IDF's soldiers nor on their armored tanks. One sequence, very late in the film, features an interview with Uri Ariel, a settler at Kokhav HaShahar, which is on the northern West Bank and was founded in 1979. Working through a translator, Lanzmann engages Ariel in a long conversation as he and some Arab employees proceed with their construction work, enlarging the settlement before our eyes. Ariel defends the notion that he is entitled to build and live on this site based on the idea that the Jewish people have both legal and God-given rights to inhabit this place. In light of Ariel's point of view, Lanzmann feels emboldened to ask some provocative questions, which may come as a relief insofar as he has been a reserved interviewer throughout much of the film. Lanzmann asks: if it were determined legally that his settlement was on Arab land, would Ariel still remain there? Ariel answers that he certainly would. Although he very much understands the Palestinians' perspective, the Bible, he says, explains that it was Abraham who obtained this land, not the Arabs; the covenant between God and the Jews is incontrovertible.

The interaction between Lanzmann and Ariel seems to contain reasonable lines of inquiry, but J. Hoberman, for this reason, describes it as a kind of breakdown within the film's argumentation: "Lanzmann's use of reason is pulverized on the rock of the settler's zealotry," which is, according to Hoberman, "a defeat more profound than Lanzmann may recognize."[39] As gentle as Ariel seems to be, his answers transgress the boundaries of the other responses in *Tsahal*; he takes recourse to the law when it suits him and explicitly invokes his prerogative to build, regardless of any contradictions that his position entails. Lanzmann's response, at their conversation's end, is to show Ariel affection, drawing him close and physically embracing him. On its surface, Lanzmann's gesture would be unusual in a documentary film because it violates most pretenses of objectivity. Regardless of whether the embrace suggests that Lanzmann shares his interlocutor's point of view, most viewers would understand this gesture to mean that Lanzmann welcomes Ariel's perspective and that he is glad to have him voice it in the film. His gesture may also be seen as an echo of a moment in *Pourquoi Israël* in which Lanzmann embraces

39. J. Hoberman, "Never again," 48.

Figure 2. Lanzmann embraces Léon Roisch in *Pourquoi Israël* (1973; top) and Uri Ariel in *Tsahal*. DVD capture.

Léon Roisch, the curator of the Dimona Museum, who had become emotional while explaining to Lanzmann the impact that his migration to Israel had on him and his wife. Lanzmann's embraces not only bring the director closer to each of these interviewees, but they also draw the first and last parts of the trilogy, released twenty years apart, nearer to one another.[40]

Following in the same vein as Ariel, Ehud Barak, in his interview with Lanzmann, presents Israel's military story in terms of its two-thousand-year-long history. Barak appears here with Lanzmann several years before he became Prime Minister. He was first appointed Minister of Internal Affairs in 1995 and became Prime Minister four years later. At the time of the interview, he was a highly decorated soldier. Barak asserts that the Holocaust, alongside Israel's twentieth-century wars, allowed for what he describes as the re-emergence of fighting Jews. He then offers an understanding of the IDF that is rooted in ancient history, repeating the nearly two-thousand-year-old tale of Yohanan Ben Zakkai, a sage from the period of the Second Temple who escaped from the Romans as they were destroying Jerusalem. Barak explains that Ben Zakkai's escape enabled him to continue teaching and thus permitted rabbinic Judaism to survive the Romans' assault; it allowed, as Barak explains it, for the continuity of the Jewish people. Lanzmann strategically places the story of Ben Zakkai at the close of *Tsahal*—were it not for the presence of Ben Zakkai "in us," Barak explains, Israel would not survive the millennia.

Fourteen years later, after his Prime Ministerial term had come to an end, Barak met with Lanzmann for a follow-up interview, the 40-minute-long film released under the title *Lights and Shadows*. The film adopts its title from a metaphor for Israel proposed by Barak, who likens his country to a nation that had a baby's face when it was born; Israel had no shadows on it—there were no wrinkles, no signs of age. Barak explains that the nation now has shadows, presumably the marks and blemishes that have been carried over from the difficulties in its recent past. Lanzmann does not take Barak to task over his own possible role in the accumulation of these shadows, and in view

---

40. The outtakes to *Shoah* also contain at least one moment in which Lanzmann physically embraces an interview subject: Lanzmann lowers his head into the chest and hands of the Holocaust survivor Itzhak Zuckerman in an interview he conducted in Jerusalem in 1979. Jennifer Cazenave describes this outtake as a "reversal of roles." See Cazenave, *An Archive of the Catastrophe: The Unused Footage of Claude Lanzmann's* Shoah (Albany: State University of New York Press, 2019), 99.

of Lanzmann's comments about the IDF soldiers ("You can see their faces, you can see that they are soft, they are very tender"), Barak's point of view seems surprisingly open to accepting the flaws in the IDF's tactics. But Barak is still a politician (he was, at the time, leader of the Labor Party), and he concludes the interview on a positive note, reminding Lanzmann that the Israeli national anthem, which was officially adopted in 2004, is called "Hope" (*Hatikvah*). He acknowledges the existence of shadows but still holds out hope, which serves as a contrast to the position taken by David Grossman in *Tsahal*. Grossman argues that it is characteristic of Israelis that they have trouble imagining the future. They cannot envision a future because they are not sure they will have one. When explaining his perspective to Lanzmann, Grossman says that it is almost impossible to imagine Israel in 2025, adding that Israelis are not allowed to think so far ahead, owing to the fear of annihilation with which they live.

Although Lanzmann appears to conclude *Tsahal* with Barak's story of Ben Zakkai, this is not the very end. He shows us footage of tanks moving across the landscape, kicking up dust and, following these long shots, moves in for a medium shot of a soldier astride a tank, followed by a zoom and, eventually, a close-up of the tank operator's face. The film spends nearly 30 seconds observing him, accompanied by nothing but diegetic desert sounds. The soldier had been identified to us earlier as Adam Ben Tolila, who now sits astride his Merkava, an Israeli-developed tank which he dubbed "a monster of iron." In this final shot, Lanzmann blocks out the rest of the desert, eliminating nearly all of the landscape and stripping away the image of the monster of iron.[41] Only the face remains, extracted from its relation to its setting. Like the *Life* magazine cover that featured only Ben Hanan, here we see only a soldier, who, in his youthfulness, may seem to us to be nothing other than gentle and reflective. There is neither a mortal opponent, nor Goya's quicksand, nor an eternal struggle. Images such as this—the young soldier, called to fight when he would surely prefer not to be—in the absence of other, critical voices, serve an iconic function. In terms put forward by Cornelia Brink, such an image might be "accepted as straightforward and un-

---

41. Tobias Ebbrecht-Hartmann also interprets this same closing shot in Ebbrecht-Hartmann, "*Tsahal*: zwischen *Shoah* und *Sobibor*," in *Le regard du siècle: Claude Lanzmann zum 90. Geburtstag*, ed. Susanne Zepp (Tectum Verlag: Baden-Baden, 2017), 175–92; here, 175–76.

Figure 3. The final shot of *Tsahal*: a close-up of Adam Ben Tolila atop a tank. DVD capture.

ambiguous reality," one that "make[s] a moral claim to be accepted without questioning."[42]

While the image of this soldier's face in isolation may seem iconic, and it might be meant to stand in for the boyish kindness of the Israeli soldiers, the shot's prolonged silence also lends the image an air of uncertainty. Just as Ben Hanan had been aware of the ambiguity of his *Life* cover, one here becomes quite conscious of the abstruseness of these images. And Lanzmann, too, may have been attempting to call their ambiguities to mind. Brink reminds us that photographic icons may become readable, but their meanings can shift "according to the context in which they are shown and looked at." She adds, "The documentary value of a photograph is not always reliable, *nor is its reception just as one would like it to be.*"[43] It is entirely possible

42. Brink, "Secular Icons: Looking at Photographs from Nazi Concentration Camps," *History & Memory* 12/1 (2000): 135-50; here, 135-36.
43. Ibid., 149. Italics added.

that Lanzmann meant for his film to say one thing: that the soldiers who appear in the film would prefer not to be there, and that a long road led to creation of the IDF, whose work is necessary because of all the wars that Israel is compelled to fight. Seen through one lens, all those contentions may be true. Images, however, do not always do the work that photographers or directors would like them to; not only is there a surfeit of absent voices throughout *Tsahal*, but the ones we do hear are sometimes in conflict with themselves, and even singular, static images may produce conflicting meanings. With *Tsahal*, Lanzmann wanted a conclusion to his trilogy, but documentary films, like individual photographs and even magazine covers, are not always reliable, nor is their reception always as one would like it to be.

MICHAEL G. LEVINE

"Yes, this is the place": Lanzmann between *Napalm* and *Shoah*

More than thirty years separate Lanzmann's 1985 masterpiece *Shoah* from *Napalm*, released in 2017 and the last of his films that is not based on outtakes from it. Whereas *Shoah* is a monumental nine-and-a-half-hour work that fundamentally alters the way we think about cinema and the act of bearing witness to the murder of European Jewry, *Napalm* is a much smaller, decidedly more personal film focused ostensibly on the director's amorous encounter with Kim Kum-sun, a woman he met during a 1958 trip to North Korea. That the story told in *Napalm* nevertheless marks a privileged moment, if not a watershed, in Lanzmann's life is suggested by its placement at the very center of his autobiography, *The Patagonian Hare*, and by the extensive detail in which it is discussed. Its significance is further underscored by the fact that it is the only incident in the 500-page memoir to be accompanied by images: the front and back of a postcard he received from the woman months after his return to Paris.

57 years after his encounter with Kim Kum-sun, Lanzmann returns to Pyongyang to film *Napalm*. Standing at the exact spot on a bridge where he had met her following their initial embrace in his hotel room, he suddenly switches from French to German. Now speaking not only in another language but in the voice of another person, he cites words uttered by the Holocaust survivor, Simon Srebnik, upon his return to Chełmno in the opening scenes of *Shoah*: "Das ist das Platz [sic.] [Oui, c'est le lieu. Yes, this is the place]." (Fig. 1)

Repeating words spoken toward the beginning of *Shoah* at this moment in *Napalm*, Lanzmann suggests that his 1985 film may have had its own beginning in this encounter on a Pyongyang bridge in 1958. Nothing will have come of the one-time meeting with Kim Kum-sun. An affair that remained unconsummated, it seems nevertheless to

YFS 141, *Lanzmann after "Shoah,"* ed. Levine and Stark, © 2022 by Yale University.

123

Yes, this is the place.

Figure 1. (1:10:20) (*Napalm*)

have stayed with Lanzmann, its utter uniqueness, compactness, and unrealized possibilities haunting him for the rest of his life. He would return to North Korea two more times over the years, never again meeting the woman or even seeking her out. Toward the end of his life, however, now in his late eighties, Lanzmann takes a final trip to make a film dedicated to her.

Many—among them leading Lanzmann scholars—have criticized *Napalm* as pure self-indulgence, as the embarrassing display of an old man's nostalgia for a charged moment, an impossible attraction that, in light of the prevailing political conditions, could go no further.[1] It is certainly a very different Lanzmann one sees in this film and one indeed wonders why he chose to make it. Examining the strange prominence given his encounter with the North Korean woman in *The Patagonian Hare* and the citation of Srebnik's words from *Shoah*

1. Stuart Liebman. Personal communication. Additionally, Peter Bradshaw calls the film a "flawed, self-indulgent but still fascinating effort," *The Guardian*, May 21, 2017; while Ben Kenigsberg describes it as a "disappointing documentary" in which "memories of lust" take the place "of what could have been a serious inquiry," "Cannes 2017: 'How to Talk to Girls at Parties' and 'Napalm'," RogerEbert .com May 23, 2017. https://www.rogerebert.com/festivals/cannes-2017-how-to-talk -to-girls-at-parties-and-napalm, and Richard Porton, co-editor of *Cinéaste*, describes it as "brazenly narcissistic." Cited in David Hudson, "Cannes 2017: Claude Lanz-mann's *Napalm*," *The Daily*, May 23, 2017. https://www.criterion.com/current/ posts/4587-the-daily-cannes-2017-claude-lanzmann-s-napalm

at a pivotal moment in *Napalm*, I want to ask what it might have been that remained so fully other, so thoroughly unassimilable about the meeting in 1958. Beyond its patently erotic dimension, what may have driven Lanzmann to return to it and embroider incessantly around it?

Clues are provided by the film itself in which Lanzmann speaks repeatedly about time at a standstill. The repetition suggests a non-linear, traumatic time frame in which one unassimilated moment is superimposed on another, each serving in its turn to hold time open and at a standstill.[2] Among these moments are scenes of boating that link the time with Kim Kum-sun to the opening scene of *Shoah*. In the famous opening sequence of the latter, a long tracking shot follows Srebnik, now 47 and sitting at the front of a small skiff, being ferried down the Narew River, performing the same Polish folksong, "A Little White House," that German guards had made him sing as a boy. (Fig. 2)

In *Napalm* a key scene on which I will focus at length in what follows also takes place on a boat. Here the little white house of which Srebnik sings finds an echo in the little white purse Kim Kum-sun loses as the boat she and Lanzmann had rented suddenly capsizes. More important, however, than this moment of loss or even the capsizing is what transpires on the boat itself. Lanzmann meticulously constructs the scene, rehearsing it verbally in *The Patagonian Hare* before staging it cinematically in *Napalm*.

So idiosyncratic is the scene that it must be read on its own terms. Ultimately, this will mean viewing it less as a central moment toward which the film builds and around which it turns than as a puncture wound in its temporal and narrative fabric. Standing open in this way, it marks not only a moment of traumatic rupture, an enduring moment of time held open and at a standstill, but also a primal scene of witnessing. I want to argue, in short, that Lanzmann will have encountered in this scene a certain fascination, a preoccupation that will never have left him, a question that will have repeatedly addressed him and which he himself seeks in a necessarily belated manner to address. It is in many ways the guiding question of his life and work: the question of witnessing.

---

2. On the notion of time at a standstill, see Walter Benjamin, "On the Concept of History," Theses XVI and XVII, in *Selected Writings*, vol. 4, trans. Harry Zohn (Cambridge: Belknap Press of Harvard University Press, 2003) 396.

A little white house...

Figure 2. (4:56) (*Shoah*)

It is for this reason, I want to argue, that he returns to North Korea in his last film. Unlike *Shoah*, *Napalm* makes extensive use of documentary footage. The majority of this footage pertains to the Korean War and is culled from American and North Korean sources. The film also makes use of home movies and stills shot during Lanzmann's trip to Pyongyang as a member of the first Western delegation invited to visit the country. (Fig. 3)

In addition to traveling back and forth between the three trips Lanzmann made to the country in 1958, 2004, and 2015, *Napalm* stitches together scenes recorded during the last trip with an interview subsequently filmed in Paris. In the latter scene the traditional Lanzmannian roles are reversed as the filmmaker now casts himself as the witnessing subject. Even during the filming in Pyongyang, Lanzmann uncharacteristically focuses attention on himself. This is nowhere more dramatic—or rather self-dramatizing—than at the moment he reaches the bridge mentioned earlier. Abruptly turning on his North Korean handler and extricating himself from his grip, he cries: "Let go now!" (*Lâche-moi!*) (Fig. 4) "I'm playing . . . I'm in my

Figure 3. (35:16) (*Napalm*)

role of cinematographer!" (*Maintenant je joue la . . . je fais du ciné-matographe!*) (Fig. 5)[3]

In addition to such moments of Lanzmann playing Lanzmann, the film takes pains to single out and visually highlight his use of particular words. One such term is *querencia*, taken from the language of bullfighting, which he uses to describe the position of safety he sought to stake out in his hotel room while receiving an injection under the watchful eye of government officials derisively referred to as *les casquettes*. In the image accompanying his account and illustrating his *querencia*, a bull is shown pressed against a wall of the ring, a bright red flower easily mistaken for a bloody gash, clearly visible on the back of its neck. (Fig. 6)

Whereas the bull's *querencia* is visible to all protagonists and spectators of the *corrida*, Lanzmann's is described as the blind spot (*l'angle mort*) (47:12) into which he draws Kim Kum-sun, the nurse administering the shot, so as to escape the intrusive gaze of the *casquettes*. Casting himself as a bull being gradually and ceremoniously stabbed to death, Lanzmann connects the *piqûres* received at the hands of the nurse with the mortal thrusts delivered by a matador and his entourage. This is not the only place where the erotic and the

3. Throughout, unbracketed ellipses indicate ellipses in the original (interruptions or pauses in speech), while bracketed ellipses indicate my omissions.

Figure 4. (59:48) (*Napalm*)

Figure 5. (59: 50) (*Napalm*)

lethal converge, a point to which I will return shortly. Before doing so, I want to note how the term *piqûre*, repeated throughout the scene, is itself enmeshed in a chain of signifiers that runs from the blows inflicted on the bull's neck to the *piqués foudroyants* (Katz 56),[4] the

4. Corine Katz, "Sur *Napalm* de Claude Lanzmann," *Les temps modernes*, 5/696, (2017): 56-63.

Figure 6. (44:54) (*Napalm*)

dive-bombing American planes captured in archival footage descending on the civilian population during the Korean War, to the countless *piqueniques* Lanzmann is forced to attend as a member of the Western delegation: "*usines et piqueniques*," "factories and picnics," he repeatedly laments. Given the discursive context, it is difficult not to hear in the term *piqueniques* echoes of the *piques-nuque* or piercing blows to the back of the neck in bullfighting.[5]

As Lanzmann notes in the opening chapter of *The Patagonian Hare*, such blows were an "abiding obsession" of his life, stressing in particular how he himself has no neck, having drawn in on himself over time so as "to leave for the blade of *la veuve* . . . no convenient place and no opportunity for it to make one."[6] Of special relevance to *Napalm* is the opening of the chapter in which he first tells the story of his meeting with Kim Kum-sun.

---

5. "I've always loved, I still love bullfighting and the running of the bulls." [Moi, j'aimais bien, j'aime toujours la tauromachie et les courses des taureaux], Lanzmann tells his interviewer (46:30).

6. Recalling a particularly haunting photograph from *Paris Match* of a Chinese woman about to be executed, he writes of a "hand that, with overpowering force, pushes her head down to expose her neck but also to compel her to die in the position of a penitent." Claude Lanzmann, *The Patagonian Hare: A Memoir*, trans. Frank Wynne (New York: Farrar, Straus and Giroux, 2012), 8. Hereafter all references will appear in parentheses in the body of the text as *PH* followed by page number. All references to *Le lièvre deed Patagonie* (Gallimard, 2009) will henceforth appear as *LP* followed by the page number.

1958, I am thirty-three. For me, this is the year of "Le curée d'Uruffe," of Général de Gaulle's return to power, of my trip to China and North Korea, and of the presentiment [. . .] that my relationship with [Simone de Beauvoir] had to take a new form. What links these moments in my life is something much deeper than mere chronological confluence. (*PH* 267)

What those links were Lanzmann does not say, going on instead to explain how the curate of Uruffe had "put a bullet through the neck of Régine Fays, a member of his flock, a girl of twenty, pregnant by him and about to give birth; then, having murdered her, he cut open the belly, delivered the baby and put out the child's eyes with a penknife" (*PH* 267). Covering his trial for *France Dimanche*, Lanzmann recalls spending the whole of the proceedings "as close to the curate [. . .] as possible, two metres behind him, staring fixedly at that scrawny neck [*mon regard intensément fixé sur sa maigre nuque*] that, I was sure, was destined for the guillotine" (*PH* 270, *LP* 393).

In what follows I propose viewing the scene on the boat to which I referred earlier as itself a kind of *piqûre*—not a blow to the neck or an injection in the buttocks but a kind of Barthesian *punctum*. Such a puncture wound in time and in the narrative fabric of the film is highly overdetermined: standing apart from its surrounding context, it not only brings Eros and Thanatos together in one shot, but conjoins them around the word "napalm." The title of the film, "napalm" is itself a term that, as we shall see, does not quite belong to its context, a part that remains fundamentally—or rather abyssally—apart.

Before turning to this *punctum*, it is necessary to sketch briefly the part played by napalm in the mass destruction inflicted upon the North Koreans by the United States and its allies (including France) between 1950 and 1953. In addition to 520,000 North Korean soldiers and 320,000 Chinese volunteers who died in the war, four million civilians out of a population of thirty million were killed. On the capital, Pyongyang, with a population of 400,000, 428,000 bombs were dropped, more than one bomb per person. On the country as a whole, the U.S. dropped three million liters of napalm.[7]

Lanzmann shows the devastation inflicted, taking care not to mix the perspectives of the footage shown or the sources from which it is drawn. The shots of the bombers thus have an abstract and dis-

---

7. For a detailed discussion of the use of napalm during the Korean War, see Robert M. Neer, *Napalm: An American Biography* (Cambridge: Harvard UP, 2013), esp. 91-104.

tanced feel while the view from the ground is impossibly close, showing burning buildings, charred bodies, and naked, frantically jump-
ing children. Yet, it is not just the destruction on which Lanzmann
dwells but, also and above all, on the war's aftermath. Indeed, what
seems to concern him most is that there is no "after" *per se* since
time itself will have stopped. The film, he says,

> is an unsparing critique of a totally anti-democratic dictatorship. Yet I
> also didn't want to forget the American's savage bombardments [. . .].
> Because if we ignore them we understand nothing of the current situ-
> ation particularly with regard to relations with the Americans. It's
> also a rather complicated film because it shows time at a standstill.
> The country is a paradox: the North Koreans are in a constant state of
> military preparedness, 10 million people are mobilized for a war . . .
> without war, locked in a constant battle without battle.[8]

Time at standstill is thus a kind of movement in place, an impetus
without outlet, without the possibility of moving forward. Even the
rebuilding of Pyongyang in a monumental style seems, in Lanzmann's
words, only to accentuate "the original void" (10:08). The more one
tries to move forward, the more one finds oneself stuck. This repetition compulsion, this experience of time at a standstill, no doubt has
something of the thanatotic. It is therefore telling that such language
is used by Lanzmann to describe the movement of the other boats
among which he and Kim Kum-sun find themselves in the scene referred to earlier. In order to grasp its strategic framing, it is necessary
to dwell first on Lanzmann's description of the circumstances under
which they first met.

A self-described health nut at the time, Lanzmann had brought
phials of Vitamin B-12 with him to North Korea should he suffer from
fatigue during the trip. When the moment came for such injections he
was told to remain in his hotel room rather than go to a nearby hospital. The shots were administered by Kim Kum-sun and the manner
in which she delivered them is described in exquisite detail. Each day
for a week she would come to his room, at first accompanied by the
delegation's translator, Comrade Ok, and five *casquettes*. With each
passing day there was one fewer government official until on the last

8. Interview with Céline Lussato, "Claude Lanzmann: 'Napalm' est une critique
très dure de la dictature nord-coréenne,'" *L'obs cinéma*, September 4, 2017. (Trans.
mine)   https://www.nouvelobs.com/cinema/20170904.OBS4190/claude-lanzmann
-napalm-est-une-critique-tres-dure-de-la-dictature-nord-coreenne.html

day, a Sunday, the nurse and patient were left entirely alone together. One is never quite sure what kind of set up led to this surprising circumstance or whether Kim Kum-sun was herself a state agent positioned to win the confidence of the foreign delegate.

Seen through Lanzmann's eyes she is incredibly beautiful, her gestures slow and precise, the injections she administers gentle and pain-free. On the last day she arrives, having exchanged her nurse's uniform for European clothing and wearing her hair, formerly plaited in two long braids, gathered up in a chignon. Lanzmann does not conceal his pleasure. "I was astounded, dumbfounded, bewildered" (51:25). They leave the door open and retreat as usual to the blind spot of Lanzmann's *querencia*, where she administers the last shot. "*Elle me pique*," he recalls, now shifting into the present tense, "plunges the syringe very, very, very slowly" (*enfonce le syringue très, très, très longuement*) (53:53). They then embrace "passionately, hungrily" (*férocement, bestialement*) (56:08). Knowing things can't go on like this, Lanzmann steps back and asks her to meet him a few hours later at the aforementioned bridge.

When he arrives, she is already there waiting for him. They continue on to the boats, hoping to row to a place where they can once again be alone together. Able to rent one, they set off only to find themselves all at once "trapped in a turning circle of boats." "There were 300 boats carrying families turning in circles" (1:08:48), Lanzmann recalls. At the corresponding point in *The Patagonian Hare* he further reflects: "'They're going round in circles,' I said to myself, 'they're going round in circles'—to me the circle seemed the very image of prison, the convict endlessly circling the prison yard, his cell—cut off from his plans, from his future" (PH 288).

This incessant turning is the spatial equivalent to the notion of time at a standstill mentioned throughout the film. Yet, it is within this movement in place that something transpires, that something happens within the boat itself. Unable to move away from the mass of vessels in which they are trapped, Lanzmann has no choice but to beach the skiff (1:09:43). Stranded on a bank, literally a tongue of sand (*langue de sable*), and encircled by the centripetal forces of inertia, Lanzmann pulls out a notebook and pencil and, as he himself describes it, "invents a language" (1:09:53).[9]

---

9. "J'ai sorti mon calepin, mon crayon, mon truc, et puis j'ai inventé un langage pour pouvoir parler avec elle."

Tellingly, the narrative breaks off at this point as a conspicuous cut shifts the scene from the story being told to the locus of narration itself. Gesturing to the place where he is now standing on the bridge, he says, "but it was right here. And that's very, very moving. I am at the exact place .... At the very spot where it happened. As they say in *Shoah*. As Srebnik says in *Shoah*, '*Das ist das Platz.*' Yes, this is the place, this is the place" (Figs. 7, 8).[10]

One begins to get a sense of the extent to which Lanzmann is "playing the cinematographer" here. For, thanks to the cinematic cut, the place to which the deictic "this" points is ambiguous. On the one hand, it refers, at the level of the narrating subject, to a place on the bridge, "the very spot where it happened." On the other, it may indicate, at the level of the narrated story, the scene on the boat broken off precisely at the point where Lanzmann claims to have invented a new language. Unable to decide where exactly the place is, we are invited to read the one place in terms of the other. This not only involves reading back and forth between the scenes, but mapping them both onto a place that will have opened between scenes, between speakers, and above all between languages in the shift from Lanzmann's French to his citation of Srebnik's German. As Lanzmann surely knows, the phrase "das ist das Platz" is grammatically incorrect and this is no doubt also his point. For what will have opened in the shift between places, speakers, and languages is precisely a between-space of linguistic error. In thus allowing the non-native speaker of German, Srebnik, to speak with and through him, Lanzmann effectively gives place to a different notion of linguistic inventiveness, a *language of testimony* foreign to any and all mother tongues.[11]

---

10. Citing Srebnik, Lanzmann suggests that *Shoah* may have had its own beginnings in the encounter with Kim Kum-sun. Indeed, the language he will later speak with Srebnik is in some sense learned in his encounter with her. About his meeting with Srebnik in Israel, Lanzmann recalls, "Straightaway I told him that I had just come back from Chelmno. I had prudently brought paper and pencils so that we could both sketch our memories of those places. Just as Kim Kum-sun and I had done twenty years earlier in North Korea, Srebnik and I invented a common language" (*PH* 437). My thanks to Jared Stark for bringing this passage to my attention.

11. Such foreignness is a key aspect of the innovative theory of testimony developed by Shoshana Felman in her pathbreaking essay, "The Return of the Voice: Claude Lanzmann's *Shoah*" in Shoshana Felman and Dori Laub, M.D., *Testimony: Crises of Witnessing in Literature, Psychoanalysis and History* (New York: Routledge, 1992), 204-283. See also Jacques Derrida on the idiomatic, idiosyncratic language of witnessing.

Figure 7. (1:10:20) (*Napalm*)

Figure 8. (8:19) (*Shoah*)

Almost immediately after this carefully staged linguistic performance, Lanzmann returns to the scene on the boat with Kim Kumsun. Yet it is no longer exactly he who speaks; that is, we now see him walking along the banks of the Taedong conversing with one of his handlers, the bridge still visible in the background. But the voice we actually hear is offscreen. Voice and speaker are then quickly reunited as the scene shifts to an interior space in Paris where Lanzmann continues his account.[12] Now, however, it is Kim Kum-sun who has taken the notebook and pencil in hand and begun to draw. In response to his suggestion that she might be from the south, she draws a map centered on the Manchurian-Korean border. Above the Yalu River marking this border, she sketches airplanes dropping bombs (1:13:31).

The passage from spoken language to silent drawing, a passage having taken place under the sign of linguistic invention, is now taken a step further. "She makes a gesture that is at once incredible and incomprehensible," he says. "With all the domesticated pleasure seekers turning around us and able to see everything, she does something with a swiftness . . . with the speed of a prodigious lightning bolt. She opens her blouse" (1:14:06). "Very quickly," Lanzmann continues,

> she uncovered her breast, a firm, full, heavy breast. I wanted to touch it. Under the breast was a thick black strip (une grande barre noire) of burned flesh. And she says just one word: napalm. And that was a word I understood. As I said, it was a lightning apparition as she immediately closed her blouse so that the passersby didn't see it. It meant that she was a victim of the American bombing raids on North Korea's northern border. I was completely overwhelmed (Moi, j'étais complètement bouleversé). I wanted to kiss this burned flesh, there where the burn really was . . . . What she did was incredible and I wanted to kiss that. It really was an act of love . . . . I went mad. At that very moment, I loved her. I loved her so deeply, I truly loved her, you understand. I loved her for having dared to do that and for having done it for me. It was in truth very intimate. I loved her for what she had suffered too. It was a mixture of all those things. She was overwhelming and I was . . . overwhelmed. (1:14:08-1:16:15)

The English term "overwhelm" does not quite capture the nature of the interaction. In French, Lanzmann says, "elle était bouleversante et j'étais . . . bouleversé." Both find themselves, in other words,

---

12. This interior is the part of Lanzmann's apartment he used as a study or home office. My thanks to the film's producer, François Margolin, for identifying the location.

capsized, turned upside down, turned literally into symmetrical inversions of one another. So unsettling, so *bouleversant*, is this moment that it momentarily spins itself free from its surroundings, from all the boats circling around them and the stagnation and sense of time at a standstill with which they are associated. These circular returns are the true locus of the death drive, the very embodiment of a silent and silencing force of repetition. If the erotic and the lethal may be said to stand in the most intimate proximity in this scene, it is to be sought not merely in the closeness of the bared breast to the charred flesh directly below but in the relationship between the vital burst of Kim Kum-sun's "incredible and incomprehensible" gesture and the fatal monotony of the boats circling endlessly around it. The moment passes in a flash. Yet, its lightning apparition is precisely what acts as a *piqûre* or Barthesian *punctum* to prick its surroundings, piercing them not only as an ever-so-fleeting opening but as one that gives place to a singular scene of witnessing.

A word passes between them, a word Lanzmann understands. Yet, it is not so much its meaning as its impact that makes it a word of testimony, that impels us to view testimony itself less as the communication of first-hand knowledge than as a gesture that, in its very incomprehensibility, sears its addressee, setting him aflame and driving him mad. "I loved her," Lanzmann recalls, "for having dared to do that and for having done it for me"—or, to be more precise, "for having done it *to* me, *à moi*." And it is in this sense that testimony must be understood first and foremost as an address, as an act that pierces its addressee. If it pricks Lanzmann like a syringe or like Eros' arrow, it does so in a way that not only makes him fall in love, but also makes us ask with renewed urgency and incomprehension what love, what testimonial love, what a love of the witness is and could be.

At the very least, I would suggest that such love involves the invention of a language, that it gives place to a language that does not yet exist and may never exist as such. For it is perhaps first and foremost a language of the in-between, a language of inadvertent slips and mercurial gestures, an act of testimony whose idiom, mode of address, and relationship to the addressee can never be known in advance. It is an act that must be inventively performed each time as if for the first time. I would suggest that it is this testimonial love that overwhelms Lanzmann time and again and that leads us in the end to view *Napalm* as a last testament and a final *éloge* of this love.

III. Lanzmann par lui-même

FRANÇOISE MELTZER

Time and the Hare: Lanzmann's Autobiography

Claude Lanzmann's autobiography, *Le lièvre de Patagonie* (2009) (*The Patagonian Hare*, 2012), provides a curious problem: the book in its original French is not the same book in its English version. I don't just mean by this that the translation itself is what changes the experience of the book—though that is to some extent the case with any translation. Rather, the type of book that is *Le lièvre de Patagonie* is suffused with so much French culture, events, politics, French proper names (particularly famous ones), the Parisian environment, attitudes, and so on that an entire setting and atmosphere will be mostly lost on the average English reader. Even the reviews in the U.S. strongly diverge from the ones in France (more on that below). The first reason for this divergence is that Lanzmann is mainly known in the States as the director of *Shoah*. In the France of the 50s, 60s, 70s, and into the late 80s, however, Lanzmann was known (and well known) as a journalist and essayist: he was on the board of the important literary journal *Les temps modernes* (founded in the 1940s by Sartre and Simone de Beauvoir), for which he also wrote and which he was later to direct. And he regularly contributed articles to *France dimanche*, *Elle*, *France observateur*, *France soir*, *Le monde*, and others. Frequently, his articles were written under a pseudonym, mostly for *Elle*. The name for one of these "writers," whom Lanzmann calls his "double," was inspired in him by what he calls a "brutal fit of Christianization"—Jean-Jacques Delacroix. The last name a Christian reference, or a reference to the painter? Lanzmann doesn't know. But he adds that he is embarrassed by none of these texts signed "J.-J.D." Articles signed by the latter were mostly "commentaries on psycho-sociological relations concerning love and

YFS 141, *Lanzmann after "Shoah,"* ed. Levine and Stark, © 2022 by Yale University.

sex."[1] Several articles that were considered a bit too "*hard*" for the readers of *Elle* were placed in *France observateur*, under Lanzmann's real name. He was also, for a time, the ghost writer for Jacques Cousteau, the explorer and naval officer, filmmaker, and so on.[2]

Lanzmann wrote furiously and mostly at great length, and he wrote, as we have seen, for popular journals as well as for the most intellectual ones. He wrote about politics and celebrity profiles, reviewed books, commented on various political and social scandals, traveled extensively (such as to North Korea and other parts of Asia), and wrote about what he saw. He wrote on writers and on writing: Jean-Paul Sartre, Claire Etcherelli, Françoise Sagan, Albert Cohen, Simone de Beauvoir, and many more. He hung out with and then wrote about meeting and/or interviewing the likes of Brigitte Bardot, Catherine Deneuve, Simone Signoret, Yves Montand, Pierre Cardin, and a host of other famous people.

Lanzmann had the opposite of writer's block; he could write all night if necessary and, by his own admission, almost never failed to keep to a deadline. His style was always trenchant and highly literary (he is the master of metaphor and of literary allusion)—a style that can be characterized by an exuberance and near total memory (as Lanzmann himself points out to his reader in *Lièvre*), combined with intensity and acuity of thought. In the 50s, 60s, and 70s, he was at the center of the heyday of French thought, existentialism, and famous critical theorists. He was also known to be Simone de Beauvoir's lover (he lived with her for seven years, with Sartre's blessing). Hobnobbing constantly as he did with the intellectual luminaries of the day (such as Deleuze, Sartre himself, Cousteau, Cocteau, Butor, Tournier, Fanon, Ponge, and so on), he achieved the role of a famous writer and journalistic star. It is not surprising then, that *Le lièvre de Patagonie* is a work of superb writing. It is full of literary tropes, humorous asides, gripping anecdotes, tragedies, incredible adventures,

---

1. Claude Lanzmann, *Le lièvre de Patagonie* (Gallimard, 2009), 369. Throughout this essay, I will be referring to the French original of the book in the parenthetical references. English translations are mine.

2. It is worth noting that Lanzmann was in the Resistance while in high school in Clermont-Ferrand (as was his father, initially unbeknownst to the son). In *Hare*, Lanzmann strongly argues against Marcel Ophül's film *The Sorrow and the Pity* in which, it will be remembered, Clermont is presented as a hub of collaboration during World War II. Lanzmann's response is emphatic: "[T]o make of Clermont-Ferrand, as the film suggests, a city that is the symbol of the collaboration is a heresy . . . . Clermont, on the contrary, was an important site of the Resistance in Auvergne and in France" (40).

celebrities, and personal confessions. Lanzmann knows how to tell a story, to say the least. His narrations frequently read like thrillers; they are spellbinding. His energy is riveting (in his life and in his prose). Moreover, Lanzmann had studied philosophy, and *Lièvre* is filled with philosophical asides and commentary.

The French press was almost unanimous in its positive view of the autobiography. I will give a few examples, and ask the reader to note how much these French reviews emphasize Lanzmann as a *writer*. "This is a very great book (*un très grand livre*)," writes *Le monde*, one that is, in fact, "a collection of several books: that of an adventurer of life, a combatant, a warrior, a partisan, a lover, and of a singular cinematographer. And then the book that unites them all, that of a writer."[3] In another essay, *L'express* describes *Lièvre* as a veritable literary and historic event. *L'express* had several reviews, one noting that the book is of an uncommon egocentrism and is thus both "insupportable and fascinating." But, it continues, "The book is great because of the writing."[4] It adds that the memoirs are hard to classify, given that they alternate between memories and anecdotes on the one hand, and literary and philosophical remarks on the other. Another *Express* reviewer exclaims, "Not a second of boredom!" and adds that the book "has been applauded unanimously by the press."[5] The life of Lanzmann, concludes the review, is itself a novel.

The center-left *Libération* didn't like Lanzmann's behavior (or that of most of his entourage) on his 1958 trip to North Korea.[6] But it says nonetheless that the film *Shoah* is a creation, "the work of an author."[7] Philippe Sollers, in the *Nouvel observateur* says *Lièvre* is "a book in which there are more than ten unforgettable portraits."[8] The narration, he continues, is one of montage, coupled with moments of

---

3. *Le monde*, March 20, 2009, "Livres."

4. Josyane Savigneau, "*Le lièvre de Patagonie* de Claude Lanzmann: Claude Lanzmann sur tous les fronts," *L'express*, March 20, 2009.

5. Marianne Payot in *L'express*, March 26, 2009, "Livres."

6. The first Western delegation to visit the country. Sartre admired Lanzmann's reporting on North Korea. But it should be added that the argument between Sartre and Lanzmann over the state of Israel was to create a rift between the two close friends, as we shall see. Sartre, one of the founders of *Libération* (quite left leaning at the time), was strongly pro-Arab and anticolonialist; the paper viewed Israel with (political) suspicion. Sartre had great hopes for the Communist state of North Korea, and felt that Lanzmann's admiration for Israel was somewhat of a political betrayal.

7. Iegor Gran, "Lanzmann lièvre ouvert," *Libération*, March 12, 2009.

8. Philippe Sollers, "Les cent vies de Claude Lanzmann," *Le nouvel observateur*, March 5, 2009.

instantaneous visual memory. Thus, Sollers ties Lanzmann's textual style to his filmic technique, without eclipsing the fact that Lanzmann is a gifted writer, whose films are in a sense informed by his style of writing. *Lièvre*, writes Sollers, is a "metaphysical event." The blurb for the French edition of *Lièvre* says it is written "in a magnificent and powerful prose." It adds that "The memoirs of the author of *Shoah* say everything about the liberty and horror of the 20th century." In other words, while none of these reviews forgets that Lanzmann is the "author" of *Shoah*, they all review him in this autobiographical context as a writer of talent and importance, whose style and narration are exceptional.[9] That was how they knew him for the decades before *Shoah*, and that is the context in which they review him, even as they pay homage almost in passing to the film.

In the American context, the situation is quite different. To begin with, there is no general knowledge of Lanzmann as essayist, reviewer, and political and social commentator—in short, of Lanzmann the writer before *Shoah*. Nor is the myriad of French celebrities scattered throughout the autobiography necessarily recognizable (with obvious exceptions) to the American reader. So too, when Lanzmann writes of the advanced degree he received in philosophy—and lists the array of famous philosophers in France who were his teachers—again, for the most part, the English reader does not recognize these French luminaries of the day. Simone de Beauvoir and Sartre, of course, are widely known. But a good majority of the names in the book are not; they are names that were part of the intellectual and social star system specific to France. No doubt this is why the French edition includes a huge index of proper names, while the English edition has no index at all. One surmises that the translator (Frank Wynne) must have seen the general futility of such an index in the English translation. (It should be added that Lanzmann was reportedly displeased with Wynne's translation.) Similarly, one wonders how many Anglo readers catch Lanzmann's literary allusions. For example, when he thinks of large families, Lanzmann writes that everything about them seems to him "ordre et beauté, luxe, calme et volupté." This direct quotation from Baudelaire's "L'invitation au voyage" is left unexplained by the English translator. I am personally agnostic about explanatory footnotes—particularly when they are overly present—but this might

---

9. It should be noted that Lanzmann referred to himself as the creator, director, and author of *Shoah*.

have benefited from a reference. Or perhaps not. It is, of course, absurd to imagine that translations can convey everything about the culture of a given text.

The covers of the French and English editions of *Lièvre/Hare* demonstrate the extent to which there are two images of Lanzmann in the two contexts. The English *Patagonian Hare* has a cover featuring a black and white close-up photograph of Lanzmann looking through a camera lens. The French edition is the classical Gallimard cover—no photograph, with just the author's name, the title, and the French custom of naming the genre; here, "Mémoires." No coincidence that the back cover of the French edition refers only briefly to *Shoah*, and to Lanzmann as its "author," thus emphasizing Lanzmann's literariness.

American and Anglo reviews of *Hare* break down into two approaches: those that are focused on *Shoah* and make passing reference to the autobiography, and those that take the book a bit more seriously. What is striking is the extent to which the American reviewers emphasize Lanzmann's (admittedly healthy) ego. David Rieff in *The Nation* calls *Hare* "simultaneously compelling and repelling" because at the age of 86, "Lanzmann . . . [is] still in love with Claude Lanzmann," and the "temperature of his self-involvement seems only to have risen in the passing decades."[10] But then, adds Rieff annoyingly, "self-deprecation has never been much prized in French intellectual life." Rieff admits that Lanzmann is a major figure who has written a major book, but the work lacks a beauty of style and profundity. The main reason *Hare* is important is that in it "Lanzmann recounts the making of *Shoah* . . . and his thinking behind the choices he made in the film" (Reiff, 36). *Hare*, concludes Rieff, "is neither an easy read nor a pleasant one" (Reiff, 42). Whereas more famous memoirists write books that "are fundamentally works about their time refracted through their own eyes," Lanzmann's great subject, declares Rieff, "is Lanzmann." "*Shoah* is a work of genius," he concludes, whereas *Hare* "is a failure humanly" (Reiff, 42). Lanzmann is guilty of a "childish egotism," and with that the book is dismissed while the film is revered.

Carlin Romano (*Chronicle of Higher Education*) thinks more of *Hare*, but notes that it is a mixture of "Self-knowledge, loyalty, braggadocio, and moral activism." *Hare* is "full of ego" but also displays

10. "Books and the Arts: A Vast Choir of Voices," *The Nation* (July 2/9, 2012), 35.

a "becoming modesty" about the nexus between Lanzmann's memories and the facts.[11] Adam Shatz (*London Review of Books*) announces
that "Self-flattery is characteristically Lanzmannian," but he does
take the autobiography seriously, even if the context of *Shoah* and
other Lanzmann films are his main focus.[12] In 2012, Paul Berman
reviewed *Hare*.[13] He is one of the rare reviewers I have read who does
not concentrate on Lanzmann's "egotism." In retelling the stories and
anecdotes of *Hare*, he remarks on "tasteless" passages therein: both
Shoah and *Hare* are "abrasive," he concludes. Alan Stone's review of
the book, on the other hand, has an unambiguous title: "In Love with
Life—and Himself."[14]

Most other Anglo reviewers equally foreground and insist upon
Lanzmann's egotism. There is no reason to cite them all here. I suspect that the French press was so much more enthusiastic concerning
Lanzmann because, as I have noted, he was such a well-known figure in France, was associated with so many celebrities, and wrote for
widely-read journals and magazines. I would add that the majority of
the French public has read Rousseau's *Confessions* in school. If ever
there was an autobiography (before the term was coined) motivated
by egotism (and paranoia), that work by Rousseau would surely be
it. As a speculative aside, I would suggest that the French reading
public might therefore not be particularly surprised by an ego-driven
autobiography, even if we were to agree that this describes *Lièvre*. (On
the other hand, what autobiography is not ego-driven?) Other works
come to mind as well: Stendhal's *Vie de Henry Brulard* is an autobiographical work (by way of a pseudonym), as are his more undisguised
(and to the point here) *Souvenirs d'égoïsme*. Sartre, of whom Lanzmann was a devotee, is the author of a best-selling autobiography, *Les
mots*. Lanzmann of course read (and reviewed) the book but needed
no prodding from it to tell the story of his own life.

It may be recalled that the word autobiography does not appear as
an adjective in French until the 1830s or as a noun until 1842. This
seems surprisingly late. Philippe Lejeune has written extensively on

11. Carlin Romano, "Portrait of the Artist as a Glamorous Existentialist," *The
Chronicle of Higher Education*, March 16, 2012.

12. Adam Shatz, "Nothing He Hasn't Done, Nowhere He Hasn't Been," *London
Review of Books*, 34/7, April 5, 2012.

13. "The Abrasive Spirit and Brazen Confessions of Claude Lanzmann," *International Harald Tribune*, August 17, 2012.

14. *Moment Magazine*, May/June 2012.

autobiography, diaries, journals, and other such facets of the genre. His foundational book, *Le pacte autobiographique* (1975) covers two centuries of autobiographies in Europe, beginning earlier than the term's usage in French—in 1770. His definition is precise: an autobiography is "A retrospective, prose narrative that a real person produces on his/her own existence. The author accentuates his or her individual life, particularly the story of his/her personality."[15] Lejeune excludes, however, a number of neighboring genres that do not fit all of his categories, the first being memoirs. The latter, he says, fits only one category, that of the "subject treated": an individual life and the history of a personality. And yet *Lièvre* does in fact fit the other three of Lejeune's categories for an autobiography: a prose narrative; an author whose name refers to a real person and is the narrator; a narrator who is identical with the protagonist. The problem is no doubt the term *mémoires*, chosen by the publisher Gallimard for Lanzmann (and presumably not with Lejeune's definition in mind). Perhaps Lanzmann agreed with—or even suggested—this designation. But let us agree that even by Lejeune's account, *Lièvre* is an autobiography. I would add that the choice of the label *mémoires* directs the reader's experience of the book, much as do captions under a photograph, chosen by the journal or magazine in which the image appears.

A few things to note about *Lièvre*. It is mainly written in two tenses: the present and the *passé simple*. This is a rather fascinating combination of "old school" writing on the one hand, and modern writing-to-the-moment on the other. Old school because, as Roland Barthes pointed out, a continuation of the *passé simple* after the revolution of 1848 is symptomatic of history viewed as well behind one, as finished and therefore as fully ready to be dissected. Flaubert, argued Barthes, was the first to drop that tense and to emphasize the imperfect.[16] Lanzmann, in using the historical past, is presenting himself as a classical writer. The present tense, conversely, stresses the drama of the many harrowing episodes that he describes in his adventure-filled life. This counterbalance and its implications—the historical past with its classical, conservative overtones, as against the present with its roots in modernity and its insistence on immediacy of action—is

---

15. Philippe Lejeune, *Le pacte autobiographique* (Seuil, 1975), 12. My translation. Unless otherwise indicated, all translations are mine.

16. Roland Barthes, *Le degré zéro de l'écriture* (Seuil, 1953), 29, 48, and 57: "Between Balzac's third person and Flaubert's, there is a whole world (that of 1848)."

not one that exists in English. Such a counterbalance is thus another way in which *Hare* produces a different reading experience than does *Le lièvre*.

Lanzmann the filmmaker continues his connection to Lanzmann the writer and to the textual. In 1985, the same year *Shoah* was released, Lanzmann published a book version of the film.[17] The book boasts an introduction by Simone de Beauvoir, who calls the film "a pure masterpiece" (*Shoah*, 10). Beauvoir sees a similar mixture of tenses in the film that I noted in *Le lièvre*: "Like all the spectators, I combine the past and the present. I have said that it is in this confusion that the miraculous aspect of *Shoah* resides" (*Shoah*, 10). Lanzmann begins his brief introduction to the book: "I am here presenting the reader with the full text—words and subtitles—of my film, *Shoah*" (*Shoah*,11). There follows a discussion of the book's typography: how to convey the difference between questions posed and answers given in the film version; the subtitles and how the speakers' cadences and emotional states can be conveyed through text; how to distinguish typographically between the interviewers' questions and Lanzmann's occasional interventions; the insistence on the fact that the time of decoding and reading must remain invariant; and the complexity of providing translations for the multiple languages in the film. Subtitles, says Lanzmann, are born and die almost immediately on the screen. As such, they are "inessential." But, adds Lanzmann, when you collect the subtitles into a book—as the text of the book *Shoah* does—they change from the inessential to the essential, and are given "another status, another dignity, and something like a seal of eternity." The subtitles, when in a text,

> have to exist alone, to defend themselves alone without any indication of staging, without an image, without a face, without a landscape, without a tear, without a silence, without the nine hours and thirty minutes that constitute *Shoah*. (*Shoah*, 12)

Reading the text of the film leaves Lanzmann with strong emotions:

> Incredulous, I read and reread this bloodless and naked text. A strange force passes through it from time to time. The text resists, it lives its own life. It is the writing of disaster (*l'écriture du désastre*[18]) and that is for me another mystery. (*Shoah*, 12)

17. Lanzmann, *Shoah* (Fayard, 1985).
18. Clearly an allusion to the book by Maurice Blanchot, of the same title.

The text lives its own life, and that is a mystery. This is the writer (and philosopher) speaking. Of course, he is obsessed by the film (twelve years in the making), but here is the writer, the one who describes the word "Shoah" as a signifier without a signified,[19] who writes with ease and elegance, who uses literary allusions and metaphor, who meditates on philosophical issues and thinkers, who produces "at least ten unforgettable portraits," as Sollers put it.

Moreover, the famous contrapuntal moves of the film are at work as well in the autobiography. The book is emphatically nonchronological, and moves freely among Lanzmann's adventures, obsessions (such as the guillotine, for example), lovers, childhood, adulthood, and writings. These are stylistic traits also to be found in Lanzmann's journalistic works, so that one begins to wonder whether the writing style to some degree affected the film(s), and not the other way around. The visual and the narrational merge in *Lièvre*, just as they do in *Shoah* and, I would argue, in all of Lanzmann's films. In *Lièvre* the narrator is Lanzmann, ever present and in rigorous control; in the film he lets others narrate and yet, like the narrator of Rousseau's *Julie ou la nouvelle Héloïse*, there are times when Lanzmann breaks into the conversations, interrupting for clarification or more information.[20] *Julie* is, of course, a novel and *Shoah* is meant to be the emphatic opposite of a fictional world. I am simply pointing out that at times both authors, despite their different genres, break into the narration that is putatively not meant to be interrupted. Shall we chalk this up to egotism, as many Anglo critics of Lanzmann have proposed? Or is it rather a need for tight control, as in *Lièvre*?

Israel also poses a problem for Lanzmann, according to many critics. Lanzmann feels a sudden love affair with the country, but it is less than obvious how a leftist such as Lanzmann could be so enamored of Israel and so unwilling to see any fault in Israel's treatment of the Palestinians.[21] The autobiography largely elides any explanation of

19. Lanzmann, "Ce mot de 'Shoah,'" *Le monde*, February 25, 2005.

20. Rousseau, however (unlike Lanzmann) makes moral judgments and commentaries in his footnotes, thus breaking the fictional pact, as it were. "Miserable young man," begins Rousseau's attack on Saint Preux's behavior, for example. "Sweet Julie," introduces his conclusion that there is much she doesn't know: "Good God!" he concludes, "what do you know!"

21. Lanzmann's idealization of Israel in the forties, fifties, and even sixties is understandable, of course. It was a view shared by many. But the autobiography is from 2009, such that one wonders why there isn't more of a critical retrospective.

such an apparent contradiction, rather concentrating on Lanzmann's complete delight upon the first of his many visits to the Promised Land. Lanzmann goes to Israel for the first time in 1947, by way of the *Kedmah*, a refugee ship. His elation with Israel is instantaneous:

> I knew very little about the country, but what I counted on finding there . . . was the *desert*. Israel had to be a desert, a virgin land to be conquered, in which each man would be the first man and would begin the world anew with naked hands, in a fraternity and equality as yet unknown. (*Lièvre*, 221)

He adds that most of the *Kedmah* immigrants with whom he spoke on board "shared that ideal" with him. It is an odd "ideal" to share, carefully (or willfully?) erasing the Palestinian population from the "virgin" land. It also relies on a type of renovated Book of Genesis, combined with a modern myth of origin (without women, it would seem). The Jewish immigrants will be the first men, and will build a new world in fraternity and equality (shades of the French revolution). The desert will bloom, in other words. Lanzmann later admits that he discovered Israel not to be, in fact, all desert, but "it is without any doubt a promised land" (*Lièvre*, 223). This from a man who was anticolonial during the Algerian war (1954-62), and who spoke at length with Frantz Fanon about politics. The meeting with Fanon, writes Lanzmann, "shook me, shattered me, subjugated me, with profound consequences on my own life" (*Lièvre*, 351). He adds that both he and Fanon had been deeply influenced by Sartre's *Reflections on the Jewish Question*. Fanon's work also influenced Lanzmann, who allies racism with antisemitism. When Sartre and Lanzmann visit Fanon for three days, Sartre does no work of his own (an unheard-of occurrence), and does nothing but listen to Fanon. Lanzmann call him "a prophet" and is devastated by his death (*Lièvre*, 362). In this light, Lanzmann's view of Israel is all the more perplexing.

The question of nationalism emerges here; several prominent Israelis urge Lanzmann to come live in Israel. After brief flirtations with that idea, he concludes that he is French, not born and bred, but by chance. When Lanzmann shows his film *Israel, Why* in New York City on October 7, 1973, the Yom Kippur War has just begun. A reporter asks Lanzmann, "Finally, monsieur, what is your country? Is it France? Is it Israel?" Lanzmann says he answered without hesitation, "Madame, my country is my film" (*Lièvre*, 244). Thus, nearly two decades after his first trip to Israel, Lanzmann finds an answer to the fraught question of where he belongs—an evasive if intriguing one at that.

When *Lièvre* discusses attacks in Israel, or war, rockets, and any other hostility, Lanzmann frequently brings up the number of Israeli deaths, but almost never Palestinian ones. This stance of Israel-can-do-no-wrong clearly angered Sartre, who was, given his strong leftist stance, very much pro-Arab. Lanzmann's almost blind support of Israel, together with his leftist tendencies and anticolonialism combine to form a contradiction in Lanzmann's political logic that the autobiography neither addresses nor acknowledges. Lanzmann was on the side of the Algerians during their war with France. But shortly after Algeria was liberated from colonial rule, it announced that it would send 100,000 soldiers to liberate Palestine. "For me," writes Lanzmann, "it was over. I had thought one could want independence for Algeria and the existence of the State of Israel, both at the same time. I was wrong" (*Lièvre*, 364).

And yet, few critics have pointed out that Lanzmann is, albeit on rare occasions, more nuanced in *Lièvre* concerning Israel. In his capacity as one of the editors of *Les temps modernes*, Lanzmann organizes a special issue on the Israeli-Palestinian conflict. The issue was to be comprised of Arab and Israeli writers, equally distributed. In preparation, in 1967, Lanzmann undertakes a trip to Egypt and then to Gaza with Sartre and Beauvoir. A visit to Israel was to follow. Sartre was increasingly unhappy with the idea of going to Israel and finally agreed to go only if he could meet with nothing but people from the Israeli left. Moreover, Sartre refused to come face-to-face with anyone connected with the Israeli military.[22] Lanzmann, meanwhile, becomes increasingly worried about the danger in which Israel finds itself, and this concern about the future of Israel seems to have blocked out his concern for Arabs or colonialism. The rift between the two close friends is thus established, and Lanzmann will never again be as close to Sartre as he had been.

The special issue of *Les temps modernes* appears the same year as the voyages, one month after the Six Day War.[23] Nearly a thousand pages long, it is introduced by Sartre, in a text titled "Pour la vérité,"

22. For a description of Sartre's unhappiness in Israel, and his eccentric behavior, see *Le lièvre*, 396-404 and 412-17.

23. *Le conflit israélo-arabe : Dossier*, ed. Sartre (Paris, Chantenay, 1967). Special edition of *Les temps modernes*.

and presented by Lanzmann. Both the Arab and Israeli points of view are represented, each with a large number of writers (though Lanzmann notes in *Lièvre* that the Israelis write much longer articles than the Arabs). This discussion—of the trips, the growing distance from Sartre, the political difficulties, the work of producing the issue— is the most significant passage for understanding Lanzmann's view of Israel and the Arab conflict (cf *Lièvre*, 396-410). And while Lanzmann is clearly pro-Israel (quite willfully and even blindly so), he is nonetheless aware of the suffering imposed on the Palestinians. The documentary *Pourquoi Israël* rethinks Sartre's *Reflexions sur la question juive*, which had been such an important influence on the filmmaker. In *Lièvre*, when Lanzmann discusses Israel and its conflict with the Arabs, it is as if his leftist politics occasionally come to the surface, only to be quickly repressed.

This division in Lanzmann—between his love for Israel and his ethical (if fleeting) impulses with respect to the Palestinian situation— appears in another passage as well. Lanzmann writes about how, in 1987, Yitzhak Rabin asked Lanzmann to make a film on the Israeli War of Independence. Rabin had seen *Shoah*, and greatly admired the film. But Lanzmann refused the new project because "There are in fact two possible narratives on this war, the Israeli one and the Arab one. And it is impossible to go into the reasons on both sides at the same time, without making a very bad film." Lanzmann instead proposes making a film on "the re-appropriation of force and violence by the Jews of Israel" (*Lièvre*, 58). The film *Tsahal* (1995) is the result.

Tsahal (the acronym for the Israeli Defense Force) begins with an odd series of assumptions and generalizations. After Auschwitz, Lanzmann writes, "the destruction of Israel was inconceivable; and if it happened, I could not, for my part, live any longer" (*Lièvre*, 45). Israel thus has a position of exceptionalism for Lanzmann, in light of the Holocaust. The Israeli army is unsurprisingly, then, unlike any other for him. The soldiers "do not have violence in their blood," he declares twice, on the same page. The Israeli soldier, he continues, "knows how to give his life, but does not put it into play for honor, for display, for remaining faithful to a gesture or to the traditions of a social class" (*Lièvre*, 45). The film is frequently seen as propaganda. "Israeli paratroopers are of a different breed from French ones," Lanzmann announces to an interviewer in 1994. And the further proof for this, he adds, bizarrely, is that "they have their hair" (Ibid.). This surprising claim extends to women in the army as well as men. The fact that "they keep their hair" changes everything for Lanzmann: "on their faces, the serious is in conflict with the sweet, humanity with ascesis, anxiety with confidence" (*Lièvre*, 46). Lanzmann goes so far as to write to the Commander of French forces to demand that French soldiers too be allowed to grow their hair. The Commander's indignant response nevertheless eventually leads to a polite correspondence between the two.

What's interesting about this little anecdote is that it demonstrates first, of course, what Lanzmann sees as the exceptionalism of the Israeli soldier—sweetness combined with seriousness, humanity with discipline. Of equal importance is how central the visual detail is to Lanzmann in everything he does, including writing—and not just an obvious detail at that (hair, e.g.). In 1958, during a trip to North Korea, Lanzmann falls madly in love with a young nurse there, Kim Kum-sun. It is a love that remains unconsummated, despite the erotic passion that obsesses both him and Kim Kum-sun. It is a searing and ardent encounter, albeit brief. The North Korean regime is such that the would-be lovers can only meet in secret and publicly (that is, they are left with attempting to disappear among the crowds, which they fail to do). The narration of this episode is as compelling and sensuous as anything out of *Madame Bovary*. The writing, in other words, is brilliant, and the *récit* itself reads like a thriller (the couple is constantly pursued by the North Korean secret police), combined with steamy descriptions of erotic desire. The would-be lovers are left with making passionate love with their toes, on a row boat.

Decades later, Lanzmann imagines a film about this "brief encounter" with Kim Kum-sun. He will use the voice off technique, he writes. There will be no actor, no actress, no reconstitution of the "brief encounter," only his voice, telling the story, remembering.[24] The film, *Napalm*, was indeed produced and released in 2017. It was Lanzmann's second to last film, and released a year before his death. In *Lièvre*, the idea of this future film elicits a significant passage on the relation between word and image: the proposed film, he writes, "will have to be a very meticulous and sensitive telling of the past in image and speech, silence and words, their distribution in the film, the points of insertion in the narration of the past within the presence

---

24. Such an approach is oddly, if in an entirely different context, similar to Lanzmann's decision for *Shoah*: no archival works, including photographs and texts, and no survivors.

of the city [Pyongyang]; discordance and concordance that would culminate in a unique temporality, in which speech unveils itself like an image and the image like speech" (*Lièvre*, 342). It is out of the question, says Lanzmann, to turn this film into a fictional story: "I felt a deep repugnance, something scandalous, about turning to fiction" (*Lièvre*, 341).

Pyongyang is almost unrecognizable to Lanzmann when he returns to North Korea in 2005, and he decides not to look for Kim Kum-sun because he wants to remember her as she was, not as she must now be—an old woman. Like Proust returning years later to the Bois de Boulogne, where he had long ago seen the young Odette strolling with her courtiers, Lanzmann decides that the return to a remembered place cannot bring back the past. And yet narration and images can elicit the past to some degree, each unveiling the potency of the other, argues Lanzmann. We can conclude that for him there is no hierarchy of word and image; both serve to recapture some of what is lost, much as the spoken words in *Shoah* suggest horrific images of the Holocaust.

Lièvre is comprised of words that motivate images, just as Lanzmann's films narrate as well as show. And yet both words and images are at the mercy of memory and a search for the real. On the last page of *Lièvre*, Lanzmann reflects on the fact that although he is "gifted with a rare visual memory," the spectacle the world or the world as spectacle always makes him think "of an impoverishing disassociation and of an abstract separation which forbid astonishment, enthusiasm, and render unreal (*déréalisent*) both the object and the subject" (*Lièvre*, 546). The connection between a name and a place, between a name and a person, as Proust (again) had noted, is often elusive, if not simply impossibly unreal. Yet there are instants that capture the real. In Milan at the age of twenty, Lanzmann is only able to make the name Milan "mean" when he is there by reciting to himself the opening lines of Stendhal's *The Charterhouse of Parma*. Years later, Treblinka comes to "mean" for Lanzmann when he sees signs for the town and at the train station. These markers in Treblinka are the "discovery of a cursed name on the ordinary signs of roads and the station, as if nothing had happened over there" (*Lièvre*, 546). That is when the name "Treblinka" becomes real for Lanzmann. And during a trip to Patagonia, when he sees that "mythical animal"—the hare—in his headlights, that's when he knows that he really is in Patagonia. The hare "literally stabbed my heart with the fact that I was in Patagonia, that at that moment Patagonia and I *were real together"* (*Lièvre*, 546; emphasis Lanzmann's). Thus the title of the autobiography is born of a moment of near epiphany, when a place name takes on a reality that is otherwise elusive. In another, nearly identical passage evoking the Patagonian hare, Lanzmann adds, "I am neither blasé nor tired of this world; one hundred years, I know, would never tire me of it" (*Lièvre*, 192). It is the image (in this case, of the hare) that brings Lanzmann to feel the reality of place and of being.[25]

The image—filmic or real—is motivated by memory, and vice versa. The text elicits and shapes images, and allows at times for the real. The Patagonian hare, caught in his headlights, allows Lanzmann a feeling of "incarnation." Incarnation here does not mean the divine become human, but rather the recognition of being-in-the-world, of feeling real, of connecting places, people, and names. The experience is also linked with time: "I was close to seventy," writes Lanzmann of his meeting with the hare. "But my entire being leapt with a savage joy, as it did when I was twenty" (*Lièvre*, 546). Lanzmann writes that he never speaks about things being "in my day." He lives now. He doesn't know what it means to grow old, and his youth is the guarantor of the world's own youth. Time is suspended for Lanzmann, which is why he could spend so many years making a film. "[T]ime has never stopped *not passing*. If time flowed, how could one work for twelve years to produce a work?" (*Lièvre*, 545). Alluding to Kant's idea of inner sense, Lanzmann writes that time has now begun to pass somewhat for him: "very slowly, convalescent. " But he still has trouble believing that it passes. The two great aspects of his life, he writes near the conclusion of *Lièvre*, have been capital punishment and incarnation (in his sense). He wonders if there is a contradiction between the two, or if they are different aspects of the same thing.

I have been considering the last pages of *Lièvre*, and turn now to the opening of the book, in which Lanzmann discusses his early (and life-long) fascination with, and terror of, the guillotine—and of the death penalty in general. He is obsessed with the gaze of the condemned prisoner: among the Nazis, in China, during the French revolution, in an Australian museum, in Goya's painting "The Third of May, 1808"—to name a few. Georges Bataille, Roland Barthes, Sartre

25. There are two other hares in the book: the epigraph from Silvina Ocampo's *La Liebre dorada* (*The Golden Hare*), and the hare that can crawl under the gate of a concentration camp, thus attaining the liberty that the prisoners lack (256).

of *Le mur*, and many other writers have of course been equally obsessed with the instants before certain death. Barthes writes of a photograph that is the portrait of a young man, Lewis Payne, condemned to death in 1865: "He is dead and he is going to die. "[26] But this double death is not what fascinates Lanzmann.

Lanzmann is firstly left to wonder about the fact that, given that he himself has "no neck," the executioner might have trouble decapitating him (*Lièvre*, 17). He is also concerned with the "barbarism" of capital punishment and the photographic records that demonstrate such barbarism freely. But mostly, he is fascinated (and horrified) by the gaze of those who face imminent death. The fact of death as an end to consciousness—that which Nabokov, for example, said he most feared—obsesses Lanzmann. Consciousness, one might say, is at the heart of his writings and, to a certain extent, of his films. In this sense, "incarnation" and the moment of the guillotine are indeed similar for Lanzmann: they are both moments of hyper-consciousness, of intense being-in-the-world, precisely because they are steeped in the inevitability of death.

What were people thinking when they lived through the Holocaust? How do they see themselves in light of the horror? In *Shoah*, Lanzmann makes clear that he wants those who talk to speak not out of memory, but rather to reexperience what happened during the Holocaust. There are no survivors of the gas chambers, notes Lanzmann in *Lièvre*, and so he explains that in *Shoah* he wanted those who lived through the murders to re-project themselves there, to return to the consciousness that was theirs when the events surrounding the horror occurred. By reenacting the consciousness that had been theirs at the time, the people in his film open up, not only their thoughts, but the question of consciousness itself, of the presence of death, and of time.

Those who lived through the Holocaust were constantly surrounded by the dead and the dying. How did that affect, Lanzmann seems to be asking, their own confrontation with mortality, with the fact of death? How did they see themselves both as mortal beings and as exempt from being murdered or as witnesses of the murdering? To what extent, in other words, does the consciousness of death, the witnessing of death, contribute to the notion of consciousness, including self-consciousness? These thoughts follow all the more urgently upon

26. Barthes, *Camera Lucida: Reflections on Photography*, tran. Richard Howard (New York: Hill and Wang), 95.

the deaths of Simone de Beauvoir and Sartre—how, asks Lanzmann, can they continue to live in the minds of those closest to them?

We have seen that at the end of his autobiography Lanzmann wonders whether capital punishment and incarnation are in contradiction each to the other (*Lièvre*, 545). In this question of contradiction between the two is to be found, he writes, "the great critical moment (*affaire*) of my life." It bears repeating that during the twelve years it took Lanzmann to make *Shoah*, he felt that time had been suspended: "time never stopped *not passing*." In citing Kant's "inner sense," Lanzmann suggests that it is the inexorable passing of time but also its suspension that is at play. And even though, after the film *Shoah*, time passes again "very slowly, convalescent," Lanzmann still has great difficulty in believing that it ever passes at all. The time now is always his time now; his perpetual youth remains.

Lanzmann's idea of "incarnation" is, as we have seen, a strange one. It is the ability to "be real" with a place. When he is conscious of being at one with the hare, he declares, "That is incarnation" (*Lièvre*, 546). Such realizations of the connection between a name and a place are far better, says Lanzmann, than is viewing the world as spectacle— indeed, they are the antidote and the resistance to seeing the world as spectacle. Neither his films nor texts are meant to suggest spectacle; they are rather interrogations of time, death, and consciousness.

Thus it is not coincidental that near the end of his autobiography, Lanzmann alludes to Kant's notion of inner sense. Time for Kant is the shape of inner sense—the possibility of representation in the mind. But time, for Kant, "is the formal a priori condition of all appearances in general," both inner and outer. If all outer appearances are in space and are determined a priori according to the relations of space, "then I can quite generally say on the basis of the principles of inner sense: all appearances in general, i.e. all objects of the senses, are in time and stand necessarily in relations of time." Whether in his films or in his texts, Lanzmann attempts to be in a now and, to return to an earlier citation, in "a unique temporality, in which speech unveils itself like an image and the image like speech." Image and narration are interchangeable as representation; they are inner sense in different forms, as are inner and outer sense for Kant. Both *Lièvre* and the film *Shoah* are the attempt to relive experience, to live in a manner that allows for the suspension of time and thus the reliving, with intense consciousness, of all nows.

CLAUDE LANZMANN

Self-Portrait at Ninety: An Interview with Franck Nouchi and Juliette Simont*

Franck NOUCHI: How do you situate yourself politically? If one were to ask me, I would be tempted to answer that you are unclassifiable, and then that you are an anarchist.

Claude LANZMANN: There is some truth to that proposition but I don't like it being put so bluntly. My "anarchy" is not a simple thing. It is linked fundamentally to my idea of freedom . . .

Juliette SIMONT: But weren't you a communist?

C.L. Yes, I was involved in the Jeunesses communistes. But not at just any moment: I was one of the leaders of the Jeunesses communistes in the midst of war, from 1942, at the Lycée Blaise-Pascal in Clermont-Ferrand. I was committed, and I was a bit of a firebrand. In two months, I recruited around fifty boarders from the school for the Forces unies de la jeunesse patriotique (FUJP). I will say nothing here of the dangerous actions that we led and the military training we undertook in the catacombs of Blaise-Pascal. I have spoken about this in *The Patagonian Hare*. The real problem for the communists at the time was how to procure arms to supply the future Maquis of the Party. My father was an important member of the Mouvements unis de la Résistance (MUR) in the Haute-Loire, the ones headed by de Gaulle himself and Jean Moulin. I was unaware of his clandestine activities, as he was of mine. One day when I had left the school to spend a Sunday with my family, we opened up to one another, and when he learned what I was doing he became incredibly pale. In fact

*This interview, "Autoportrait à quatre-vingt-dix ans," originally appeared in *Claude Lanzmann: Un voyant dans le siècle* © Editions Gallimard, 2017.

YFS 141, *Lanzmann after "Shoah,"* ed. Levine and Stark, © 2022 by Yale University.

he feared for his children, his two sons, my brother Jacques and myself, and Evelyne, our sister.

The result of all this was an agreement between the MUR and my group. This agreement presupposed good faith on both sides. I acted as guarantor for my father and he for me. When the time came to join the Maquis and go underground, the highest officials of the Party lined up on different platforms of the Claremont-Ferrand train station and congratulated me in front of the troops. While waiting to leave for the Maquis of La Margeride, we were lodged in the château de Chabreuges, a splendid medieval fortress belonging to Count Aymeri de Pontgibaud. The Anglo-American airdrops of Sten machine-guns, Bren machine pistols, big Gamon grenades, and all sorts of fabulous munitions drenched in layers of green grease, amazed us. It didn't last long. The day after the arms delivery I was called to the gates of the chateau. Three hefty, unsmiling guys shouted: "Comrade, we've come to bring you the orders of the Party. Tomorrow morning, you steal all the trucks you can find, pile the arms into them and meet up with the Communist Maquis over by La Chaise-Dieu." I procrastinated, played for time, I spoke to my father, who immediately made sure every precaution was taken. I gathered together my group, telling them that those who wanted to leave would do so alone and without arms. Half of them left. I learned later that I had been condemned to death by the Party and that some heavies from the Michelin factories had received the order to kill me. Right after the war I went to see Jean Poperen, then secretary of the communist cell at Louis-le-Grand, and told him the whole story. Hardly surprised at all, he said, "Ah! the jerks!", promised he would sort everything out, and proposed that I join the Party. But that I couldn't do, it was asking too much.

J.S. Still, during the cold war, you remained sympathetic toward the Communists . . .

C.L. Yes, and that sympathy has never left me. I am not speaking about the French communists of today. But even when I recently went back to North Korea, I felt that sympathy again—not for the totalitarianism of the regime, but for the people I was able to meet and for the beauty of the communist idea. Look at this photograph that I've had framed: it is the return of the soldiers who liberated Leningrad. You see these fine Russian faces, those high cheekbones? Those faces move me deeply. They died by the hundreds of thousands during the siege of Leningrad. This photograph was on the front page of a newspaper, I brought it back from Russia. I was there at an event commemorating the liberation of Leningrad. But it's true, I am profoundly anarchistic. In France, everything is regulated, everything is forbidden. That's what I feel most strongly: the prohibition. I dream of the world of the forest, of the world before laws. Of the early Far West, when there was still no sheriff. I think we have no need of a State.

F.N. You tend to see the repressive and totalitarian aspect of the State. You are a libertarian. And France is a country where the State assumes particular importance. Do you feel French?

C.L. No. In a sense, however, I am completely French. It's my language, it's my culture, the idea of emigrating to Israel seems impossible to me, I would be incapable of learning Hebrew. But at the same time I don't know the Marseillaise. Clovis, Duguesclin, Saint Louis, I know all that by heart because I studied it, but . . .

F.N. But it is not your history?

C.L. How can I put it? It is my *lateral* history. I never recognized that as my own history, it never resonated with me. Don't forget, I was born a foreigner in France, in an unassimilated family. But Jewish history is not my history either. I don't know it. I never set foot in a synagogue for the holidays, I know next to nothing about that religion. I'm bizarre, I'm outside of the usual framework, really.

F.N. So how do you resolve the question of belonging?

C.L. I'll answer like this: the first time I was invited to a film festival, the New York film festival, for *Pourquoi Israël* (*Israel, Why*, 1973)— it was the first day of the Yom Kippur War—a journalist said to me: "But Monsieur, what is your homeland? France or Israel?" I answered straight off, without ever having thought about it: "My film is my homeland." There is a truth in that.

J.S. It's like what you said about the Parti communiste: sympathy, yes, card-carrying member, no. You are always at once inside and outside. It's a fundamental posture: that of the witness, of the critic. But at the same time you are very French.

C.L. I feel French when I read stories about the heroes of the Resistance, those killed at Mont-Valérien, the guys who threw themselves from prison windows so as not to talk under torture. That's why I was so close to Sartre when he wrote those plays where torture was present.

J.S. *Morts sans sépulture* [*Men Without Shadows*], *Les séquestrés d'Altona* [*The Condemned of Altona*].

C.L. That—that interests me. But it would interest me just as much if it involved a country other than France.

F.N. Yet your very particular attachment to Victor Hugo brings you back to France. Victor Hugo *is* France.

C.L. Victor Hugo is France, yes. And I love Victor Hugo. But he is not the only one. I also love Bossuet for example. And at night, when I can't sleep, I spend my time reciting poetry. In point of fact I sleep less and less. The other night I spent two hours trying to find the rhyme in a stanza from "Le bateau ivre" ["The Drunken Boat"]. "J'ai suivi, des mois pleins, pareilles aux vacheries / Hystériques, la houle à l'assaut des récifs, / Sans songer que les pieds lumineux des Maries / Pussent forcer le mufle aux Océans poussifs!"[1] It's unfathomable, no? We are in the middle of a storm, why are the oceans "wheezing" [*poussifs*]? And the "luminous feet of the Marys"—are those lighthouses? Anyway, in the night, I was searching for what rhymes with *hystériques*. I was looking for the rhyme. But the rhyme is *vacheries* and *Maries*. It took me a while to locate the caesura.

J.S. You learn poems by heart, preferably very long poems. "Aymerillot" from *La légende des siècles*, 300 lines! Why?

C.L. It's a sort of challenge. At first I did it for my son, I thought it good to learn with him.

---

1. "I have followed, for whole months on end, the swells
   Battering the reefs like hysterical herds of cows,
   Never dreaming that the luminous feet of the Marys
   Could force back the muzzles of wheezing Oceans!"
   Rimbaud, *Collected Poems*, trans. Oliver Bernard (slightly modified) (Penguin, 1987).

J.S. I know that challenge is something very important for you: to cycle up the steepest slope, to dive from the greatest heights, and so on. But all the same, there is a pleasure other than the pleasure of the challenge. The pleasure of literature, of language?

C.L. Of course. It's very important.

J.S. Who are your favorite poets? Victor Hugo, Rimbaud, who else?

C.L. Not Apollinaire, oddly. Mallarmé, I know some. "Ses purs ongles très haut dédiant leur onyx / L'Angoisse, ce minuit, soutient, lampadophore, / Maint rêve vespéral brûlé par le Phénix / Qui ne recueille pas de cinéraire amphore."[2] Baudelaire I like less, he is a bit too rhetorical and overblown for my taste. But I know some. "Les femmes damnées" ["The Damned Women"] I knew by heart. Saint-Jean Perse. Leconte de Lisle. "Viens par ici, Corbeau, mon brave mangeur d'hommes! / Ouvre-moi la poitrine avec ton bec de fer / Porte mon coeur tout chaud à la fille d'Ylmer [. . .] Et la fille d'Ylmer, Corbeau, te souriras."[3] I also know Emile Verhaeren:

> Le vent, le vent, voici qu'il vient des longs pays où luit Moscou,
> Où le Kremlin et ses dômes en or qui bouge
> Mirent et rejettent au ciel les soleils rouges;
> Le vent se cabre ardent, rugueux, terrible, et fou,
> Mord la steppe, bondit d'Ukraine en Allemagne,
> Roule sur la bruyère avec un bruit d'airain
> Et fait pleurer les légendes, sous les montagnes,
> De grotte en grotte, au long du Rhin.[4]

2. "That for these pure nails, to the very highs of their onyx
   This midnight, Anguish, sustained shade in the lamp of the street
   Many dreams have been brought down, Phoenix, by these vespers
   That for the cinerarium amphora, have failed to collect . . ."
   Mallarmé, "That for these pure nails," trans. Stephen Cudahy, *Asymptote* (3/6/2021).
3. "Come over here, raven, my fine eater of men
   and cram your iron beak deep into my heart. For here
   we shall be waiting for you when you come again
   Carry my smoking heart to the daughter of Ylmer [. . .]
   And she, Ylmer's daughter, will smile on you, Corbeau."
   "Hjalmar" ("Le coeur de Hialmar"), trans. Richmond Lattimore, *The Hudson Review* 4/2 (Summer 1951).
4. "The wind, the wind, here it comes from the long countries where Moscow shines,

F.N. What is this happiness you radiate when you recite poetry? It's as though you—who are constantly battling it out with everyone and everything—when you dive into a poem, suddenly you are at peace.

C.L. It's true that it makes me happy. I could make it into a business.

J.S. You're not answering. What is the nature of this happiness?

C.L. I might try to answer indirectly. Some years ago Arte asked a number of "personalities"—between quotes—to write and read something modeled on Georges Perec's *Je me souviens* [*I remember*, 1978]. This mostly produced stuff like: I remember the day I met my wife, where my first child was born, etc. As for me, I made a sort of montage; I didn't read it but recited it by heart on television. I'll recite it for you now, I still know it:

> I remember only what I have learned by heart.
> I remember having read, in Guadeloupe, at the Pointe des Châteaux, a poem by Saint-John Perse, chiseled into the granite surface of a panoramic map. I remember that the rock of La Désirade rose up in the distance, stiff shard of ascetic, naked stone on the Caribbean Sea. I remember that my emotion was redoubled by these verses of Apollinaire that I remembered:

> Je ne veux pas l'oublier
> Ma colombe ma blanche rade
> O marguerite exfoliée
> Mon île au lointain, ma Désirade
> Ma rose, mon giroflier.[5]

> Where the Kremlin and its domes of shimmering gold
> Mirror and toss up to the sky red suns;
> The wind bridles, ardent, rugged, terrible and mad,
> Bites the steppe, leaps from Ukraine to Germany,
> Rolls on the heather with the sound of bronze
> And makes weep the legends, under the mountains,
> From grotto to grotto, along the Rhine."
> Emile Verhaeren, from "À la gloire du vent."

5. "I wish not to forget her
   My dove my harbor
   O naked daisy
   My distant isle, my Désirade
   My rose, my clove."
   From "La chanson du mal-aimé" ("The Song of the Poorly Loved")

I remember recopying the Saint-John poem in a notebook in the fading daylight. I remember that a squall broke out as soon as I started to recite it. I remember spending the night learning it by heart. Here it is:

Ô toi qui pêches infiniment contre la mort et le déclin des choses,
Ô toi qui chantes infiniment l'arrogance des portes,
criant toi-même à d'autres portes,
Et toi qui rôdes chez les grands comme un grondement de l'âme sans
    tanière,
Toi, dans les profondeurs d'abîme du malheur
si prompt à rassembler les grands fers de l'amour,
Toi, dans l'essai de tes grands masques d'allégresse
si prompt à te couvrir d'ulcérations profondes
sois avec nous dans la faiblesse et dans la force
et dans l'étrangeté de vivre, plus haute que la joie,
Sois avec nous celle du dernier soir,
qui nous fait honte de nos œuvres
et de nos hontes aussi fera grâce
Et veuille, à l'heure du délaissement
et sous nos voiles défaillantes,
nous assister encore de ton grand calme
et de ta force et de ton souffle
Ô mer natale du très grand ordre
Et le surcroît nous vienne en songe à ton seul nom de mer.[6]

I still remember it, I will remember it until I die, I learn a lot by heart.

---

6. "O you who sin infinitely against death and the decline of things,
    O you who sing infinitely the arrogance of gates, yourself shouting at other
        gates,
    And you who prowl in the land of the Great like the growling of the soul
        without a liar,
    You, in the depths of the abyss of woe so prompt to resemble the great irons
        of love,
    You, in the trial of your great masks of joy so prompt to cover yourself with
        deep ulcerations,
    Be with us in weakness and in strength and in the strangeness of living, higher
        than joy,
    Be with us the One of the last evening, who makes us ashamed of our works,
        and will also
    release us from our shame,
    And be willing, when we are forsaken, under our faltering sails,
    To help us again with your great confidence, and with your strength, and with
        your breath, O natal Sea of the very great Order!
    And may increase come to us in our dream at your single name of Sea!"
    Saint-John Perse, from *Seamarks*, trans. Wallace Fowlie, in *Collected Poems*
    (Princeton: Princeton University Press, 1983), 565.

* * *

F.N. Let's go back to the question of belonging and non-belonging, let's speak about the Jews, about the Jewish religion, about Israel, about your relation to all this. You have said that you do not feel truly French, in spite of Victor Hugo. But do you feel Jewish?

C.L. Yes, oh that, yes! It is one of the great pleasures of my life, being Jewish. Truly! But, let me repeat, I am Jewish in my own way. I don't go to synagogue, I don't know the prayers, I'm incapable of saying Kaddish, I don't know the Bible. I read neither Rashi nor Levinas— which does not mean that one day I won't. But the fact is I have no knowledge about Judaism and I even think that I *need to not know*. I am not at all integrated. I explained this in *The Patagonian Hare*. One day, in Israel, I wandered around a small provincial town, Afoula, it was Shabbat, everything was deserted, shuttered, I was skulking around, lost, I did not dare enter the synagogues, it was horrible, I felt repelled by my own people, I couldn't go back to Tel Aviv, there were no means of transportation. In truth it's difficult, my life, my way of never fully "belonging," I am extremely alone.

F.N. Can you tell us some more about this great pleasure of being Jewish? Does that have to do with your personal history, your family history?

C.L. First of all, I encountered antisemitism before the war. I experienced it deeply. At the Lycée Condorcet I saw how guys got beaten up, thrashed. There was a big red-headed kid called Lévy, he was the whipping boy. I kept a low profile. Even if I played Shylock in a production of *The Merchant of Venice*, saying with conviction, "One pound of flesh," even if a certain Perez hissed at me one day, "You, you're a dirty little Jew," I still managed to remain pretty much unnoticed and I was cowardly, I didn't dare defend Lévy. I suffered from that and I never forgot it. Then there was the war, the first racial laws. My father wondered what we should do, if we should obey or not. To obey was to declare yourself, to mark yourself. At the start, he thought it was necessary to obey. Then that became intolerable for him; for me and for my brother as well. So we went into hiding. Those are not things that you can forget. The pride in being Jewish comes from there obviously. What is very bizarre, all the same, is that despite being so little assimilated into that culture, so ignorant, so minimally Jewish in a sense, I spent so many years of my life having to deal with it. It's the great mystery of my life.

F.N. Indeed, it can't be said that your culture is Jewish.

C.L. It isn't at all. And certain members of the Jewish community, in return, really don't like me. I recall at the time *Shoah* came out—and it really did create a stir—an offensive led by M. Schumel Trigano. He said, in essence: the Holocaust, that's enough, we need to turn the page, give some positive content to Judaism, we need to go back to religion. And so I found I had some enemies.

F.N. It is not only your relation to Judaism that is a mystery, but also your relation to Israel. You are deeply Sartrean, deeply close to someone like Frantz Fanon, your history is very linked to anticolonial struggles. And at the same time you defend Israel tooth and nail. That too is difficult to understand.

C.L. No, I don't think so. I wanted independence for Algeria, I support independence for Israel. It was Maxime Rodinson who invented this fable about Israel, the Colonial State, and with my support, since I was the one who in 1967 put together the enormous special issue of *Les temps modernes* devoted to the Israeli-Palestinian conflict, and his text, with the title "Israël, fait colonial," opened the issue. I knew Israel, after the Six-Day War for example, and even before, living a sort of idyll with the Palestinians, and vice-versa. The Palestinians came to work in Israel, they earned their living like Israelis, they had social security, guarantees, they were assimilated and happy to be so. They learned Hebrew, just as some Israelis learned Arabic. There has always been, since the birth of Israel and even before, war, wars, violence. But there have also been periods of near-fraternity between Arabs and Israelis. Moreover, a considerable number of Arabs remained in Israel.

F.N. You claim not to support the State. Does it not bother you to speak of the Jewish State?

C.L. Not only does it not bother me, it delights me. First of all, I think that in a certain way the Jewish State, precisely, escapes the general system of States, which indeed I detest. Everything is different in Israel. To make war in and for this country, for example, has nothing to do with our wars today, these distant wars where we police the world with military "strikes." Then there is this, which few people understand: pride. Pride in being Jewish and in having a Jewish State. This pride has to do with the history of the Jews.

F.N. Let's go back to antisemitism. When you read Céline, does it disgust you and you stop, or do you see his literary genius and that's what matters?

C.L. As it happens I have not read much Céline. I have read *Voyage au bout de la nuit* [*Journey to the End of the Night*] and *D'un château l'autre* [*Castle to Castle*]. And I don't think that the paucity of my Célinian readings has to do with his antisemitism. Let's leave Céline there. But as regards antisemitism, you have to understand this: when, as happened to me, one has experienced antisemitism during childhood, it is so internalized, has entered so far into one's bones, that it becomes a natural phenomenon. How can I put it for you? Antisemitism, it's *normal*. As if it were part of human nature. As if it were eternal, in the manner of the return of the seasons. It doesn't stop, it comes back in new guises. It's not that I am resigned to it, not at all, but I don't tend to react with indignant words and stances. At bottom, antisemitism, for me, is outside of language. The answer to antisemitism is as well. When governments rise up against antisemitism, they don't say what needs to be said.

F.N. Meaning?

C.L. I think that they don't grasp the extent of the horror of the thing, they do not really know what they are talking about. They settle for fine words. It turns into pompousness, rhetoric. The Jews, moreover, speak very poorly about antisemitism.

F.N. Who speaks about it well?

C.L. Sartre spoke about it very well. *Réflexions sur la question juive* [*Anti-Semite and Jew*] is truly a masterpiece. But there are all sorts of antisemitisms. There is the old, French antisemitism of the right, the extreme right, there is also the antisemitism of the extreme left, which has always existed. As for Arab antisemitism, you just have to have been to Gaza, Ramallah, Bethlehem, where I have been often, in the schools . . . To me, it's hopeless: Israel doesn't exist, it is wiped off the map.

F.N. Do you equate anti-Zionism with antisemitism?

C.L. Yes. Today antisemitism can only be anti-Zionism. If you are antisemitic today, that's the angle you come from.

F.N. But can one imagine an anti-Zionism that is not antisemitic?

C.L. No. To be anti-Zionist, that doesn't mean anything. What does it mean? That Israel should not exist. How could one think that without being antisemitic?

F.N. In Israel there are orthodox religious people who are anti-Zionist.

C.L. They are anti-Zionist, but they live over there. It was a big surprise, when I first arrived in Israel in 1952, and when I discovered these people. I said to myself, it's difficult to live in Israel, they are getting along as best they can.

J.S. We also need to talk about your relation to religion. You are an atheist, the consolations of religion are completely foreign to you, you do not pray, you don't go to synagogue. And yet there is that scene in *Israel, Why*, where you are conversing in an orange grove with a religious Jew—you are explaining to him your ignorance about things religious and your atheism. And he replies to you with a smile that any Jew is a good Jew, even if some are better than others. In *The Patagonian Hare* you speak about your first trip [to Israel] in 1952, and of the discovery of a yeshiva, of the sharing of dried herring between the master and his students. And in these shots one feels on your part a profound fraternity with these men who are nonetheless so different from you.

C.L. They are my brothers, yes. No doubt I couldn't stand to be one-on-one with them for twenty minutes, but they are truly and profoundly my brothers. And at the burial of my mother, who was nevertheless an even more radical atheist than me, I wore a kippa, which would have sent her into a rage or made her laugh. That's the way it is. Don't hope to resolve my contradictions. They are many, and I hold to them.

F.N. You have read Heidegger. Is there a mystery for you in the attention he is getting today?

C.L. No. There is no mystery. But yes, we don't know if he understood the gas chambers, that's mysterious. But at the heart of his thinking there is "Blut und Boden," blood and soil. For me, the fascist kernel of this philosophy is very clear and I don't doubt that Hitler appeared to him as a messiah. Moreover, we were already discussing Heidegger's political allegiances back in 1946 in *Les temps modernes*. All these Heidegger "affairs," all this fuss today around the *Black Notebooks*, is a publishing coup. Discovering one or a few clearly antisemitic passages in Heidegger's prose doesn't change a thing.

*   *   *

F.N. You receive us today seated in your director's chair. Have you always had such a chair, since you have been making films?

C.L. No, not at all, it's very recent, it dates from *Le dernier des injustes* [*The Last of the Unjust*]. That's the only film for which I used this chair.

F.N. Why did you wait so long? Did you doubt that you were a director, in the American sense of the term, with the attributes of the profession?

C.L. Not at all. It's simply that this business of attributes of the profession leaves me completely indifferent and cold. I'm not attached to such symbols. Now that I have adopted this chair, I like it, and when I think about all those who have had their name on the back of their own chair, it excites me a little. But all that remains very inessential.

F.N. Would you like to have the imprint of your hand or your foot on the sidewalk of Hollywood Boulevard, like some actors and filmmakers do?

C.L. I do, in Haifa. In Los Angeles, it would not displease me. But honestly, I'm not very attached to such symbols.

F.N. Still, you like honors, you like to be recognized and even being celebrated. You sometimes wear in your buttonhole the Golden Bear that you received at the Berlin Film Festival for the totality of your work.

C.L. The Golden Bear, yes, I like it because it is truly a distinction in cinema. That pleases me more than the Legion of Honor.

F.N. Would you have liked to become part of the Académie française, wear that outfit?

C.L. Wear the outfit, no, become part of it, yes. I love the French language more than many who are in the Académie now.

J.S. Your relation to honors is very paradoxical all the same. Be honest, you like rosettes. Your anarchism and your taste for the gilded paneling of the Elysée palace, how do these go together?

C.L. Honors, I call them rattles. It's a game for me.

F.N. I think there is something deeper. Aren't these distinctions a way for you to be accepted by the French, to be a legitimate, full-fledged Frenchman?

C.L. Yes, you could say so. I told you, I was born foreign in France. Maurras writes this shameful sentence that Sartre quotes in *Anti-Semite and Jew*: "Never will a Jew understand these lines [from Racine]: 'Dans l'Orient désert quel devint mon ennui.'" I grew up with this scorn, with this antisemitism. Only the well born, the French "of pure stock," can allow themselves to disdain these marks of recognition from the State.

F.N. Let's talk about cinema, if we may. You have produced a cinematographic œuvre comparable to none other, you have been interviewed a lot about it. But you have not said much about other filmmakers. Are there directors who have influenced you in your own work? Or did you draw everything out of yourself?

C.L. Difficult to say. I see a lot of films, in the cinema or on DVD. I like a lot of films, there are directors I revere. And at the same time I think that no one influenced me, that I brought out of myself everything I have done and the way I did it. What I have done does not come at all from my knowledge of cinema. Perhaps my lack of cinematic knowledge even helped me. Having said that, before cinema, I did several things for television, in particular a program directed by Daisy de Galard, *Dim, Dam, Dom*. As a journalist, I've done things I liked a lot, notably, for *Panorama*: a program with Olivier Todd, a show about the war of attrition in 1968-69 in Israel, on the Suez Canal, on the Syrian and Jordanian borders. It frustrated me not to edit the images myself, I wasn't happy at all. Those were good shows, but I would have done them completely differently. Bit by bit I realized that what I liked above all was montage, and in a sense it was montage that led me to cinema.

F.N. When you speak of this taste for montage, didn't it come from films you had seen in which the montage struck you as very well done?

C.L. No. I liked it, but I did the montage in anguish, because I did not know the rules of montage: I had to reinvent them. I do think that, really, nothing influenced me. That's not boasting.

F.N. Does the fact that you were not influenced come from your fierce desire for freedom, for independence?

C.L. I don't know. Independence, yes, it's vital to me. But there is no cause-effect link here. Just because I am independent doesn't mean I haven't had any influences, I don't think. It's too simple to think like that.

J.S. And what directors do you revere?

C.L. Jean-Pierre Melville is one of them. I loved all his films. I met him before *Israel, Why* came out. He saw the film and adored it. He invited me to his place. He received me in his office, with his hat, his big black glasses, and his funny face. He was very sweet with me. There was a ritual: I came over, we talked—in fact, we didn't talk that much, to tell the truth. He was very important in my life.

He introduced me to credit cards. He took me out to the bistros of Les Gobelins, he paid with a credit card, it was miraculous for me. Then we took his Rolls (it was leased, though I didn't know this). He brought it out cautiously, we went 20 kilometers on the motorway, came back, he put the Rolls away and we went into the projection room—he had a private projection room. And the two of us spent entire evenings watching his films, only his films. But did he influence me cinematographically? I don't think so. I like Tarantino enormously. I read one day a long interview with him, one of the best interviews with a filmmaker I've ever read. I was struck by his knowledge of culture, which is immense, by his extreme intelligence, by his sense of humor. He taught me a lot of things. He is an intellectual and a writer. I like the greats, the classics, Eisenstein, Poudovkine . . .

J.S. With Melville you saw his films and only his films. You recount something similar in *The Patagonian Hare* about your visits with Albert Cohen, which consisted in part in reading sessions of his own books. What does that mean?

C.L. Quite simply that I am capable of admiration, which isn't so common. I admired both of them, I admired their works.

F.N. Are there films that are like bedside reading for you, that you watch endlessly, that have stayed with you over time?

C.L. I watch and re-watch all the submarine films, the war films. The last submarine film I saw was a splendid German film, *Das Boot*. I love *The Enemy Below*, with Curd Jürgens as captain of a U-boat and Robert Mitchum as captain of a destroyer seeking out submarines.

F.N. What is it that you like in war films?

C.L. Difficult to say.

J.S. Isn't it your epic and adventurous side that makes you like those films? Plus, you knew war. Is that the reason?

F.N. I don't think so. I think that these films evoke childhood, toy soldiers.

C.L.: But I never had that, toy soldiers! My childhood was absolutely without toys. Yes, I am sensitive to heroism. I also adore aviation films. I saw *Only Angels Have Wings* three times with Sartre. We were both in tears.

J.S. Are you sentimental at the movies? Do you like melodramas?

C.L. Yes, "Vive le mélodrame où Margot a pleuré,"[7] that's me all over, truly. I cry at the movies, my tears are boundless, I bawl. I've seen *Only Angels Have Wings* at least ten times, and every time I cried. *Brief Encounter*, same thing. I like rewatching what I have liked. I'm not very adventurous in cinema. I like the films of John Huston, *Asphalt Jungle*, *Beat the Devil* . . . I love the films noirs from after the war, *Double Indemnity*, *The Postman Always Rings Twice*, *The Big Sleep*, *The Killers*, and so on. Sartre spoke very well about these films. You know right away that things will turn out badly, but you have to follow the road that leads to the catastrophe, drink it to the dregs; you know the catastrophe is coming from the start and that's what creates the suspense. Sartre called it "the tone of failure." If now, while we are speaking, you know that I am going to die in three quarters of an hour and I don't know, there is incredible suspense for you; for me, what will happen to me will simply be an accident.

F.N. Someone once asked Hitchcock how long he could make a kiss last. He answered: "20-25 minutes." The questioner exclaimed, "But that's very long!" Hitchcock says, "Yes, but before the kiss begins, I will have placed a bomb under the sofa."

C.L. Yes, that is also a function of cinema: films fill up time.

J.S. What you are saying there, that films fill up time—or give shape to time, it's the same thing—makes me think of Sartre. You remember in *The Words* he recounts that as a child his mother would take him to the cinema; for the duration of the film, it was as though time was supplied with meaning. When he left the cinema, he re-entered the disjointed time of ordinary life, and it's this contrast, he says, that made him feel intensely what he would later call "contingence."

---

7. "Long live the melodrama where Margot wept," a line from Alfred de Musset's "Après une lecture." TN.

C.L. I remember that passage from *The Words*. This feeling of full time, this feeling of suspense that is at the same time the feeling of a necessity—of destiny, of what has to come about—is linked to my love of the detective novel. Sartre moreover also liked noir fiction. I have read all of the "Série noire." I like James Hadley Chase, he's a genius. *No Orchids for Miss Blandish* is terrific. The book as much as the film.

F.N. Do you sometimes go to see a film for an actor or an actress playing in it?

C.L. There are actors I adore, yes. Sterling Hayden, I adore him. I could go just to see him. Robert Mitchum. Bogart is also in my pantheon.

F.N. *Casablanca*, is that a film you like?

C.L. That I adore, yes. With that enormous guy dressed all in white who kills flies, Sydney Greenstreet. I also loved *The African Queen*, with Katherine Hepburn. *Sunset Boulevard* as well, I've seen it an incalculable number of times.

F.N. Are there filmmakers you have known very well? With whom you maybe had long discussions about cinema? Comrades? Chris Marker?

C.L. No, with Chris Marker I didn't discuss cinema. Not at all. I knew him in North Korea, in 1958, during the trip that I write about in *The Patagonian Hare*. At first, we hated each other cordially. Then, over the course of the same trip, we became buddies. He had failed in all his attempts to get financing from the Chinese for a film he wanted to shoot, in China, about the legend of the monkey king. I could appreciate his sadness. Chris Marker's jaw was blocked by a sort of prognathism. Coming back from a visit to the Great Wall of China I suddenly heard, through his clenched teeth, this sentence: "I adore complicity, I do." That moved me and we became buddies. But I didn't much like his films. There are films where he talks all the time. He talked far too much. He made associations. The rue de Rennes, reindeers . . . He was very affected.

F.N. What about the filmmakers of the Nouvelle Vague?

C.L. Truffaut I met at the festival in New York. Met him in passing, not privately, and he looked down a little on me. I have seen his *Jules et Jim*, adapted from a book by Henri-Pierre Roché that Mitterand had lent me. Mitterand used to have me come to his bedroom at the Elysée, he was mortally ill with cancer, he loaned me books, among them *Jules et Jim*, which he adored. He asked me questions that made me very uncomfortable. "Lanzmann, what is death?" I replied, "It's an absolute scandal, Monsieur le Président." That's what I think, but my answer, addressed to Mitterand who was suffering a lot, seemed very inadequate to me. To come back to Truffaut, I haven't seen many of his films.

Godard is another matter. There are films by Godard that I just can't see, that bore me terribly, and others that I liked a lot: *Breathless*, *Pierrot le Fou*. He's funny, Godard. I was present at the filming of *Pierrot le Fou*. He has a maverick way of filming. All of a sudden he has a white wall repainted in white because the white wasn't exactly what he wanted. I would see him sometimes, we were all at the same hotel, Belmondo was there too, he was hilarious. He was so funny! And since he was famous and rich, he did whatever he wanted. I remember he would take hold of stacks of plates, throw them to the ground. Then he'd pay for the damage. As for Godard, he was in the process of getting ditched by Anna Karina, who went off to Italy every weekend. He would read Elie Faure, all alone at a table. Whenever he underlined something, you could be sure it would turn up in the film the next day.

F.N. But with Godard, did you have long discussions?

C.L. Yes, we had dinner together several times at the Hôtel Raphaël. It was Bernard-Henri Lévy's idea. Godard wrote me I don't know how many letters at that moment. There was a project for a film. It started out from declarations Godard had made, you know the ones, "If I set about it with a good investigative journalist, I'll find images of death in the gas chambers." Lévy wanted to have us in dialogue and for the dialogues to be made into a film. We had several meetings, at the offices of Arte. I realized that the project was in fact for each of us to make a film. Godard wanted to show that he was more of a filmmaker and more of a poet than me, which seems obvious to me. But I had no desire to measure myself against him in that way. At one point I said in front of Jérôme Clément and others who were present, "I don't quite understand what you want from me. Enlighten me." And what does Godard do then? He gets up, he goes over to the light switch, he turns on the lights. He is odious. I think he has seen all my films.

J.S.: In the exchanges that you had with him was there anything that interested you?

C.L. It was never one-on-one. Lévy was always present. That distorted things.

F.N. And Spielberg? You ended up being friends, I believe.

C.L.: Yes, indeed, we became friends. You remember the controversy following *Schindler's List*? I said that in that film he had not reflected enough about what the Shoah is, nor about what cinema is, even less about how they can be related, the way cinema can treat the Shoah. When *Schindler's List* came out, I realized that some people hated *Shoah* and were delighted with Spielberg's film because he brought them back to familiar territory, to the ordinary measure of things. I saw them, during the screening of the film, I was invited. There was such happiness on their faces!

In Spielberg's film there was that scene that I couldn't stand, a "suspense" scene. The Jews were going into what we thought was a gas chamber, we were expecting tragedy, then, relief, water started coming out of the showers. That relief, that old cinematic device, had something unworthy about it for me, because for 99.9% of Jews it was in fact gas. With such a subject, I find that one does not have the right to resort to "tricks." I haven't changed, I still think that.

But on the other hand I've seen films by Spielberg that I have liked. He is a very skillful filmmaker, in his films there is always some piece of breathtaking bravura . . . Time passed, we met again three years ago, he had read *The Patagonian Hare*, he liked it. And he also understood the deep reasons behind our previous disagreement. Wait, let me read you the end of one of his letters: "I'm so proud that we have become friends!" And the beginning of another: "Claude, my hero, my inspiration, my muse . . ." It's like in Hegel: the conflict produced its *Aufhebung*.

F.N. You have made films, but also written a lot. There are very few filmmakers who are both filmmakers and writers.

C.L. Nor are there many writers who are filmmakers.

F.N. Cocteau?

C.L. No, Cocteau is transgeneric, he escapes all categorization.

F.N. Pasolini?

C.L. I don't know him well. I saw a terrific film by him along with Sartre and Simone de Beauvoir, *Medea*, which makes you understand what the sacred was at that time. I saw *120 Days of Sodom*, which I didn't like at all. He has an odd mug, Pasolini. Nasty looking, rather.

J.S. You tend to group people according to their looks, their "mug." For you, everything is on the surface of the face, there is no interiority.

C.L. Yes, I think that's true.

F.N. Then can you speak to us about your criteria for beauty and ugliness.

C.L. It's not so simple. There are people who are ugly, but who are beautiful, who have human mugs. I like human faces. It's outside of beauty and ugliness, in the end.

F.N. Do you look at a woman and a man in the same way?

C.L. I'd say yes. Except as regards desire.

F.N. When you look at women you're thinking that they might be objects of desire?

C.L. Oh yes! But I am also sensitive to the beauty of men, aside from all desire. Not to their model-like beauty, to the human side of a human face.

F.N. Do you like to seduce?

C.L. I hate that. It's a waste of time, it's pointless, it's Don Juanism. Albert Cohen speaks very well about seduction. In *Belle du Seigneur*,

Solal presents himself to Ariane with fake broken teeth, two teeth painted black, to give the impression there are gaps. "I am worth no more than two canines," he says to her, to denounce the masquerade of seduction. I'm like him. Sartre also talks about this comedy in *Being and Nothingness*. The girl at her first rendezvous who pretends not to know the intentions of her partner and who leaves her hand in his while she draws him towards the heights of spirituality through her conversation. It's an example of what Sartre calls "bad faith." It disgusts me to have to resort to playacting to get a woman into bed. I used to hit on women with Cau, when we were classmates. But on the whole we preferred to stay with one another rather than split up for the sake of a woman, even a very attractive one. They interested us less than our conversation, we usually dropped it and walked around Paris together.

F.N. Are there women who for you have remained dreams?

C.L. Certainly. I was in love with the wife of an American gangster.

F.N. Was it reciprocal?

C.L. No. And she was drop-dead beautiful. She lived in the same hotel as me, in the Batignolles. I was swept away right from the start. She took me out to bars around the Opéra, bars frequented by the underworld. I was petrified. One day—my room was very close to hers—I heard her making love with one of those guys from the bars. I waited as long as I had to, till she was alone. Then I went in, I was violent. She was terrified.

F.N. Are you a jealous person?

C.L. Very.

J.S. How old were you?

C.L. Twenty.

*   *   *

F.N. And today you are over ninety . . .

C.L. It's a nasty business. One day I realized that I was going to be ninety, I turned ninety, and since then I live in permanent fear.

F.N. Fear of what?

C.L. Of death. I've realized that I can't escape. I have never been easy-going as regards death, but ninety years old, it's like a barrier, a limit, that made it very real to me all of a sudden. The situation I'm in is truly unbearable. Death is there, it can happen at any moment. One dies because one is that old. Statistics are against me. It's very bad. I'm always surprised that people speak so little about it. Perhaps to protect themselves.

J.S. But your attitude is very peculiar! There are people who are really serene and who, when they reach that age bracket when the statistics are "against them," see that as the completion of a natural cycle and not as a scandal.

C.L. Well, this non-scandal scandalizes me.

F.N. Is philosophy of no help to you?

C.L. No. On the contrary, I'm very annoyed with the philosophers. They have shown so little interest in that.

J.S. Heidegger, whose work you know, says that death is man's own-most possibility. For him, animals do not die, they cease to live, only man dies and that is his grandeur.

C.L. Those are fairy tales. Animals die. He never saw up close the death throes of a dog or a cat. And dying has nothing great about it. On the contrary, it's the end of the possibility of being great. The impossibility of every possibility.

F.N. I don't think you are afraid of dying. I think you don't want to die.

C.L. I absolutely don't want to die. And it is very painful to see a whole generation disappear. The number of more or less close friends who have died in the last few months . . .

J.S. Michel Tournier . . .

C.L. And others . . . Not necessarily friends, but people who traveled with me or who I traveled with for the whole of our respective lives. Decaux, for example, it's not that I was thinking of him or that I saw him a lot, but he was there. Gilles-Gaston Granger, whom I knew at the Lycée Blaise-Pascal in Clermont . . . People of my generation, there aren't many of them left.

Speaking about people of my generation, I'm going to show you something. You remember in *The Patagonian Hare* I speak about my friend Rouchon, who was a boarder like me at Blaise-Pascal. He was doing philosophy, I was in *hypokhâgne*[8]. He was an adorable fellow. His mother sent him *clafoutis*, sweet things that gave him flatulence, and so we called him "Gaz." He was killed in the course of the first ambush at Pas de Compaing. I was a total coward. Two men were mown down trying to get to him, it was impossible, the Germans were sweeping the area with machine guns. And I didn't go. I hesitated for a second, a second too long. I would have been killed, there was no chance it could succeed. And then just the other day I receive a letter, from a Dr. Serge Singer, former teaching fellow of the Faculty, consulting physician, a rheumatologist in Alsace, in Vendenheim. Singer, for me, is a Jewish name.

> Dear Claude Lanzmann,
>
> In *The Patagonian Hare* you describe your adolescence in 1944. You devote a long passage to André Rouchon, killed at Pas de Compaing. Your description of the combat is remarkably accurate.
>
> I was very moved. André Rouchon was my friend. Together at the Collège de Rion, we joined the Resistance through the FUJP (Forces unies de la jeunesse patriotique), then, recruited by Marcovici, we made our way to the Col de Néronne, where we lived in a stone hut.
>
> You were a loader for a man who wanted to avenge his father, who died in the war of 1914-18. That was my friend Alex.
>
> Our lives crossed. During the combat I was to your left, spraying with my machine gun the two Citroëns and the truck you speak about.
>
> Every day I have thought about that day, the 7th of August 1944.
>
> I wanted to share with you these moments that have marked us.
> Respectfully,
> Serge

8. Preparatory class for the entrance examinations for the Ecole Normale Supérieure. TN

I recount all that in *The Patagonian Hare*. Not only the ambush at Pas de Compaing, but also how at Blaise-Pascal I recruited guys for the FUJP—we've already talked about that. There were two terrible days in the Blaise-Pascal schoolyard. I hadn't told my recruits, who had signed up out of patriotism, that the FUJP was a communist organization. Marcovici, a Jew and member of the Armée secrète, a show-off, and who had wads of money for recruiting, came along and poached my guys by revealing to them that the FUJP had been infiltrated by the Party. I tried to retain them, about forty remained with me, all communists. Rouchon was among those I had recruited and who left me for Marcovici.

F.N. That letter really speaks to some things about you. The concern with accuracy, with detail. What is a "loader"?

C.L. That refers to English machine guns parachuted in, with a curved magazine that contained the bullets. I was the "loader," meaning when the magazine of the machine gun was empty—and it then made a recognizable noise—I was ready to remove it and replace it immediately with a new magazine. I didn't know Singer. We must have been together after the debacle of La Margeride. We suffered a heavy defeat, we didn't know what to do next, and along with some of my guys I had joined up with Marcovici's men, whom we knew, since I was the one who had recruited them in the first place. It was better not to be alone.

F.N. You were speaking of a generation that is disappearing. Of whom could one say, of that generation, that he was a long-term fellow traveler?

C.L. This isn't just about the Resistance, it defines contemporaneity. This loss of people who have died in the last two months is the destruction of my contemporaries.

F.N. Then with whom, today, do you share this old contemporaneity?

C.L. With Tournier it wasn't that at all, even though he was a contemporary. We were together in *khâgne*, we met up again in Germany . . . But this little letter from Singer is much more intimate for me than my relations with Tournier ever were. Even if it comes from someone

I don't know, we shared that ambush. It's very moving for me, to find someone again in this way. And for him, to come across that story recounted by me, me who all the same became a bit famous, that must have been touching too. I called him, we talked. And indeed I was not mistaken, he is Jewish.

It's complicated, this business of contemporaneity. In truth it's not simply a matter of generations. I'll speak about this in my next film. I'll say that the men of the Valley of the Kings along the Nile, the Charioteer of Delphi, the Doric temples of Paestum are our absolute contemporaries. For me that's clear. If I say "absolute," it's for emphasis, since we tend to believe that they are not our contemporaries.

J.S. That means that for you the function of art is to immobilize time? You're speaking about works of art. So, do you see *Shoah*, ideally, as the Charioteer of Delphi?

C.L. Yes, you could say that.

J.S. We have gone far beyond the idea that contemporaneity is represented by a generation.

C.L. Yes. The tombs of the Valley of the Kings at Luxor are at once deeply moving and completely mad. They have recreated the apartments they inhabited during their lifetime, with the same foodstuffs, the same spatial arrangement. That says a lot about what the scandal of death meant to those people. For me, contemporaries are not in fact merely men who are my age today, like Tournier. The Charioteer of Delphi, in a certain way, is more my contemporary than Tournier.

J.S. That connects with your very unusual vision of time. In order to spend twelve years making a film, don't you have to have the ability to suspend the flow of time?

C.L. Yes. There has in fact been in my life a suspension of time. If not, making this film would have been impossible. I said to myself, "I'll have finished by next year," in the same way as one says, "Next year in Jerusalem." I was lying to myself, I knew perfectly well that I was lying to myself and I needed that lie to have the strength to go on; I needed some sort of hope. But in truth I had stopped time.

The question of time is at the heart of *Shoah*. The film is a struggle with time, against time, for time as well, from beginning to end, and even still today. You'll remember the film opens with a liminal text. The first sentence of it is this: "The action takes place in our time." What does "in our time" mean? It's very mysterious. Does it refer to the past into which the film plunges us, the time of the events properly speaking, let's say the year 1942, although I shot the film decades later? Or does it refer to the moment I shot the film? Or again, the moment the film is seen? For me, it's the moment the film is seen. "In our time" is thus *always*. I wanted it that way, and that's also the reason the film doesn't age.

There's another thing, another reason for this present, which has to do with the very nature of the image: every image worthy of the name has a crushing presence, it abolishes, in a sense, what has preceded it. That's why cinema is an art in which there is no concessive proposition. In a film, one cannot say "although," and then come back to the principal proposition. That's the underlying reason for the circular and symphonic construction of *Shoah*: there had to be recurrences, echoes, so that one image didn't abolish another, so that everything remains present.

And the question of the films that came after *Shoah* but that came in part from material shot for *Shoah* is linked to this as well. When *The Last of the Unjust* came out, when the public learned that a film shot in 1975 was being released forty years later, I was often asked, why wait so long? The same question was put to me a few days ago in the Grand Auditorium in Amsterdam. It's a very good question, which made me reflect deeply on what my approach had been. It made me become conscious of this: in truth, I cannot say that in 1975 I was shooting for *Shoah*, in order to make a film. I filmed Murmelstein in 1975, for an entire week, afternoon, evening, and often in the morning as well. Was I mad? Or was I not? There isn't a film producer in the world willing to invest money in such an undertaking.

What I realize today with great lucidity is that I was putting together a *treasure*, in the Greek sense of this word. All those years as I was accumulating an immense quantity of material I was a kind of archeologist, completely possessed and fascinated by what I was discovering. That discovery did not really have as an end the making of a film. What I wanted above all was for everything to be gathered, saved, saved from time, which passes and causes everything to be forgotten.

But Murmelstein couldn't be integrated into *Shoah;* it would have been a concessive proposition. Same for Lerner. Same for Rossel and Karski. Their presence could not be integrated into the time of *Shoah.* Or else I would have needed hours and hours more.

And yes, you are right, it is within this same relation to time that I remember Egypt, which I saw with Sartre and Beauvoir. Greece too. Time stopped, they are both entirely present.

F.N. Are you concerned with posterity?

C.L. Yes. I think about it. I would be enormously displeased if *Shoah* were to be forgotten.

F.N. Posterity, it's *Shoah?*

C.L. No, not only.

F.N. I'll ask you the question differently. Claude Lanzmann, director of *Shoah?* Or something else? Stendhal thought about his own death and he left very precise instructions. He wanted written on his tomb "I lived, I wrote, and I loved." And that's what you find on his tombstone in Montparnasse cemetery, in Italian. About you, one might say that you filmed, loved, wrote. In what order?

C.L. Since you are pushing me into the grave, I need to tell you that before that I intend to do a certain number of things. Dive from a height of 10 meters.

F.N. Have you already done that?

C.L. No. From 5 meters, I've done that.

F.N. That's already high. Weren't you afraid?

C.L. Yes, I'm absolutely terrified of heights. But when I am at the end of the diving board I no longer see any possibility of turning back. In Positano I saw an Italian man, a simple man of the sea, very handsome, dive from very high up, maybe 20 meters; it was sublime. Someone has to teach me how to do that. Perhaps not from 20 meters, but from 10. I'd like to do everything that scared me throughout my life. A parachute jump.

F.N. Do you like to put yourself in danger? Do you like the feeling of fear?

C.L. I don't like the feeling of fear, I like doing what makes me afraid, it's different. Overcoming my fears. I tell myself that if I don't do it, I'm a coward. It can happen that I remain a long while on the diving board before deciding to jump. This doesn't apply to the fear that men inspire in me, which is much more difficult to overcome.

F.N. You don't have confidence in men?

C.L. No, I don't have confidence in them. But it's above all in myself that I don't have confidence. To fight some guy, I don't like that, I'm afraid. Man is a murderer. Things, things are dangerous, but they don't mean you any harm. If you behave properly with them, it should work out. I flew in a Phantom and in an F16. I wasn't the pilot but they are impressive machines, I wasn't afraid.

J.S. Is it the challenge you like? The diving, is that a challenge you give yourself?

C.L. I don't know, it's complicated this issue of fear. I'm not at all a reckless person, a daredevil, a guy who fears nothing. Rather I'm afraid of everything. A daredevil is a guy who is not conscious of the risk of death. Read *Eastern Approaches* by Fitzroy Maclean for example. He talks about men who went on raids in the desert, who went deep behind the German lines, and he says of this one or that one that they had remarkable courage. That's something I couldn't say of myself.

It depends also on who is around me, that's very important. For example, when I filmed *Tsahal*, I wanted to have as many real experiences as possible. They took me to see the parachutists, I saw them jump. I asked them how they trained. They have a tower, called "Eichmann." You go up in a sort of lift to the top of a hundred-meter tall tower, you see the people all tiny down below, and you have to go, you have to jump. You're in a harness, with straps that go under your arms, around the waist. But there is that moment of decision.

F.N. But didn't you do that?

C.L. Yes, I did it. My team was down below. They were depending on me, I was the director and they were my Israeli "employees." They were challenging me a little. "Will he dare to do it?" I was very afraid.

F.N. If you fail, you die.

C.L. If the straps give way, yes. But they aren't supposed to give way, and it wasn't of dying that I was afraid. I was afraid of the void, it's very intimidating. You jump, and right away you are at full speed. And then you are violently brought up by a shock, your fall is stopped by "Eichmann," except that you don't have a rope around your neck like Eichmann, but straps under your arms. You continue to descend, slowed down but still too fast. I really hurt myself on landing. I landed too quickly. I admire the Israeli trainers a lot. If not for them I might not have done it. It's true that I do things that I know are dangerous, yes.

F.N. Let's talk about a completely different kind of danger, if we may. Terrorism is a question you have already talked to me about, in a way that I think is linked to your relation to death. You gave an interview in *Cahiers du cinéma* about your film *Sobibor, October 14, 1943, 4:00 p.m.* The interview took place as it happened on September 11, 2001, and news of the attack interrupted it. We continued it a few days after. You took the measure of what had happened right away. Do you see a continuity between 2001 and what we are living today, or does the situation today seem to you very different from what happened in New York?

C.L. To me, it's something different. First of all, in 2001 it was the first time, at least for us, in the West. For the United States there had been Pearl Harbor and then this, the Twin Towers. It was an act of pioneers. I have thought a lot about the journey of Mohamed Atta and the others . . . They traveled from an airport in Maine to Boston, in Boston they changed planes. The weather was splendid, we all remember the blue sky. They took a plane for another city, not New York at all, San Francisco maybe, or Los Angeles, I can't remember. There was this unheard-of idea of having them learn to fly these airplanes. I took the same flight from Boston to New York, three weeks later, on a similarly bright morning. I thought of them. My first thought was for them. Of them carrying out a very precise ritual (which moreover no doubt helped them forget the imminent horror they were about to inflict on themselves), their toilette, Mohamed Atta tying up his balls according to the rules of what they believe to be the Koran. They had astonishing sang-froid and determination. They killed a flight attendant, took over the plane, they tied up or killed the pilot and co-pilot, we will never know, then they flew. And then the final *Allahu Akbhar*. It fascinated me. I thought of course of the horror it was for the victims, the people who were in the plane, in the towers. It was appalling.

F.N. How is that different in your eyes from the kamikazes diving into their targets?

C.L. It's very different. The Japanese kamikazes were real soldiers, they didn't want to be doing it, there was no volunteering. They had to do it, they were obeying a military order. If they didn't do it, they would die in any case.

J.S. And why do you say that what is happening today is completely different from what happened in 2001? Because it was a technically complicated operation that required great preparation, whereas today terrorism invests little in minimally qualified and easily replaceable human materiel?

C.L. Yes. For them it was an exploit that grew out of weeks of training in the United States. The organization of attacks today is much less meticulous. And then there was their solitude during that trip. I wondered what was going on in their head during the flight, just before the flight, and when they saw the towers getting closer. Today, that solitude no longer exists. It's as though that surprising act of taking lives by taking your own life has been mechanized, automated, banalized. There are numerous candidates, there's a waiting list. And the enigma of the solitary relation to death, which astounded me, I think it has disappeared, that those suicide-killers no longer have the time to ask questions of themselves. They do everything so that they kill themselves and others without even thinking about it. I think that, deep down, they no longer even have any relation to death. That's even more frightening.

F.N. Have you always confronted your fears, have you always met challenges? Were you already like that as a child or an adolescent?

C.L. Oh no! As a child, I told you, when I saw Jewish school children getting beaten up at Condorcet I didn't step in to defend them, I was afraid. My manner of exposing myself to danger is perhaps linked to that, to that childhood cowardice, which was difficult to bear. I was very unhappy because of it. During the war I did things that were objectively dangerous. I did them and it was linked to that childhood fear. I know it, but I can't express it any better.

J.S. So those challenges would be a way of overcoming your original fear?

C.L. Yes, I think so.

F.N. There is perhaps something else, there is your absolutely incredible feeling of freedom. You don't like to yield. Not before fear, either. Sollers said to me, about you: of all the men I have met, Lanzmann is the most hardline (*le plus irréductible*). Then he added, upon reflection: I knew another hardliner, Jacques Lacan. Did you know Lacan?

C.L. I didn't know him, but I met him, and in comical circumstances. On the Boulevard Saint-Germain, near Odéon, there was a trendy shop that sold ski clothes and that belonged to two brothers, the Pépin brothers—I knew them well. The fashion then was for stretch ski pants. I saw Lacan there, trying on stretch ski pants in front of Sylvia. To test their elasticity, he rolled around on the ground, in the shop, for quite a period of time. Apart from that, I went to two lectures by Lacan, of which I didn't understand a word.

F.N. You were never tempted by the idea of doing an analysis?

C.L. No.

F.N. You never felt the need?

C.L. Yes. Once I needed it. The psychoanalyst that I went to see was very pleasant, intelligent. I wanted him to stop me from killing my wife. He understood me, and, in fact, he stopped me from doing it. But I did not pursue it further. I had achieved my goal.

F.N. You resist psychoanalysis because psychoanalysis is the Law. When Sollers said, Lanzmann is a hardliner, he meant that you would always put in first place your own freedom, your desire.

C.L. There's some truth in that. Perhaps I am the last of the hardliners. That would make a good title, "The Last of the Hardliners."

March–April 2016

—Translated by Peter Connor

Contributors

PETER CONNOR is Professor of French and Comparative Literature at Barnard College. He is the author of *Georges Bataille and the Mysticism of Sin*, and the translator of *The Tears of Eros*, by Georges Bataille, and *The Inoperative Community*, by Jean-Luc Nancy.

ALEXANDER GARCÍA DÜTTMANN teaches philosophy and aesthetics at Universität der Künste in Berlin. His latest book publications include *In Praise of Youth* (2021) and *The Hopeless* (2021).

SARA GUYER is Professor of English and Dean of Arts & Humanities at the University of California, Berkeley and the author of *Romanticism After Auschwitz* (2007) and *Reading with John Clare: Biopoetics, Sovereignty, Romanticism* (2015), as well as articles and essays on the legacies of romanticism and the state of the humanities.

JUDITH KASPER is Professor of Comparative Literature at Goethe University in Frankfurt am Main and co-editor-in-chief of the German psychoanalytic journal *RISS*. Recent publications include *Der traumatisierte Raum. Insistenz, Inschrift, Montage bei Freud, Levi, Kertész, Sebald und Dante* (*Traumatized Space: Insistence, Inscription, and Montage in Freud, Levi, Kertész, Sebald, and Dante*) (2016); *Catastrophe & Spectacle: Variations of a Conceptual Relation from the 17th to the 21st Century*, co-edited with Jörg Dünne and Gesine Hindemith (2018); and "The Persistence of the Witness: Claude Lanzmann's *Le dernier des injustes*," co-authored with Michael Levine (2020).

MICHAEL G. LEVINE is Professor of German and Comparative Literature at Rutgers University. He is the author most recently of *Atomzertrümmerung. Zu einem Gedicht von Paul Celan* (*Atomic Fission: On a Poem by Paul Celan*) (2018) and *A Weak Messianic*

YFS 141, *Lanzmann after "Shoah,"* ed. Levine and Stark, © 2022 by Yale University.

Power: Figures of a Time to Come in Benjamin, Derrida and Celan (2013). He has also published articles on film and human rights trials, translation theory, the graphic novel, and Holocaust literature, film, and the poetics of witnessing.

STUART LIEBMAN is Professor Emeritus of Film Studies and Art History at the CUNY Graduate Center. He has lectured and written extensively about Holocaust cinema in various publications, including *Holocaust and Genocide Studies, Trafic, Revue d'histoire de la Shoah* (Paris), *Archivos de la Filmoteca, L'Atalante, Revista de Estudios Cinematográficos* (Spain), and *Zeszyty Majdanka* (Poland). His anthology, *Claude Lanzmann's* Shoah: *Key Essays*, was published in 2007.

FRANÇOISE MELTZER is the Edward Carson Waller Distinguished Service Professor in the Humanities and Professor in the Divinity School at the University of Chicago. Her books include *For Fear of the Fire: Joan of Arc and the Limits of Subjectivity* (2001), *Seeing Double: Baudelaire's Modernity* (2011), and *Dark Lens: Imaging Germany 1945* (2019).

BRAD PRAGER is the Catherine Paine Middlebush Chair of Humanities and Professor of German and Film Studies at the University of Missouri. He is the author of *After the Fact: The Holocaust in Twenty-First Century Documentary Film* (2015), *The Cinema of Werner Herzog: Aesthetic Ecstasy and Truth* (2007), *Aesthetic Vision and German Romanticism: Writing Images* (2007), and monographs devoted to Christian Petzold's films *Phoenix* and *Yella*. He is the co-editor of *Visualizing the Holocaust: Documents, Aesthetics, Memory* (2008) as well as a recent collection of scholarly essays entitled *The Construction of Testimony: Claude Lanzmann's* Shoah *and its Outtakes* (2020).

JARED STARK is Professor of Comparative Literature at Eckerd College. His work on Holocaust testimony and memory includes, with Alina Bacall-Zwirn, *No Common Place: The Holocaust Testimony of Alina Bacall-Zwirn* (1999); essays in *The Yale Journal of Criticism, History & Memory*, and the MLA volume *Approaches to Teaching the Representation of the Holocaust*; and his translation of Annette Wieviorka's *The Era of the Witness* (2006). He is also the author of *A Death of One's Own: Literature, Law, and the Right to Die* (2018).

LYDIA J. WHITE is a Wellington-based German literary studies scholar, translator, and editor. Her research interests include Bertolt Brecht, Germany's (post-)colonial history, and philosophies of the Other. She is the author of *Theater des Exils: Bertolt Brecht's "Der Messingkauf"* (2019) and has been translating since 2011, above all in the fields of literary studies, cultural studies, theater studies, film studies, philosophy, and history, and was the 2021 winner of the Deutscher Börsenverein's GINT Translation Prize.

Yale French Studies is the oldest English-language journal in
the United States devoted to French and Francophone literature and culture. Each volume is conceived and organized by
a guest editor or editors around a particular theme or author.
Interdisciplinary approaches are particularly welcome, as
are contributions from scholars and writers from around the
world. Recent volumes have been devoted to a wide vari-
ety of subjects, among them: Levinas; Perec; Paulhan; Haiti;
Belgium; Crime Fiction; Surrealism; Material Culture in
Medieval and Renaissance France; and French Education.

    Yale French Studies is published twice yearly by Yale
University Press (yalebooks.com) and may be accessed on
JSTOR (jstor.org).

    For information on how to submit a proposal for a volume
of *Yale French Studies*, visit yale.edu/french and click "Yale
French Studies."